GAME, SET, CA$H!

GAME, SET, CA$H!

BRAD HUTCHINS

NERO

Published by Nero,
an imprint of Schwartz Publishing Pty Ltd
37–39 Langridge Street
Collingwood VIC 3066 Australia
email: enquiries@blackincbooks.com
http://www.blackincbooks.com

The National Library of Australia Cataloguing-in-Publication entry:

Hutchins, Brad

Game, set, cash! : inside the secret world of international tennis trading /
Brad Hutchins.

9781863956598 (pbk)

9781922231598 (ebook)

Hutchins, Brad. Tennis – Tournaments – Anecdotes.
Sports betting – Anecdotes. Gambling industry – Corrupt practices.
Television broadcasting of sports.

796.342

CONTENTS

For Pooch

TENNIS TRADER GLOSSARY

I've put together a quick glossary to get you up to speed with the terms and phrases tennis traders use.

TERM	DEFINITION
ATP	Association of Tennis Professionals (men's tour)
Back end	The team member(s) managing bets from the base computer
Bagel	Losing a set six to nil
The boot	Being caught by security for court-siding and kicked out of a tennis venue. The result can range from a slap on the wrist to trespass orders, legal action or physical threats and violence.
Choke	When a winning player folds under pressure and loses the match
Con	Wi-Fi or internet connection
Court-sider	A consultant who transmits live scores from the court-side to their back end or a computerised gambling system to take advantage of the time delays experienced by the rest of the online gambling community.

Dicked	Beaten by a large margin
Double bagel	Losing two sets six to nil – the tennis trader's Holy Grail in terms of quick matches
Heat	Pressure from security or police in the venue
ITF	International Tennis Federation (Grand Slam organisers)
Market	The online gambling population for that specific match
Oop	Order of play (the schedule of play for the day)
Pos	Our current gambling position on the match
Straights	When a player wins a game in straight sets
Tennis trader	A person who uses an 'in-play' gambling website to make multiple bets on tennis matches in real time throughout the match, with the aim of trading at opportune moments to build a profitable position.
TIU	Tennis Integrity Unit (the sport's gambling-corruption watchdogs)
Trainer	An alert to let our back end know when the physio is on court
WTA	Women's Tennis Association (women's tour)

PROLOGUE

I'm sitting on the side of court eight at the Championships, Wimbledon. I'm holding my phone in my left jacket pocket and trading a typical Wimbledon battle – five sets. The player approaches the service line. I hit 5 on my phone. He bounces the ball one, two, three, four times – as the crowd watch in silence – looks up, and throws it into the air with concentration and the strain of physical effort on his face. His serve connects and the fuzzy, fluorescent ball zings over the net and skids off the centre service line. Ace! I hit 6. The crowd applauds then returns to its reserved and respectful silence.

He serves again. I hit 5 again. This time, he loses the point. I hit 4. The score is 30 all. My phone knows this before the umpire has had a chance to announce it into the microphone, and before half the crowd has realised the point is over. The scoreboard statistician has not even thought about updating this information, but my phone has told the internet server back in . . . well, I'm not telling you where, that it's 30 all. Nobody really cares, though; the players care more about points to come, the crowd do too, and the umpire just tells it like it is. It's just another point. It's 30 all and nobody *really* gives a shit . . . except me. You see, if I screw up and get the score wrong, it could cost thousands of dollars. If I concentrate and get the score right before anyone else, it could *win* thousands of dollars.

I hit 5 as the next point begins. It's still 30 all when I realise that both the tournament supervisor and director are watching me. They sit on the other side of the court in their formal Wimbledon attire, whispering in each other's ears, watching me. They're discussing what to do about my presence on court.

In their eyes, I'm a rodent, a rat, a stain on their wonderful game, the cancer of tennis. They know I'm updating scores because they recognise me from the past three days (not to mention previous tournaments). I've been on court, alone, watching every point and hitting those numbers on my phone at just the right time. I'm no rat – I'm a court-sider. Misjudged, vilified and hunted is what I am. I travel the world with all expenses paid because I update tennis scores to facilitate lucrative online gambling profits. I'm a twenty-six-year-old Australian guy who has finally found a way to see the world without going broke. It's June 2012 and what I do is completely legal at this point in time, although the officials on the other side of the court sure won't tell you that. They like to accuse me of 'threatening the integrity of the sport', whatever that means. They think I'm corrupt. They use this facade to eject and ban me from the venues (when they can catch me).

I've never approached a player with a gambling proposition in my life. I never will either. I know a lot of other traders, and there's not a corrupt bone among us. Match fixers don't come to the tennis. They stay away and stay out of trouble. Avoid the scene of the crime, right? I live on the scene, and I've got nothing to hide. We traders should be free to do what we do because we have no involvement with illegal or immoral practices. This is where certain people beg to differ. You see, there's a clause in the ticket-purchase policy that states 'ticket holders are prohibited from collecting, transmitting or releasing any match scores or related statistical data during match play'. Okay, I'm a rule breaker – but

I'm no criminal. Court-siding and cross-border gambling are the prickly issues we're involved in. Encouraging thrown matches and influencing the outcome of the score are definitely not. Court-siding is not illegal. This is not to say they can't kick me out, though.

I'm on edge, as Wimbledon's security is second to none. I was ejected from the venue during my first match here the previous year. I returned later that week and, predictably, was caught again, this time by a police officer who slid up next to me and addressed me by name. Strike two was more serious: I was issued with a formal letter from the lawyers of the club, banning me from the venue for life and threatening trespass action if I ever returned.

That was last year.

It's Tuesday now, and so far so good, but it's sketchy. As the head of security said last year, 'Wimbledon is a very influential club with exceptional lawyers and a prestige to protect.' The only problem is, this is my job and I want to keep my job. So I queued in the morning, entered the immaculate grounds, ignored my lifetime ban and proceeded to trade away. The crowds are thick and provide good cover. However, my face is too well known. I know they have an exceedingly competent and active security team looking for traders, and I think I've now been rumbled.

The server cracks a forehand winner down the line and my thumb hits the 6 button, which in turn tells my phone that it's 40–30. Things are heating up. However, I'm more focused on the fact that the tournament director has just relayed a message into his walkie-talkie. Did he just call security? I've got spare batteries and a personal Wi-Fi unit in my bag – enough to sink me if I'm searched. I've been trading every point and I need to trade this one. It's 40–30, they're mid-rally and I'm on the edge of my seat contemplating my options when I see the blue polo shirt at the side of the court. Alarm bells! I hit 2, to pause my operation. The guy in the blue polo is not a security member, though – he's the physio. Our server wins the point then walks to his seat to receive treatment for cramps. The umpire announces a medical timeout.

People mill about the court-side. Not many care about the score now, and I'm one of them, because I've also just spotted the spotter out of the corner of my eye. It's hard not to, as he's walked up and stood directly behind me, watching over my right shoulder like a hawk. That grey, cropped hair and beige jacket are all too familiar. He's the head of security, the same guy who personally turfed me out last year. He will no doubt recognise me and knows that I'm banned for life. This is bad. I take no chances, grab the bag at my feet and swing out into the crowd. I push forward double time. Stumbling through the thick crowd, I frantically text news of the possible injury to my co-workers.

I don't look back until I've rounded a few corners and done a bit of ducking and weaving. When I finally brave a quick glance back, he's out of sight. I live to trade another match! I sneak off to the nearest toilet, where I hide in a cubicle and relay what's just happened to my associates. I'm attending one of the most prestigious and celebrated sporting events in the world and I'm hiding in a toilet. Shithouse, indeed. They need me working, though – this is my job. Wimbledon is the biggest event of the tennis year, and, despite the issue of the eager security crew searching for me, there is a whole mountain of money out there to be made.

I'm in a bit of a pickle here and nobody in the bathroom gives a proverbial shit. Hell, nobody even knows. Aside from the annoyed tournament officials and the security team they radioed, none of the other 40,000 people has the faintest idea what I'm doing. They all see me as another spectator. The people who sat next to me last match would be shocked to hear the intriguing truth about my phone and the scores it was transmitting. A fellow trader might extend a wink or a subtle nod in passing, but it's our little secret. We operate under covert conditions because we have to. It's a unique and profitable business, so we keep it as exclusive as we can. Dream jobs don't just roll around every day.

After a short debate with my associates, I'm simply relocated to another court less than a hundred metres away from where I was. I don't like my chances. I hide as best I can, moving around in the crowd and trading from my pocket. It's another marathon match. Around the middle of the third set, I spot the spotter on the other side of my court. He's making strides in my direction, and this time he has a security entourage. Once again, I take no chances. I grab my bag and push through the throng of spectators. I get to the end of the court and am feeling optimistic – this game of cat and mouse, although slightly nerve-wracking, is undeniably thrilling. Then I hear the voice.

'Excuse me, sir. Stop right there, please!'

I ignore it and try to keep walking, but a tall man rounds the corner and steps into my path, blocking the way. He's dressed in an official blazer and looks far too important to simply shrug off and run from. Besides, I'd rather not cause a scene and the security team have caught up behind me now. I'm done. I turn to the chief in his beige jacket, breathe a sigh of defeat and admit, 'All right, you got me,' with a laugh. I'm fairly relaxed, but there is an undeniable tone of apprehension in my voice. The big question is: will they take legal action against me?

1

SCORING THE DREAM JOB

Ever since I was a kid, I knew I wanted to travel. My parents had inspired the idea and often told me stories from their times spent abroad. They showed me old photos and slides, let me read their travel journals and encouraged me to save my pennies so I could spend them on one of the most valuable things money can buy – life experience. Dad worked for a large bank in the Brisbane CBD and Mum was a teacher's aide at a local school. They'd been settled into a quiet family life in suburbia for many years now, but, from their tales of overseas travels, I could tell they had enjoyed some incredible adventures and experiences in the past.

My childhood unfolded during the nineties, in a middle-class area of Brisbane, Australia, surrounded by parkland and peaceful suburban sprawl. It was a happy one, full of sport and study. When I wasn't skateboarding, swimming or kicking a footy around, I was scouring Dad's library shelves for new books to read. Both my parents were avid readers, and it was through them I discovered the classics by Wells, Huxley, Heller, Hemingway and many others, and developed an enduring love for literature.

Despite dabbling in cricket, basketball, rugby league and touch football, I never really found a sport I loved or could dedicate myself to . . . until I tried surfing. Unfortunately for me, I was already eighteen when this moment rolled around. But it was better late than never, and I became well and truly hooked.

Before the addiction to board sports took hold, tennis was a fairly prominent sport in my life, and I have some fond memories of playing it as a child. I used to prop the trampoline up on its side in the backyard and hit the ball against it over and over, practising my topspin backhands and forehands (slices were tricky as they spun awkwardly off the trampoline mesh). I'd also sit up late at night to watch the best US Open and Wimbledon matches. The time difference in Australia made this quite hard on school nights but I did my best to see all the action. Naturally, the Australian Open was where I got my fill of tennis viewing for the year. Pat Rafter was my hero, and I had the pleasure of watching him play against many of the greats – Agassi, Sampras, Safin and Chang, to name a few.

I did relatively well at school and transferred this into university while working a range of part-time jobs at local stores. By the age of twenty-one, I had a Diploma in Business Management, a BA majoring in Sociology and a Graduate Diploma in Education. I was a qualified schoolteacher but I had more in common with the kids than with the teachers. When I first started teaching, I'd skip the mundane staffroom conversations about cooking recipes and TV shows to kick a ball around with the students. Life got repetitive and I got bored. I didn't want to be another stress-ball robot grinding out the daily commute and getting home just in time to eat, zone out in front of the idiot box, sleep, then repeat. Fuck that noise. So I saved my pay, and before long there was enough cash sitting in my holiday fund for a serious adventure. None of my mates were interested in seeing the other side of the world, so in the end I just said 'peace out' and booked myself a ticket.

It helped having family in England (my first port of call). Because my old man had been born there, I was able to acquire dual citizenship and enjoyed the benefits of a British passport for work purposes. Once I took off, I didn't hold back. Between 2008 and 2011, I explored over forty countries, living between England, Australia and Canada, enjoying old hobbies in new places and picking up fresh ones along the way. The most prominent new addictions included snowboarding and scuba-diving. I ran with the bulls in Pamplona, threw tomatoes at strangers in Valencia, sailed around Croatia, danced on tables at Oktoberfest in Munich, dodged bats and spiders by candlelight in Guatemalan caves, rode a camel through the Sahara and snowboarded on a man-made ski hill in the desert of Dubai. I'd found an even more encompassing addiction than surfing – travel was not just a hobby; it was a life-style and a mindset.

In my opinion, travelling is the best thing a person can do. Everything is new. The locations, architecture, culture and food all surprise you constantly. You meet the most interesting people you've ever met, and you make some of the best friends you'll ever have.

It was during 2008, on a tour of Europe, that I met the three mates who would eventually introduce me to the mysterious world of tennis trading. We moved into a rowdy share house with five other friends in West London and I began teaching at schools around the area. The other lads needed work too. By chance, they met a local Londoner, named Nads, who worked on the tennis tour and apparently got paid to fly around the world and watch live sport. To their amazement he offered them jobs. It sounded too good to be legit, but they applied for shits and giggles, and unknowingly made a move that would change all of our lives for the better.

A few weeks later, they were bringing home fancy phones to program and looking over itineraries to far-flung corners of the globe. Apparently, they were now working on the world tennis circuit for some enigmatic gambling syndicate, getting paid to watch live sport and flying to a new country every other week. I was stoked for them but continued teaching because there was no position available for me at the time.

This didn't bother me much because I still had plenty of plans for the following year. We parted ways and I managed to explore Scandinavia, Russia and a lot of Europe's lesser-known countries. I then travelled to Canada, where my love for surfing translated directly onto the powder-filled slopes of the Rockies. Snowboarding consumed my life, and I was content to live as a happy-go-lucky snow bum for the time being.

*

About a year later, while relaxing on my couch in the scenic ski town of Banff, Alberta, I had an epiphany. In approximately six months' time, after I'd finished my season of snowboarding and completed an epic surfing road trip from British Columbia to the bottom of Mexico that two good friends and I had planned, I'd have to fly home and get a *real* job in the *real* world. This did not sit well with me. I'd been travelling for the best part of three years and had become accustomed to the surreal, stress-free lifestyle that drifting and adventure entailed. There was no way I was going back to full-time teaching in the sleepy suburbs of Brisbane. I'd seen too much, yet still hadn't seen enough. I wanted to continue this vagabonding lifestyle and explore more of the world.

The problem was, I was going broke. I had to work. That being the case, I decided I'd do everything I could to find myself a travel job. Working for a heli-ski lodge, on a cruise ship or as a tour guide were the initial ideas that popped into my head. Then the real epiphany hit me: the tennis job! It was perfect. I sent my friends an email asking if they could hook me up, crossed my fingers and continued snowboarding for the next few months.

I then fell off the map completely after smashing my Canadian cell phone in a tequila-induced haze and taking off in a van for the land of sombreros, surf and . . . well, tequila. We surfed the west coast and crossed the border for hotter weather, cheaper, better food and bigger, better waves. Three months and ten thousand miles later, after seeing most of Mexico, Guatemala and Belize I was back in San Diego enjoying some Californian comforts and high-speed internet. I had an email from Felix, one of the boys from London. There was a job opening and he'd recommended me for the position. There were no promises but I had a good chance of getting the job. With one day remaining before I flew back Down Under, I couldn't have been more stoked.

I jumped on the plane home with high hopes, reunited with my family and friends, and waited for the phone to ring.

*

'Okay, I'll give you a brief run-down of what we do.' My future manager is on the phone from England. I'm at my family home in Brisbane, where I've been waiting for the past two weeks, jumping out of my skin and trying to hide the excitement in my voice at finally receiving this call. This is the phone interview. My mates have come through for me; I've basically got the job.

'We gamble on tennis matches, point by point, in real time and send people out to these events to cover matches from the court-side. As one of our consultants, we will rely on you to provide accurate, quick scores so we can make consistent, successful bets. While you do have some long days at the beginning of the week, the workload gets easier as the week goes on. We communicate via text with you to monitor a player's performance and all we really need apart from that is for you guys to be punctual and manage yourselves on the road in different countries. There's no need to apply for work visas. I'm not sure whether our practice can be defined as work or not but it's guaranteed to open up a can of worms if we mention it each time we touch down in a new country. Last time I checked there wasn't a box you could tick on your immigration form for 'borderline legal sports gambling'. So it will be your responsibility to organise *tourist* visas for places like China, India and Russia.'

'Okay, sounds great,' I reply, 'I've got plenty of experience travelling, so that's the easy part for me.'

'Good to hear. Your wage will fluctuate depending on the syndicate's success but we'll also pay bonuses based on performance. On top of that, you will be able to claim food and travel expenses each day you work. I'll also organise flights, hotels and tennis tickets for you.'

'This sounds incredible,' I said.

'Yeah, it is a great opportunity, but obviously the job isn't for everybody as you need to be free from attachments and comfortable on the road for most of the year without going home. As flights to Australia are so expensive and time-consuming, it's best if you use your weeks off to holiday in a destination of your choice closer to the tennis tournaments. Because you'll work six days followed by a travel day, you won't get weekends off. In lieu of this, we will aim to give you a week off every five or six weeks with a few of the other lads to keep you fresh. How does that sound to you?'

Un-fucken-believable was the honest answer. I wasn't sure that was suitable phone-interview etiquette so I didn't say it in those words. I didn't have a girlfriend at the time (perhaps the only downside to a travelling lifestyle), I had no other commitments and I was thirsty to see more of the world.

'It sounds like the perfect life to me,' I replied.

'Great! Now the only real negative I've got to cover here is the occasional annoyance of run-ins with security. Unfortunately, the officials don't want us at their events, and from time to time you may have to deal with them and even be ejected from the venue. Gambling is perceived as a threat to the integrity of the sport, and their solution is to ban us rather than confront the real issues. What you'll be doing is not illegal. However, because you are transmitting live data, it falls outside the rules of the ticket purchase. This means they have the right to kick you out if they catch you. While it's not an ideal situation for us, it's just something we have to accept if we want to continue to operate.'

I'd heard about this from the boys. I was cool with it. It sounded kind of amusing actually.

'Yeah, that stuff doesn't really faze me. It's a shame we have to deal with it, but if it's part of the job then that's fine by me.'

'All right, well I think we've covered everything. Any questions?'

'Umm, hundreds, I'm sure, but none I can think of right now – it all sounds amazing to me.'

'Okay, we'll be in touch soon then.'

'Thanks, bye.'

Fist pumps, jumping and cheering ensued. A few days later, I opened my inbox to discover a job offer. I started on 2 January. The dream job was mine.

*

Yeah, you'd take it – anyone would! An expense account, flights, hotels, tickets and taxis paid for, a credit card, and a food allowance to boot. I was going to be *paid* to watch live sport and travel the world! The whole security issue was a bit strange, I had to admit, but, in the grand scheme of things, it barely came into consideration. So I took the job, enjoyed my final month of a sunny Australian summer and packed my bags once again for a whole different type of adventure.

I'd heard the odd story from my mates about the job and its perks. I'd seen photos of beachside parties in Mexico and Thailand, and heard about loose nights out in Vegas. My knowledge of tennis was mediocre but I enjoyed the sport and was even looking forward to the work side of things. The major perk was the travel, though. I would be on the road for ten months straight and travel to over twenty different countries. I'd travelled a lot in the past but always on a budget; I couldn't wait to live it up on an expense account.

2

THE MYSTERIOUS WORLD
OF TENNIS TRADING

My workmates were a group of Australian and English dudes in their mid-twenties who all loved sport, partying and travelling: the three main prerequisites for fitting into the trading lifestyle.

Mono was a blonde Englishman with such alarmingly white eyebrows it looked like they'd been bleached. As a result, he seemed constantly surprised. He was also colour blind and had an amusing habit of wearing outfits of the same coloured clothes without realising it. Sometimes, we had to stop him from leaving the hotel in his monochrome outfits and convince him to change before allowing him to step out into the public eye.

Nads also hailed from the United Kingdom, and he was our main coordinator on the 'back end' (our base, from where all bets were calculated and placed). He was a cultured Londoner with a supreme love for live music. If there was a gig on in Europe, Nads not only knew about it but most likely had a fistful of tickets too. His job was to monitor our score updates and make sure the computer program placed bets effectively.

Jethro and Felix completed the crew. They were the pair of fellow Aussies who'd scored me the job. Jethro was extraordinarily tall, and Felix wasn't exactly a short-arse either. While walking through the tennis grounds together they were often mistaken for players and asked for autographs rather than being suspected as traders.

We called each other 'court-siders' or 'traders' because, by transmitting live scores, we facilitated the practice of trading tennis matches online. Now I feel like it's time for a quick trip to the classroom, because the question most people ask when I tell them about this job is 'What is it you do exactly?'.

Sports trading. It's a very clandestine and hence exclusive occupation that most people have never heard of. Sports traders, not unlike their economically minded counterparts, follow the progress and performance of an 'investment opportunity' and trade this commodity as you would with something on the stock market. In our case, the 'investment' is generally an individual athlete or team. Hence the title 'sports trader'. This business is facilitated by online gambling websites, which, as you may be aware, allow the public to gamble on almost any legal sporting event around the world in real time.

People have been doing this ever since the turn of the millennium from the comfort of their homes. Some mathematically minded individuals eventually took their hobby to new (somewhat obsessive) levels by applying statistical data and algorithms to their gambling habits. By building a model or a system to gamble with, some of these people have enjoyed incredible success. This, however, takes time, patience and intelligence. Not to mention the capital required to test a system and ride a few bad losses if they happen to have a slow start.

Due to the odd nature of this endeavour, few people actually attempt to take on the challenge full-time. Of those who try, not all are successful. However, those intelligent and persistent enough, with sufficient capital, can discover a way to turn a tidy profit with nothing but a few clicks of the mouse and taps of the fingers. These select few become their own bosses. They work the hours they want to, gamble as much money as they're comfortable with and make smart bets when they see value in a situation – all from their favourite armchair. While they are self-employed success stories, they can't win all of the time. Their system doesn't have to, though. As long as they're winning more than they're losing, then they stay in the green. If they generate enough green to turn a respectable profit, and maintain a positive yield, they continue to work from home for themselves.

When I say 'system' I'm talking about a calculated method for gambling. Each trader might operate under different rules or habits, but each system should be based on mathematics and statistics. It's a numbers game, and there is no room for emotion or hunches. As soon as the score update comes through, traders will run the numbers, plugging them into a matrix, using software, algorithms or their own set of governing rules, and act immediately to make bets. Time is definitely money in trading. With the constant fluctuation of odds during 'in-play' gambling, the quicker you can act on information, the sooner you can take advantage of new odds that appear after each point is played. If you're first to get the score updates, you'll be first to take advantage of the odds.

In gambling, no legal method can be foolproof. There is simply no way to guarantee wins all the time. The best you can hope for is a system that returns a high rate of success and curtails loss to a minimum. Tennis is an unpredictable game, and the most unusual or unexpected swings in momentum can occur at any time. Losses are inevitable. Having said that, tennis is also one of the most predictable sports in terms of its uniform scoring structure. This means it's easy to predict odds in advance by knowing the possible outcomes that will unfold. A major difference between tennis and other sports is that tennis has no set time limit. There must be a result. Without the limitation of time, gambling becomes even more intricate. You have to know the players, understanding how they will respond to pressure, how they will perform in certain situations and locations, and their strengths, weaknesses and habits. This is where obsession comes in. The more you watch and learn, the better your understanding and skill will be when finding the delicate balance between using calculated odds and trusting your intuition of a player's temperament.

I want to clear up some popular misconceptions straight from the get-go. I never worked for Betfair, Bet365, the TAB, Sportsbet, Ladbrokes or any other bookies, the ATP, Sky Sports or any live-update website. I never even gambled from the court-side myself. I was simply the monkey hitting buttons. I worked for freelance gamblers and relayed live scores from tennis matches so my syndicate could place online bets. I was never involved with any large organisations and simply lucked into a rare position with a group of very clever and innovative professional gamblers.

*

Early in the year, I was given my schedule for the first six months. It's a wonderful thing to look over a work roster that shows you travelling to locations such as Acapulco, Miami, Monte Carlo, Rome, Madrid and London – all in the space of a few months. After letting the initial excitement subside, I began mapping out sights to see and nearby friends I might get to catch. What famous attractions are there to tick off? Can I surf, snowboard, scuba-dive or wakeboard somewhere nearby? Where are the best bars in town and will any of my mates who live there be able to meet up and party on the weekend? It was the same basic thought process I went through every time I was heading to a new destination.

*

As fate would have it, my first stop turned out to be the least exotic of them all: Brisbane, Australia. My home town. I met the gang on the Monday morning and introduced myself to the few I had not yet met. Jethro then gave me my equipment for the year: two phones, five batteries, a few chargers, a travel adaptor and a couple of USB connections. I was ready to trade.

*

An hour later, I'm lying on the grass beside court two of the Brisbane International. It's a relaxed tournament for both men and women, located about ten minutes' drive from the city centre. The weather is hot and humid, and the venue is surrounded by greenery. I'm calm and optimistic as I settle into my first day of a new career. This phone feels foreign in my hand, and I'm trialling different ways to hold it without looking obvious. My old friend Jethro is showing me the ropes.

'Keep your eye on that umpire,' he says, pointing across the court. 'She's usually chilled but you can never be too careful.'

Jethro's been booted out more than anyone else on tour – it's hard to fit in when you're six foot eight. I'm not worried about being kicked out, though. I'm a fresh face and they have no idea who I am. I'm more worried about putting my scores in accurately and getting the basics right.

'As soon as the player moves towards the service line, you need to be paying attention,' Jethro schools me. 'If you're in a bad spot and can't hear the calls properly, you might think a let is a second-serve fault. That would cause us to make bets on a point that hasn't actually happened and could be costly. So, as soon as the ball is in play, you need to be watching and listening to everything on court. Watch the line judges' signals to make sure you've heard the call right, then check the umpire's reaction to make sure it hasn't been overruled or replayed.'

We watch the ball fly back and forward in a rally. Eventually, it spoons up and one of the players runs into the net. 'Hit,' whispers Jethro, 'winner for sure,' before the racquet has even hit the ball. I hesitate and wait for a clean connection before hitting the button. It's an easy winner. Jethro's eyes have been fine-tuned to the intricacies of this sport.

The next point is quite quick and this time the ball balloons into the air for what would appear to be an easy overhead smash. I'm about to click in anticipation when Jethro stops me. 'Wait for it!' he urges. I do. The player sets herself, one arm pointed at the falling ball, the other bent behind her head, ready to smash it . . . when she misjudges the shot and dumps it into the net. In a moment of bewilderment, I freeze, then move my finger from the button it was on and hit the opposite one. My heart rate jumps a bit. That was close. 'You'll be amazed how often they fuck up an overhead smash, mate. It's not as easy as it looks – so never go early on those ones unless it's one of the top players who doesn't make mistakes.' Sound advice.

A few officials in white polo shirts with beige pants wander through the crowd, checking all is well on court and keeping an eye on proceedings. 'These guys are the ones to watch out for,' Jethro says. 'They're the tournament officials, and if anybody is going to call security on us it's likely to be them.'

I'm nervous for a moment and push my phone under my leg

and out of sight. They wander by without even casting an eye over us and my heart rate finally returns to normal.

*

As my first covered match as a trader finishes, I put the match point in and relax for the first time in two hours. The match was a typically mundane first-round scrap. It was okay but nothing special. More promising tennis looms as Jethro and I move to centre court to cover a clash between Andy Roddick and Lleyton Hewitt. This match is an exciting one for me – I've never seen either of these champions play live and I've grown up watching both of them valiantly battle legends such as Sampras and Agassi (occasionally emerging victorious) at Grand Slams over the years. I'm alert and stimulated during the first set and begin to quiz Jethro about trading techniques in an attempt to get my head around the numbers. Numbers are not my favourite subject – I'm more of a words person – but numbers are the key to trading. Jethro breaks it down into simple terms for me.

'Okay, so now Roddick has the advantage point to break Hewitt's serve, and is paying 1.50 to win the match. The next point will either result in game to Roddick or back to deuce. Judging from how the market has been reacting during this match and using experience in these situations, I estimate the payout on Roddick to win the match will change to roughly 1.20 (game) or 1.85 (deuce). This helps us immensely when trying to beat the scoreboard and place bets ahead of the market.'

'Yeah, but we're using our computer model to make our bets, aren't we?'

'Well, you're right, but some traders operate as "scalpers", which means they buy and resell stock on a player for small, quick returns. They do this throughout the match and gradually build a profit without any considerable risk. They see the point go against Roddick and immediately buy into him at 1.50 before the market knows it has happened and has time to react. Then, knowing the price will change to 1.85, they sell what they bought back for an inflated price and the difference is profit. Over the course of a day, week or year, this can amount to enormous sums for very little risk.'

'What are we talking here, tens of thousands? Hundreds of thousands?'

'Millions, mate.'

'So why don't we just do that?'

'Well, we do, to an extent, except we have the added advantage of the computer model to guide our decisions. Every time we hit a button, it goes through the model's matrix. The model makes a purely mathematical assessment and then places a bet. While the scalpers might be a bit quicker than us, we make accurate and profitable gambling decisions on a regular basis because of our model.'

'Genius,' I muse, while watching A-Rod execute a backhand drop shot that displays an equally impressive yet different brand of brilliance.

*

'So, if it's that simple,' I say during the next break in play, 'then why don't we go trade cricket matches in the Caribbean or football matches all over Europe?'

'There are plenty of other popular sports that people bet on online. Football, rugby, cricket, darts and basketball are a few. I've even heard of dudes trading badminton and volleyball matches before, but all these markets pale in comparison to the tennis market. Tennis is perfect because of the dynamic nature of the game combined with its structured scoring system and the fact that people all around the world love to gamble on it. Deuce allows for maximum swings in momentum. Break points are concise and pivotal moments of focus. You'll learn soon enough that tiebreaks are the ultimate heart racer: in the space of minutes or even seconds, matches can swing from match point for one player to set point for the other, and then back again, and again. Each point constitutes an incremental change in the match. Each change constitutes a predictable move in odds and an opportunity to profit. This is why tennis is the perfect sport to trade, and why it is the sport of choice for the betting market. A goal in football will alter the odds drastically, but it's only likely to happen a couple of times per match.'

'If at all!' I add. 'I suppose in tennis you're guaranteed opportunities to bet because players *have* to score to progress through the game.'

'Exactly,' agrees Jethro. 'Likewise for points scored in rugby. Cricket is even more ambiguous because of its fickle nature and the way in which wickets can influence a match. Badminton, volleyball and darts are well structured but don't have the same media exposure or fan base. While all sports offer undeniable betting opportunities, none have the same dependable structure or market liquidity as tennis.'

'This is pretty impressive stuff, mate!' I remark. 'You've really got your head around this trading business.'

'Two years on the job will do that to you, pal. Don't worry, you'll get there too.'

In London, Jethro was a bit of a wild man – he travelled most of Europe with me and we had some epic benders together. He was renowned for his excessive, comical behaviour and erratic shenanigans. I knew he was an intelligent guy but two years in the trading business has given him an air of expertise and authority that I've never seen before.

*

Sitting on centre court, I realise how much easier it is to trade in the stadium. It has big-screen replays, big scoreboards and a dense crowd to blend into. Jethro and I are laughing as he recalls one of his craziest stories from the road last year. He awoke in a Cincinnati hospital on a double drip with no recollection of the previous night. Apparently, the police had found him lying in a ditch, unconscious. He'd failed to make it home after a heavy night of drinking and dancing on the bar and had ended up with severe alcohol poisoning. Not only did he make his flight the next morning, he was in better shape than all of the other lads, as he had a solid sleep under his belt and zero hangover thanks to the drip purging every drop of alcohol from his system.

Things are going smoothly when, all of a sudden, disaster strikes. Halfway through the second set, we are faced with a major obstacle that prohibits us from trading. The Betfair server has gone down and all markets are suspended. Our phones are rendered useless in our hands and there is nothing we can do. Until the website's server is back up, we cannot bet. We are suspended from trading and we haven't even had a security run-in. We stay on court and cross our fingers, hoping that things are back up sooner rather than later. The pitfalls of technology.

'Why don't we just use Bet365 or one of the other gambling sites?' I ask Jethro.

'Because Betfair is *the* online gambling site when it comes to trading. They invented it. They were the first online gambling company to facilitate in-play betting, and, because of the enthusiastic gambling population in the UK, it took off, and is still growing with astounding numbers. With such a huge and consistent market, Betfair is the ultimate gambling tool for traders. Without it, we don't trade.'

'I know Betfair is massive in the UK, but how did it get so popular in the first place?'

'Dude, I thought you'd know at least some of this stuff – you've really got to get your head around it so you understand what we're doing here.'

'What can I say, mate? I've never been much of a gambler. I'm all ears now, though.'

Jethro is amazed that he has to explain so much to me. On the other hand, I am astounded by how much there is to take in about this unique industry. As we watch Roddick rain down aces, Jethro explains the intricacies of Betfair to me.

I learn that Betfair is different because the market sets the price instead of a bookmaker or pricing index. It effectively operates as a betting exchange rather than as a bookie or betting agency. You're gambling your money against another gamblers. There's no 'house' or bank to break. It's simply your money against another punter's. If somebody wants to put a bet on a horse to win the Melbourne Cup and thinks the bookie is offering too steep a price, he or she can offer it on Betfair and wait to see if it's 'matched' by another punter. For example, if the bookmaker has Pharlap to win at 1.30 and average Joe punter thinks 1.50 is a more accurate value, he can put any amount (say $10) up on Betfair at 1.50 and see if anybody takes it. If somebody sees that price and thinks it is reasonable, they can match the bet by taking those odds against Pharlap. This is called laying. When you think a tennis player is going to lose, instead of betting on the other player, you may actually find a better price by laying that particular player. If the price is reasonable, then average Joe stands a good chance of having his $10 matched, because the exchange constantly fluctuates with different prices as people match each other's bets.

Traders use Betfair because:

- You can gamble on every single point of the match while it is live.
- You can get different odds from a range of different people on the market.
- You can back or lay players as often as you like during the match to improve your profit or calculatedly build one up.
- You can guarantee yourself a win–win outcome *if* you trade at the right time(s) during a match.

The bottom line is if Betfair didn't exist, online sports trading wouldn't exist and we wouldn't be sat on court crossing our fingers for their server to come back up. I learn there and then that Betfair is our lifeblood and without it our industry would not exist.

As if on cue, our phones finally reconnect to the server we've been bitching about. We're back online and it's as quick as that – all systems go. I stop asking questions and focus on the match. We've got precious gambling time to make up!

*

Despite the home crowd's support, Lleyton loses to Roddick, and we head back to court two to relax on the grass and await the start of our next match. This time, it's a women's match. The mixed tournaments are cool because you get to switch from the power of men's tennis to the grace and skill of women's tennis (and, yeah, let's face it, I much prefer the view when the women are playing).

The match begins and I concentrate on the action rather than the view. The routine is becoming automatic already. Each player has a specific button and after a few points your brain is programmed to react as soon as they win a point. Your eyes tell your brain, which tells your thumb, which in turn tells the phone who won the point. The rest all happens in cyberspace.

I look up and, to my surprise, clock a few familiar faces in the crowd. A couple of old mates from school have walked in with beers in hand and are watching the same match I'm trading. They're not close friends but guys I used to hang out with at school and surf with a bit. They don't see me and my first reaction is to call them over. I want to tell them all about this amazing new job I've scored and explain that I'm actually *working* right now. But I quickly reassess and realise it's not really an option. I need to be focused on points and I'm also supposed to be keeping a low profile. It's not a job you can broadcast to the general public. We operate in a covert manner for a reason, and it has to stay that way.

Jethro notices my brief distraction and jumps on it. 'Concentrate, bro. You need to be getting those scores in quick smart.'

I ignore my old schoolmates and focus on the point being played. 'Okay, no worries,' I assure him. 'But why is there such emphasis on being quick?'

'You know how I told you there are other traders you'll get to meet during your time on the road?'

I nod. He has mentioned that guys from England, Italy, France, Switzerland, and even Russia and Estonia also work on the tour.

'Well, Brizzy is a pretty low-key tournament so you won't see them here this week, but at the bigger tournaments you are going to have to compete with these guys. If you're working on centre court at a Grand Slam, there could be up to twenty other traders gambling on court.'

'Holy shit! I had no idea there were that many traders out there.' I feel a sudden surge of pressure. At least I'll have a few weeks' practice before the Australian Open.

Jethro continues his lecture and I soak up every bit of it – this information is crucial to my future as a trader and I want to be the best I can be at this job.

'At Grand Slam events, there can be up to twenty different courts running at one time, which leaves plenty of room for everyone. Outside courts have less media coverage and attention. However, this usually results in a smaller amount of money being traded on the market. So most guys will head to centre court for the big bucks. While it offers the most potential profit, it is also the most competitive market. If you make a mistake on a big match, your money is gone. Somebody will swoop in and take it in the blink of an eye. When courts are competitive, speed becomes the key. Everything in tennis happens so quickly that you need to have lightning reflexes to take advantage of the lag. If everyone gambling at home is watching a television feed that is delayed by five seconds, you have just five seconds to take advantage. That's plenty of time to log a point, right?'

I nod. I've been getting the points in comfortably within a second or two so far.

'Say you hit the wrong button by accident: our computer will throw money on the player who has just lost the point instead of the player who just won the point. A few seconds later, the general public will see the point and make their bets. If your money hasn't already been taken by another court-side trader, then the market will snap it up.'

This has not yet happened to me, but, as Jethro explains it, I feel another burden settle on my shoulders.

'If all the other court-siders are using superior technology and techniques, then they will clean up every point and there will be no money left for us to take. As more traders come on court, the competition intensifies. A bet is placed with Betfair as soon as our server receives your submission. If you're watching a match that five other traders also happen to be sitting on, it becomes a challenge to consistently be the quickest.'

'So that's why we sit behind the baseline – for the best view?' I ask.

'Yeah, that's right. Best view equals best reaction time,' Jethro confirms. 'Generally, you'd expect to enter a point about a second after it's been decided?' he asks.

I assume this is a rhetorical question, so I nod. I'm wrong.

'This is far too slow,' Jethro explains. 'There are a lot of guys out there all vying for the first hit. All traders watch enough tennis to understand and premeditate the construction of a point. They're putting points in half or even a *tenth* of a second after each point is decided.'

This blows my mind. I thought it was easy. In truth, I'm pathetically slow.

'If a big server is playing, then you need to be ready to cash in on those aces. If one of the super-fit and flexible guys is playing, never hit too early on a drop shot – chances are they'll get to it and maybe even turn the momentum of the point around. If a ball spirals up for a simple overhead smash, never hit.'

'I've learnt that one already,' I assure him.

'When a number of traders are all on court premeditating points and hitting as quickly as possible,' he continues, 'things are broken down into fractions of a second. If you are 0.01 seconds slower than the guy two rows in front of you, then too bad. You miss out and he cashes in. Most of the money traders win often comes from other traders. They are the ones constantly pumping money into the market, after all. During a long day, mistakes are almost inevitable and there will almost always be another trader there to make a profit from your loss.'

'It's a cut-throat game,' I say, beginning to comprehend.

'Sure is, and *that* is why we need to be focused and quick.'

It's clear now that my job is to reduce that transfer time between eyes, brain, thumb and phone, and be as accurate as possible. I'm going to have to train my brain to be constantly focused on the action if I want to be a good trader.

*

The server frames the ball and it shanks off in an unexpected direction. There's no way it's going in. My thumb jerks in response and I've hit the button without even thinking. That one was definitely my quickest reaction yet – well under a second.

'I think I'm getting the hang of this,' I say.

'Yeah, that was quick, mate. Now try doing that every point for five matches and see how your brain feels when you finally get back to the hotel.'

It's a fair point. While this job sounds amazing, it is also going to require a certain degree of dedication.

'Bring it on,' I say. 'I can't wait, man. I'm really looking forward to this year.'

'Yeah, you'll have the time of your life,' agrees Jethro. 'Except for in situations like the one Felix is in right now. Don't look too obviously but he's just been dragged out by the cops.'

'Shit!' I steal a glance just in time to see my new co-worker being walked out the door by a group of security guards and policemen.

'Occupational hazard,' Jethro shrugs.

I stare in shock. I've been far too blasé about the threat of security guards kicking us out. There are a lot of things I've underestimated about this 'simple' job. It is going to be an interesting year indeed.

3

A DAY IN THE LIFE

I roll over in bed and check the time. Eight a.m. Sydney time. No rush. Our workday generally starts a bit later than most people's. Play doesn't commence until 10 or 11 a.m., and in some of the hotter locations it can start as late as 3 or even 5 p.m. – suffice to say we never have to wake up to an alarm clock. Most mornings, we'll make our way down to the hotel breakfast between eight and nine. It's not unusual to see tennis players, coaches or officials at breakfast. Some of them know what we do, while others are oblivious. It's funny when you see a player do a double take or visibly recognise you from another location. I guess most of them just assume we're following the tour for a media company or in some other capacity. Close enough.

I roll out of bed, throw some clothes on, wake up Felix and head down to the buffet, where I see Australia's next big hope, Bernard Tomic, ordering an omelette. I don't talk to him as I line up for my own serving of eggs. I've never bothered celebrities when I see them, and tennis players are no exception. There is no reason why our lives should intersect. Like all famous and outspoken players,

Bernie has stirred up quite mixed opinions from the Australian public. Regardless of my opinion, I take my fill of breakfast and sit with my co-workers to enjoy it. At the end of the day, players are just people. I think they deserve their own space.

Once we've eaten and read the schedule for the day (this is called the 'order of play'), we get our gear ready. We make sure our batteries are charged and our phones are set up, ready for trading. If you're going to spend twelve hours at the venue, you'll need a few other things too. Depending on the type of tournament I'm at, my bag will generally contain: two phones (one for internet, another for texting if necessary), three or four spare phone batteries, a Mi-Fi unit (as in a mobile Wi-Fi hotspot, which also needs a few spare batteries), a bottle of water, some snack food, sunscreen, a book, a jacket for those cold nights when you don't move for three hours, and sunglasses for the glare off the court.

You can never predict how long your day is going to be. If you have four matches, you could get three straight-setters and a retirement and escape with a four-hour day. Conversely, you could cop four three-setters full of tiebreaks and trudge back into the hotel room twelve hours later! As a result, you always have to come prepared. It's not much fun sitting on court at 1 a.m. when it's eight degrees and you're wearing a pair of shorts and a T-shirt (which seemed completely reasonable that afternoon when it was thirty degrees and sunny).

*

The working weeks start off busily for both players and traders. Players have rigorous training routines to follow, singles and doubles matches to play, and media and sponsorship commitments to fulfil. Depending on the size of the tournament, the first few days can consist of ten- to twelve-hour days for traders but by Thursday (finals time) the workload diminishes and we get some downtime. This allows us to go check out the sights, explore the city and wind down with some beers before hitting the bars on the weekend. After watching up to thirty matches of tennis during the week, surviving on snacks and quick meals, and crashing in a sterile hotel room of a night, the best cure is mixing it up and sampling the nightlife with a few good mates. Depending on how far they progress in a tournament, the players can also explore the sights in their downtime (although this often involves a promotional photo shoot and additional sponsorship duties). I doubt 'hitting the town' is ever pencilled into their agenda.

There's not always time for gallivanting around the countryside and sipping fine ales, though. Some weeks, we get slammed with huge hours, day after day. I can think of a few occasions where I worked a seventy-hour week, and a thirteen-hour shift is not unheard of when covering a day's tennis. Our diet isn't the best during these weeks – consisting of snacks from vending machines and fast-food stalls, and late-night binges in hotel rooms. Conversely, most of the players have premeditated diets, prescribed to them by nutritionists or coaching staff. They will eat bananas on court and sip energy drinks to provide them with extra isotope hydration for improved performance. Their snacks, meals and workouts will all be calculated and followed religiously to give them the best possible preparation for match days.

*

On this particular day in Sydney, we have a late start. So, once we've let our food digest and organised our gear, we head down to the local tennis courts to have a hit. On our way, we see Bernard jogging with a mate as part of his morning exercise regime. It's a frustratingly comical thing to try and play tennis after watching the pros all week. We get on court and think we can belt the shit out of the ball too. Why not? Everyone else seems to be able to do it. However, those sizzling down-the-line forehand winners I have planned in my head regularly turn into framed fizzers in the physical world. We play for an hour and on our way back the pros are still jogging.

*

In the hotel room, I'm trying to get a good internet connection on my phone before setting off for the day. Organising our bearings, tickets and phone connections can provide major headaches in new destinations. We have to be resourceful and resilient to get things done and put up with the constant challenges of navigating through country after country. In Sydney, it's no big deal. But adjusting to different languages, remembering flight details and hotel names, and finding tennis venues or phone shops can range from simple chores to arduous burdens depending on where in the world we are. Then we have to plan our transport to the event, making sure we arrive with plenty of time to get set up before play commences. It pays to be organised – Jethro once had to run into the middle of a busy street in Moscow and literally stop traffic to convince a driver to take him to the airport in time to make his flight.

After the players have had breakfast and completed their morning stretches, exercise and warm-ups, they are picked up and chauffeured from their hotel by tournament cars. They have VIP areas inside the venues for training, eating and socialising. They are given a schedule for the tournament and provided with access to interpreters, food, drinks, towels, racquet services, gym facilities and practice courts. Our days diverge even further from this point on.

*

After setting up our phones, Felix and I pack our gear, meet up with a few of the other traders and head off to the venue. In Sydney, the tournament is held at Olympic Park, so the train is the most rational option for transport. This route requires us to walk, train, shuttle bus and walk again. It takes a little longer than a VIP chauffeur. When we arrive, there is a large crowd making the most of Sydney's fine summer weather. The air's abuzz with the chatter of excited spectators and it's shaping up to be a good day of tennis for all.

I grab a seat on court four, set up my phone ready for trading, keep an eye on security and watch the action unfold. I'm feeling pretty quick on the buttons today and the back end informs me we've had a small win on the first match. Bernard plays in the second match and looks to be in good form. It seems we're both having a good day.

*

Because we can't tell people what we do, we often end up looking like friendless tennis geeks, sitting on court all day, soaking up the action like we live for it. I enjoy chatting to people in the crowd, as you often meet friendly, happy folk who are having a fun day and are in a good mood. A bit of conversation helps the day go by, but it can also get distracting (like when somebody borrows your sunscreen) and even a little awkward (when somebody asks if you've got the tournament's app and updates on your phone there). I've had to excuse myself and leave a perfectly good seat to avoid talking to perfectly agreeable, albeit curious, spectators because of the nature of my job. It's just not worth the risk, so instead we generally sit there like solitary nerds on court and let people think we are just that.

Their opinion of us must swing to alarm when we're dragged from our seat by an angry security crew. 'The lonesome loser' becomes 'the curious criminal'. Luckily for us, neither description could be further from the truth! Hours later, we have the opportunity to laugh about our awkward on-court escapades with mates over dinner and beers.

*

One of the first questions people ask when they're talking to me about tennis is 'Who's your favourite player?'. It's a funny question – almost seems a bit childish – but people enjoy different players' styles, techniques and temperaments, and they like to compare opinions. You may find my answer slightly predictable and tiresome. It is without question Mr Roger Federer.

In Rome, while Feds was dismantling an adept Andreas Seppi (who was in good form on home soil), I once heard a spectator shout in broken English, 'Roger, from what planet are you?' I laughed along with the crowd. It was a valid question considering the unearthly display we were all witnessing. His stroke play, flair and aptitude are all unmatched, in my opinion. He has such timing, natural talent and effortless style, I can't think of anyone I'd rather watch. Nadal, Djokovic and Murray may have trained hard enough to find the physical advantage over Federer, but I don't think any of them could have conquered him in his prime.

Apologies to all those Nadal fans out there but in all honesty his style of play generally bores the shit out of me. I'm not denying he is a champion. After reading his book, *Rafa*, and gaining an insight into his incredibly motivated and tenacious psyche, I have all the respect in the world for Rafael Nadal. Mentally, he's probably the toughest player to have ever picked up a racquet. He's also modest and fair. But he's boring. Not because he wins often. I have nothing against prolific success. He works hard for his wins and he earns them. But that's the thing. He admits he's not quite as naturally talented as some other players on tour, so he finds a way to win regardless. He grinds players down. He plays safe, defensive, monotonous tennis. He runs around his backhand to use his overpowering forehand. He bounces the ball sixty-eight fucking times before serving and goes through his superstitious routine every single time. Imagine watching that ball bounce for five hours straight. Imagine sighing in exasperation after watching that routine for the eightieth time in a day, as one of Rafa's ball tosses goes astray and you realise you'll have to sit though it yet again. Now you might understand why I get bored while watching certain players on court.

I honestly believe the greatest and most pivotal moment in Rafa's career was his decision to play left-handed, knowing this would give him the advantage over the majority of right-handed players. (Kudos to Nadal for making this adaptation even though he was a natural right-hander.) In my opinion, he never could have matched Federer if he'd played right-handed (that massive forehand topspinner into Federer's backhand is just too much of a weapon). But I won't wax lyrical for too long – Fed's track record says it all. He is undisputedly the greatest of all time, and it is an honour to watch him whenever he walks out on court. Most importantly, he comes across as a gracious, appreciative winner and a true gentleman for the young'uns to idolise.

Other favourites include: the unpredictable Latvian Ernests Gulbis for his unflinching attitude, powerful shots and classic sense of humour; diminutive and agile Ukrainian Alexandr Dolgopolov for his unique style, deceiving power and ability to outplay guys much bigger and stronger; and Frenchman Gaël Monfils for his raw athleticism, talent and showmanship. I also love a comeback story and thoroughly enjoyed following the returns of German legend Tommy Haas and American Brian Baker after their absence from the sport. It was heart-wrenching to see Brian Baker tear his meniscus (a debilitating and painful knee injury) on court at the Australian Open in 2013. He went down awkwardly and collapsed after trying to stand on his injured leg. He was also a set-up and on his way to the second round of a Grand Slam but instead had to retire hurt. Given his shocking history of injuries and extended absence from tennis, it was a miserable thing to witness.

*

As tennis aficionados, traders spend so much time on court we end up going through epic battles, struggles and ordeals on a daily basis with players. We're like invisible teammates, willing players on and cheering from the sidelines. We get to know their temperament, mentality and headspace from certain telltale signs. It's impossible not to notice these things if you spend as much time as we do on court. It's also our business to know. If a player has a recurring injury or isn't fully committed to a tournament because of personal issues, then it's imperative we are aware. While computer models and gambling systems can be very quick and beneficial, they are still computers. Without human intervention they will gamble on injured players, hence our 'monitoring' of player performance is an equally critical aspect of court-side trading. If there is an injury we need to be there to suspend all bets. This is where having a second phone is essential for communicating with the back end. You don't want to be throwing money on a player who is not hungry or fit enough to win. You don't want to back a player who struggles with mental pressure either. Certain players choke when it comes down to the nitty-gritty, while others take it in their stride.

In his 2000 article in *The New Yorker* entitled 'The Art of Failure', Malcom Gladwell uses the 1993 Wimbledon final between Jana Novotná and Steffi Graf as a case study for choking. Ahead 4–1 in the final set, Novotná let the gravity of the occasion get to her, and her composure imploded. Her natural game dissolved. She double-faulted and mis-hit her way out of a commanding lead. Ten minutes later – to the shock of the crowd – she had lost the Championship 4–6. It is widely recognised as one of the greatest chokes in sporting history.

Gladwell reasons that people respond to pressure by either not thinking enough (panicking) or overthinking (choking). In tennis, the choking response is prevalent because of the crowd presence and the pressure players put upon themselves to perform in an individual sport. After watching countless matches, I couldn't agree more with Gladwell when he suggests the true champions are separated by their rare ability to detach themselves from the crowd's expectation and perform consistently regardless of the occasion. As Gladwell states, 'Choking is a central part of the drama of athletic competition.' It is an integral and pivotal part of the game, and one we must have a firm understanding of to be successful traders.

It's a risky situation for traders to bet on a known choker. You'll often hear the phrase 'Just fucking serve it out!' uttered in dismay when a player looks like he or she might choke what should have been an inevitable win. This is just another example of how nothing is guaranteed in the gambling world – you are always taking some sort of risk when you place a bet. However, the more we know, the better. And there's no better way to build comprehensive knowledge of tennis players than by sitting on court.

It raises the question: how many people on earth would know more about tennis and the players than we traders? Well, I can only speculate, but, aside from coaches, other players and a few officials, you'd have to assume the answer is not many. We know which conditions players prefer, what their history is at certain tournaments (it's amazing how often players have repeat wins at tournaments), how they perform on different surfaces and what type of form they are in. It's a lot like horse racing, except you have the human element of emotion and 'the choke' to consider.

*

Bernard Tomic may be many things according to the Australian media or public, but, from my experience, he's no choker. His match is over in two succinct sets. I'm grateful because it gives us another small win and reduces the amount of hours I have to spend in the stand. After my matches on court four are finished for the day, I head back to the hotel and relax for an hour. I pop down to the gym for a workout before dinner. Lo and behold, Mr Tomic is in the pool. I can't get away from this guy today! He seems to be winding down after a day of exercise and competition. My friends call me and organise dinner at the hotel trattoria at 7 p.m., so I head back to my room and get ready.

*

'Guess what Azarenka is paying against Ivanovic?' Felix asks me, as we down a few beers in the hotel room before dinner.

'Umm, well, she'll be favourite, obviously,' I state, biding time until I can make an accurate estimate. 'Say 1.3. How's that sound?'

'Not bad, mate. She's 1.28 at the moment.'

'Nice!' I'm impressed and a little disturbed by my bizarre knowledge of this niche. This is a common pastime between the lads, guessing what the odds will be and testing ourselves against the market. How good is our perception?

'That seems a little short' or 'Shit, that's long' are often heard during these conversations. Followed by comments like 'Yeah, the market have no idea, I'll be throwing some cash on that' or 'I'm steering well clear of that match; they must have an injury we don't know about'.

We place side bets and give each other different odds to the market just for fun, and almost always back a winner for the tournament. It adds an extra element of investment to keep us interested while at the tennis. At the Grand Slams or Masters, one of the most challenging bets is to pick the 'singles double' – the men's and women's tournament winners. If you can pull it off, the odds are handsomely rewarding.

'I think Ana's going to win it, though,' Felix decides, knowing it will be a controversial opinion. 'I'm throwing a tenner on her – you'll see.'

'You're mad,' I declare. 'There is no way Ana is getting one over Vicky tomorrow.'

We're still arguing about this when we meet a few of our mates in the foyer. As tragic tennis nerds, they all chime in with their opinions. Felix is well outnumbered.

At dinner, we are sat at a table right next to – yes, you guessed it – Bern and his team. It's almost uncomfortable. He must be starting to worry that I'm some sort of obsessed psychopath. As his team toast to victory, my mates and I enjoy some Italian food and plan our night out on the town. Here is where our lives vary drastically: we go and do what we want, while he is bound by routine and responsibility. By the time we get in a taxi to head out, he will probably be heading to bed (despite his rowdy reputation in the media I never saw him out on the piss). Admittedly, we will be jealous of his clear head and healthy vibe the next morning while we nurse our hangovers and attempt to cure them at the breakfast buffet. But at least it will be my choice, while he will already be planning every detail of his day around that single word that runs his life and fuels ours: tennis.

*

That night, we go to a local pub and down some beers over a few games of pool. An American guy comes over and asks if he can challenge the winner. We get chatting to him and discover he's a hitting partner who also follows the tour. His name is Rick and he's worked on the tour for the past year. While he was never good enough to make it competitively, he's still good enough to give the pros a decent warm-up. It seems he's got an enjoyable life-style carved out on the road. Because he doesn't have to compete in the morning, his routine isn't anywhere near as strict as the players'. He prefers to enjoy himself in a similar style to us, and joins us for a few beers. When it comes to the tricky terrain of explaining what we do, we opt for the sneaky white lie. 'We work in the media, for Sky Sports channel' is the cover. This seems to suffice, and we continue talking about his duties on tour.

'I mainly hit with the girls,' he explains. 'The guys will gladly hit with each other if they have the opportunity but many of the girls prefer a guy to hit with instead of another female player.'

'Why's that?' Felix asks, lining up the eight ball.

'Well, half the time it's because they want somebody who can hit powerful, consistent shots to them, but sometimes it's because of their attitude problems. Some of the girls are such bitches none of the others want to hit with them!'

I remember seeing Maria Sharapova hit before and noticing how powerful her groundstrokes were. Even though she was hitting with a guy, she was still too good for him. The poor bloke was blasted off the court. So this revelation doesn't surprise me. To be honest, the comments about some players' attitudes don't either. Some of the girls are so nasty and foul-mouthed on court that I don't blame other players for not wanting to have a hit with them.

Felix pockets the eight ball and shakes Rick's hand after a close game.

'Another round?' Rick asks.

We all look at each other and nod in agreement. 'Why not?' I say. 'It's not like *we've* got to be up early to hit the courts.'

Everyone laughs and clinks glasses in celebration of an enjoyable life on tour.

*

From what I've seen and heard of the average tennis player's lifestyle, it appears to consist of travel (often on the same flights we're on), living in hotels (sometimes the same ones we're staying in), eating, sleeping, training and playing matches. For most of his career, Nadal has trained over six hours per day. Every day. That means that, each year, he spends almost half his waking hours with a racquet in his hand.

They live and breathe tennis, and that's what it takes to be at the top these days – the level is so high. It came as a bit of a shock to me when I realised that some players are, well . . . is the word 'losers' too harsh? They spend their whole day at the tournaments training, playing and watching tennis. Then they go home, hang out with other players, watch TV in their hotel room and do it all again the next day. They're dedicated athletes so they don't drink or party often. One of my English co-workers once asked Victoria Azarenka if he could buy her a drink. She politely declined. Ouch. I've seen groups of players heading to dinner in the hotel or to a nearby restaurant together on many occasions. Because of this closed culture, most players end up dating either their coaches or other players. Roger and his wife, Mirka, met on the tennis court, as did Andre Agassi and Steffi Graf. Tomáš Berdych dated fellow Czech Lucie Šafářová, Hewitt dated Clijsters. Then you've got Ivanovic and Verdasco, Kirilenko and Andreev, Malisse and Capriati, Melzer and Benešová, Pennetta and Moyá, and the list goes on. Bulgarian Grigor Dimitrov is rumoured to have a few top female players on his hit list, and vice versa for Maria Sharapova. On top of that you constantly hear whispers about who's been shacking up with who and even begin to notice when a new admirer repeatedly turns up in a player's corner to cheer them on. Almost every player on tour has some sort of romantic history with a fellow player or coach. But let's stop there before this turns into a fucking gossip magazine. One thing is for certain, tennis players do not date traders. Most of them don't know who we are, for starters. Some probably think we're creepy stalkers following them around the world, while others would run a mile to avoid the scandal of being involved with an international gambler. There has only been one exception that I know of. Before my time on tour, an Italian trader dated one of the French girls. It was destined for failure though – once her coaching staff figured out what he was involved in, they ordered her to end the relationship.

A few mates and I once sat at a restaurant table next to Andy Roddick while he played tour guide and entertained a couple of Czech players in Memphis, Tennessee during one of these typically boring 'tennis-player-dinners'. Hats off to Andy for breaking out of the tennis circle and marrying the smoking hot actress and swimsuit model Brooklyn Decker. Although I must admit, him spotting her on T.V and getting his agent to call her agent in an effort to tee up a date is a little weird. But it worked, so I'll just shrug my shoulders in dismay and keep my agent's number on speed dial.

There are many exceptions, of course (I almost walked into Novak Djokovic while he was partying and dancing with friends one night in a trendy nightclub in Sweden – I believe he was sober, for the record – and he appeared to be having a blast), and I don't mean to be disrespectful to the players, but from an outsider's perspective it all seems quite reclusive. Then again, this is coming from the guy whom most people assume to be the 'lonesome loser', sat court-side by himself all day. So maybe I shouldn't be so quick to judge. Either way, I admire the players' achievements and life-styles but I don't envy them.

*

Players may have fame and wealth but they also have an obligatory dedication to their sport. I personally feel that fame is something the world has mistakenly overrated and become sadly obsessed with. In any case, I don't see how you can enjoy the wealth when you're a slave to the gruelling yearly calendar that tennis follows. Sure, you can afford a Ferrari, but it will sit in your garage on the other side of the world for forty weeks of the year. Once holiday time rolls around, players have the option of pointing at a map and saying 'Let's go there'. Thing is, I get to do that almost once a month in my job. Aside from the lack of physical talent, I could never have made it as a tennis player – I just don't have the drive, subservience and discipline required to follow such a lifestyle. Luckily, I've found one that suits me just fine. While it isn't that far removed, it is a very different existence.

4

MEET THE CREW

'*Ciao, buongiorno,*' says a man in his mid-thirties as he takes a seat next to me.

'*Ciao,*' I reply, '*come stai?*'

'*Sto bene, grazie,*' he laughs and gives me a nod of approval. I've never met this man but I know who he is. It appears he knows who I am too – our reputations precede us. We're in Melbourne, Australia, at the first Grand Slam event of the calendar year, so why are two strangers exchanging Italian pleasantries in the middle of a tennis stand?

Well, traders are a colourful bunch who come from all corners of the globe and range from mathematical genii and entrepreneurial masters to addicted gamblers and borderline alcoholics (often juggling all at once). It took me some time to really get to know everybody – when you're new to the scene, most traders will keep their distance until they know you're one of them. Not Arturo, though, aka 'the Godfather'. He'd wandered up the stand and nodded in my direction. I didn't know what to make of this guy but I'd heard he was an experienced trader so I returned the nod, and he came over to introduce himself.

He's a talented and jovial Italian who can also speak fluent English, Spanish, French and Polish, as well as dabbling in a little Russian and German. And that's not to mention the maths skills. While we watch the match together, he tells me how he got into the profession many years ago.

'I was working as an interpreter in the media department of the tennis tour,' he begins, 'when I realised there was so much potential for court-side gambling. So I started using the staff Wi-Fi access codes to trade matches from the stand. After doing a few trials in my spare time, I quit my job to take the gambling on full-time.'

In his first year, he made over a million euros. He's addicted not only to gambling but to the life of the tour too. After eight years of following it around the world, he's well and truly stuck in its routine. His knowledge of the world is constantly surprising (he knows most cities on tour intimately and navigates cultural conventions and dialects with ease), and his card tricks are legendary on a night out.

Arturo is one of the pioneers of the occupation that has now become my own – court-siding. As the online market became more crowded and competitive, people began to seek new means of obtaining 'an edge'. Initially, there were only a select few who had the brains, balls and bank account to initiate such an original and unusual idea.

'I would book myself a flight to the next tennis tournament,' Arturo reminisces, 'purchase good tickets, take my laptop in and gamble away while sitting court-side. We're talking circa 2006 here. Those were the good old days when we could all sit on the baseline with our laptops out and trade to our heart's content. There were only a handful of us back then. We'd compare our winnings, swap books and magazines, and talk about our next holidays. "Oh, who just fucked up?" I'd yell across the stand. One of the other traders would raise his hand and shake his head in embarrassment. "Thanks for the payday!" It was all fun and games though, I'd buy him beers that night and we'd laugh about it. Nobody had a clue what we were up to and nobody bothered us. It was all too easy!'

Most of the originals had a tennis tournament in their home town or at least nearby, so naturally the majority of them were European. These guys were true lateral thinkers, ignoring uniformity and opting to work outside society's conventions. The practice of turning up to a live event and logging scores in real time is commonly and aptly referred to in the gambling world as 'court-siding'. While many online gamblers know court-siding exists, most simply don't have the means, imagination or drive to join the party. So, while it's not a completely secret vocation, those of us who do it have been able to operate with a relatively limited amount of competition and exposure. On the whole, the practice remains largely undiscovered by the general public, and we traders do all we can to keep it that way. Invariably, new traders will pop up to try their hand on the tour. Some stay while others succumb to greed, bad luck or poor operations. One thing is for certain, though – it's a much more crowded industry than the secret society that existed back in 2006.

'If only I'd known then what I know now,' Arturo lamented. 'I would have saved more of my money!' He burst out laughing in the stand. 'We would work for a week without any stress, clear anywhere from 5000 to 30,000 euros and then take off to enjoy the spoils in a sunny location. We had weeks on end in Ibiza, the Canary Islands, Greece, the Caribbean, the Amalfi Coast – you name it. We'd party until the cash got low and then book ourselves a flight to the next tennis tournament. Easy as that.'

Why did he have to go and tell me that? I thought I had it good until I heard the stories of the golden days!

*

Sitting in the stand with Arturo this first day is a great introduction to the obscure trading society that is hidden in plain sight, right in front of me. He points other guys out to me, explaining what to look for and where to sit to avoid detection. It's easy for experienced traders to spot one of their own.

'Look for the telltale signs,' he tells me. 'If you see a guy sitting by himself or even two guys in their twenties sitting together, they're most likely trading. My friend down there' – he points towards the front of our stand – 'that's Romeo. I'll introduce you to him later. He's Italian too.'

When I get to know Romeo later, he has no trouble living up to his name. He is a textbook Italian playboy who loves his designer clothes and flaunts his success around the globe. He would regularly show me X-rated photos of his latest exploits and conquests on his phone.

'Okay. And, to the left, see the guy with glasses on? That's my friend Giovanni. He can speak many languages also. So feel free to introduce yourself, his English is good.'

Gio is another talented veteran of the tour who will go on to give me plenty of advice during matches. He even tests my speed skills on his laptop one day to see how good I am. (I score a 0.17, which I am pretty happy about.)

'Behind us, see the guy who looks like Johnny Depp?'

I turn around to see an effortlessly stylish, long-haired dude in a leather jacket and nod.

'That's Vittorio. He's from Naples, so he doesn't give a shit about security problems. There's nothing that worries him on this tour – his home town offers many more intimidating problems than we have to worry about here.'

'Yeah, I can see his hand in his jacket. He's definitely trading.'

'You're learning,' Arturo smiles. 'Tell me if you can spot Leo. He's not far from Vittorio.'

I scan the crowd between the tennis points. It doesn't take long. Another guy wearing glasses is slouched comfortably up to the back left of us. He has his right hand in a satchel, and, once I spot that, I know he is trading too.

'He's not Italian but he is a good friend. Leo is from Madrid, so his Spanish translates quite well with Italian. We all talk together and understand each other. That's not all, though. Over the other side of the court, I can just make out a few of the other guys. There are the English traders, and a few Russians too. Have you met them yet?'

I haven't, but apparently there is a horde of traders present at the event, all cruising under the radar and turning a tidy profit for themselves. If you didn't know what to look for, you'd never have guessed it. I am amazed but excited to learn I will have familiar faces and colleagues I can hang out with during my time on the road.

*

Later, once I settled into the tour, I discovered that most traders are pretty friendly guys. It's worth pointing out that ninety-five per cent of them are male. The combination of gambling, sport and single life on the road must suit men more than women, I guess.

The casual flings and one-night stands are as inherent as any other part of the trader lifestyle. We're young, energetic and ambitious. Meeting girls during our travels is inevitable. Holding on to

them is a much tougher prospect . . . and one we generally give up
on after long enough on tour. There is a glaring absence of girlfriends or steady relationships on the court-sider scene. The truth
is, you can't work full-time on the tour and expect to maintain a
healthy relationship. I watched guys try and fail time after time.
There are exceptions, of course, but, generally speaking, intermit-
tent long-distance relationships are destined to failure.

Having travelled for a few years before joining the tour, I was
accustomed to this kind of life and knew what to expect. I'd had
girlfriends back in Australia but had never really worried too
much about being settled at a young age. It wasn't until I started
travelling and began to connect with like-minded girls from other
parts of the world that I really made the most of my single life,
though. With my new itinerary, I couldn't wait to party around
the world.

After a few tournaments, some of the traders would recognise
me and extend the standard head nod or wink on court. If I
bumped into somebody between matches, we might have a quick
chat about the week and I'd find out a bit about them. Beers on
the weekend were usually a pretty popular suggestion and we
would catch up once the business end of the week had passed.
This is the way I came to meet many traders. We'd hit a bar, order
some food and drinks, celebrate a week of trading and share a
range of stories from all over the tour.

This was how I came to meet the Englishmen Doug, Angus
and Dylan. Doug was an ex-pilot who had lived and travelled all
over the world. Angus was an intellectual who had travelled South
America extensively and had a passion for anything with a Latino
influence. Dylan was a larrikin with a wicked sense of humour
who (to his displeasure) was often told he looked like Peter Andre.
They all loved tennis and a night out on the town. Their back-end

computer whizz was an ex-maths teacher with a genuine love for the language of mathematics and an addiction to online trading. Apparently, he used to drive around the English countryside playing pokies in pubs and draining them of their coins. He had the system figured out and, with his mathematical prowess, knew how to trigger a win.

On one of these late-night expeditions around the local pubs, he was pulled over by the police for a random breath test. When they saw the bags of coins on his car floor, they started asking a lot more questions. According to standard police logic, he was under suspicion of robbing a bank. He had to quickly explain his little charade and assure the officers he hadn't been involved in anything untoward.

While his fund-raising exercise wasn't illegal, it certainly wasn't a conventional way of earning a living. So he graduated to trading after recruiting my new English friends and promising them a generous commission to fly around the world and report on tennis matches. A successful gambling syndicate was born.

I met many traders during my time on tour, but these guys were the ones I spent most time drinking, partying and travelling with (apart from my own co-workers, of course). Traders share a special bond. While we're not the best of mates because we've only known each other a short time, we're all part of a unique society. Yes, we compete against each other but that is accepted as part of the game, so there is rarely any bad blood or hostility between us. It's not like there are many of us out there, so when we all get together outside of work we celebrate and make the most of our time on the road. There's a whole world of bars, beers and good times to be sampled, and we do our best to see them all.

*

Back in Melbourne, Arturo decides to extend some generosity by sharing a tip. The veteran trader fancies himself as a bit of a gambling guru. As a newbie, I'm all ears.

'I'm going to lay Vera Zvonareva tomorrow.'

'Oh, really? Why's that, mate?'

'Well, she just walked past me and she has a few pimples and her breasts looked swollen. I think she's got her period. She's definitely going to lose tomorrow.'

I cough to stifle a laugh and then laugh at him anyway. I can't help it. 'You what?' I ask.

'Yes, she's got her period. So I'll lay her and the other girl will win. That's my tip for tomorrow, my friend.'

'Um, okay. Well, good luck, buddy. I'm keen to see how that pans out.'

That was the most outrageous prediction I'd ever heard. And that was Arturo for you – a funny, intelligent guy who liked to analyse everything and tried to use any form of knowledge to his advantage. He was never a close friend but we became acquaintances and got to hang out in many locations over the next few years. I respected the guy for his sheer ingenuity and free spirit.

I told a few mates of his prediction and we all laughed about it. The beauty of it was – Vera came out the next day and absolutely obliterated her opponent. At one stage, I thought it was going to be a double bagel! I think the match was over in forty-one minutes. I have no idea if she was on her period that day but, if she was, she managed to channel some intense energy into the right aspects of her game!

While traders often take a player's form, fitness and history into account, I think studying a female player's menstrual cycle is going a bit too far. Lucky he didn't get it right – would have been a bloody good guess!

*

With the Brisbane, Sydney and Melbourne tournaments at an end, I pack my suitcase to leave Australia, knowing I won't be back for at least ten months. I've been away longer than that before but I've always had bases – places in which to relax and unwind, to stop and actually unpack my bag and get settled for a bit. This year will be different. The longest I'll spend in one place will be two weeks. Apart from that, it will all be one-week stopovers and backpacking holidays. So I pack the usual: clothes, shoes, toiletries, books, my laptop, iPod, headphones, wallet, passports, documents, and so on.

There are a few other essentials that need to be squeezed in if I am going to enjoy the year, though. First and foremost is my snow gear for weeks off in the mountains. (I am well and truly addicted to snowboarding by this stage.) Then there is my slackline. If you've never heard of slacklining, try to find a video. It's a challenging and enjoyable sport to learn. It improves your balance, core strength and is just plain fun. All you need is some nylon webbing, a few carabiners and two trees or posts to set it up between. It's like tightrope walking but more versatile. This is the perfect travel sport as you can do it anywhere in the world, provided you have a park or some trees about. People love to watch it, too, and often during sessions I'll end up teaching an inquisitive spectator or helping kids to have a go at it.

A few travel adaptors, a pocket knife, a harmonica and, of course, my tennis racquet make up the rest. Last but not least are my new phones: every trader's essential tool. They are my licence to trade. I have learnt the ropes and become familiar with the scene. Now it is time for the real test – I am ready to hit the road.

5

VIVIENDO EL SUEÑO

'Mierda!' yells a frustrated David Ferrer before smashing a ball up into the stand. I've already put the score in but look down to check it's gone through accurately: 30–40. All's well. I look up just in time to see the ball flying straight at me! Reaching forward with my free left hand, I attempt to take an awkward catch at the last second . . . and drop it like a complete butterfingers! The Mexican crowd goes wild, giving me the grief I deserve for such a pitiful effort. I shake my head in disbelief and try to concentrate on the next point when my phone vibrates.

Nads: Nice one muppet! I just saw that on TV haha!

Me: Dammit! Ah well, if that's my darkest moment of the week I can't really complain. I'm soaking up sunrays with nothing but palm trees, surf and sand in sight. Acapulco is insane!

Nads: Nice for some innit? Fkn rained all week here. It's miserable out.

Me: I'm trying to decide whether to go jet skiing or scuba-diving tomorrow . . .

Nads: Enough out of you! Just shut up and concentrate on the tennis, cabrón!

*

This job really was the dream. The road was my home for the next ten months and I liked that just fine. After leaving Australia, I got through a few more tournaments and started to feel like I belonged on tour. I could read points more quickly and easily than before. I knew which tickets would give me the best view on court and I started to get a feel for predicting matches. Hitting the buttons became second nature for me, and I felt at home in the stands watching that little yellow ball bounce back and forth.

I soon realised that one of the main challenges of the job was being able to adapt to and blend into a new environment every week. The last thing we want is to stand out (which can be pretty tough when you're the only white boy in a crowd full of Mexicans). The key is to look like you know exactly what you're doing and where you're going. You need to pretend that you belong so nobody will question you. Easier said than done. With foreign languages, alphabets and customs, you're thrown into the mix from the moment you leave the hotel until the moment you get back. Negotiating taxis, ticket sales and venue layout are all a challenge when you're rushing to get onto the right court for the start of play.

Two weeks earlier, in Memphis, I'd experienced my first security run-in. The tournament director walked up to me as I was leaving one night and said, 'Look, I know what you're doing here and it isn't allowed. There will be no more gambling at my tournament, and, if I see you again, I will personally escort you from the premises.' I played dumb but he was no fool. In the end, I just took his warning and let my co-workers trade the rest of the week.

From Memphis, we flew to a location I'd been looking forward to since I'd first laid eyes on my schedule: Acapulco, Mexico. Tournaments such as Acapulco epitomise the extravagant lifestyle the tour offers. Play started at 3 p.m. every day, so we had plenty of spare time for swimming at the beach, slacklining between palm trees, jet skiing and watching the famous cliff-divers send themselves off thirty-metre ledges. If we wanted to relax, we could chill back at the hotel. Lush gardens, lakes, pools and palm trees surrounded our resort, and the restaurants offered some amazing Mexican fare. The tennis venue itself backed onto the beach, offering a picturesque setting with beer tents and greenery all around.

I didn't learn much as a trader at this tournament, but this was the week when it really sank in for me. I was a lucky bastard and I was determined to make the most of it. To our surprise, we met a couple of Mexican traders – Carlos and Tony – who became good friends. They only worked tournaments in the Americas and were happy to act as our tour guides for the week.

On the Friday night, Carlos and Tony took us out to sample some local food and (in typical Mexican style) to drink tequila shots at the beachside bar. Tequila is the devil as far as I'm concerned. It has made me do outlandish things in my time. But I welcomed it that night to build up some Dutch courage for the bungee jump. It was right next to the bar and hung out over the ocean, staying open late to attract drunken tourists like myself. As soon as I saw it, I vowed I wouldn't leave without doing it.

An hour later, I'm standing on the platform looking out over the dark ocean with alcohol and adrenalin coursing through my veins and sweat beading on my forehead. The gentle sea breeze feels cool against my skin on this warm summer night. Disco music thumps way down below me as the moon glints off the Pacific swell. I draw in a deep breath and try to lower my heart rate. Good fucking luck! My toes are dangling over the edge and I'm all set to jump. The only thing saving me from certain death is the bungee cord wrapped around my legs.

'Let's do this!' I hear myself saying. I'm psyched and ready to go. I've skydived before but bungee jumping is definitely scarier. The mental challenge of overcoming your instincts and throwing yourself into oblivion is both terrifying and invigorating.

'Okay, look out at the camera on that pole and I'll count you down,' says the guide. 'Three. Two. One.'

'Fuuuuck!' gushes from my mouth as I swan dive off the ledge and plummet head first into the darkness below. Just another day at the office in Acapulco!

*

The next day, David Ferrer defeats Nicolás Almagro in an epic, three-set clay-court final – it's an amazing match. A battle between two top-ten players is always a spectacle to watch. Acapulco has been my favourite tournament to date. I never expected a working week to be one of the best weeks of my life.

6

KEEP YOUR EYE ON THE BALL

The text messages I was receiving from the back end read quite similarly to my thoughts: *Shit, shit, shit, fuck, shit, fuck, goddamit! Motherfucker! You stupid son of a bitch!* We'd just lost a lot of money, and it was entirely my fault. I stood up and looked over the railings at the back of the Miami stadium down to the concrete below, feeling like I was about to throw up. Thinking back to Acapulco, I remembered how I'd been so anxious to bungee jump that my mouth had dried up and a swarm of butterflies had bloomed in my stomach. That was nothing compared with the nausea welling up inside of me right now. Give me the bungee any day. I didn't even want the cord after what I'd just done.

Acapulco was a distant memory as I stood on centre court feeling utterly dejected and miserable. The weeks leading up to Miami had been some of the best of my life. Now, I'd just made one of the biggest mistakes of my life.

*

Player fitness is a major factor in a highly physical sport such as tennis, and one of the main reasons why sitting court-side and being able to see the players up close and personal provides such an advantage over gamblers at home. Some gamblers trade off internet scoreboards without even using a television feed. Others watch a television feed but still have the distinct disadvantage of telecast delay and advertisement breaks. If the camera misses a player injury or retirement, those gamblers at home are stranded in their current position. By the time they realise what has happened, they will most likely be unable to trade out of a poor position and their money will be lost. The court-siders, however, will see all of this unfold and have the edge over the rest of the market. If a player calls for a trainer to assist with an injury or cramp, then the court-siders can instantly throw money on the other player, knowing with almost guaranteed certainty that their position will improve. Even if a player grabs at a muscle or grimaces to show some sign of discomfort, the court-siders will be aware and prepared while those at home may not even know it's happened.

The importance of player fitness cannot be overlooked. Gambling thousands of dollars on an injured player is simply not an option. It is an incredibly risky if not entirely foolish one. The best way to prevent this is to simply keep your eye on the ball. Easy, right?

*

It's Saturday and I'm approaching the end of a lacklustre week of trading. I've made a few frustrating mistakes and am yet to secure a decent win at this tournament. Miami is a very cool place, so I'm enjoying the scenery, city, culture and event, but I'm feeling a bit disappointed with my professional performance.

Today, I'm on centre court, which is a treat as I get to kick back in the giant stadium and relax. There have been no security problems thus far, and I've no reason to stress. I grab a seat right up in the top tier so I can trade to my heart's content without the fear of prying eyes. Palm trees and blue water surround the venue, which sits on the picturesque isle of Key Biscayne. There's a light breeze and the sun is beating down, but the heat isn't quite as oppressive as it has been for the past few days. I enjoy a great display of tennis skills from Roger Federer as he defeats Radek Štěpánek in straight sets. I snap a few photos, reapply sunscreen and get ready for the next match.

The crowd favourite and reigning champion Andy Roddick is taking on Pablo Cuevas of Argentina in a second-round clash that also promises to be a quick one. A-Rod is currently ranked number eight in the world and I am hopeful of a swift victory so I can take another small win from a straight-sets affair.

Play commences and I trade away. Andy is playing to quite a mediocre standard but I'm not close enough to notice the subtle signs of physical discomfort. That was my first mistake. Sitting up the back may be a cosy retreat but it's definitely not the best option if you want to keep an eye on everything. So I continue to trade as per usual. Cuevas is playing quite well and manages to break Andy's serve towards the end of the first set. It is slightly unusual yet not completely implausible to see Andy in a losing position.

During the next changeover, my co-worker Felix pokes his head around the gate and waves to me. I'm stoked to see him as he's bought me some lunch. What a guy! A pulled-pork sandwich is just what I was craving, too. I've been stuck in the stand for a few hours without a break and am extremely excited to tuck into a tasty meal. While we exchange some idle chat about the day's tennis and tear into our lunch, Andy Roddick calls for a trainer and doctor to assist him on court. I'm too busy stuffing my face and hearing updates from around the grounds to even notice. I didn't realise just how hungry I was until the food arrived. Now, I can't get enough of it. I'm famished.

'This pulled pork is amazing!' I mumble through a mouthful of food.

'Yeah, figured you'd be hanging for a feed, mate. Enjoy. I had a retirement earlier due to heat exhaustion,' Felix fills me in.

'You lucky bastard! So, what, you've got a bit of spare time before the next match?'

'Yeah, thought I'd bring you some lunch and check out the action on centre.'

'You're a champion, mate. Thanks a lot. This sandwich has saved the day.'

Meanwhile – unbeknown to me – down on the court, Andy gets his pulse and heart rate checked by the doctor. The market goes wild.

'No worries, mate. What match do you have after this one?' Felix gestures towards the court but I don't bother looking up.

If I had done, I would have seen Roddick take a few tablets and inhale from a respiratory puffer. The odds are swinging like crazy. Our system is none the wiser, so we keep taking bets on A-Rod. Here's the problem with using computerised models to gamble – they don't know when a person is injured. They just do what we've programmed them to do, and, without any human intervention, they will keep on doing it. That's one of the main reasons I'm here. Apart from putting in scores, I need to monitor player health and performance. Instead, I'm chowing down on this sandwich like it's the last one left on earth.

'Umm, I'm not sure. It's a women's match but I can't remember who's playing next.'

I've missed the boat. The favourite is looking ill and the market has jumped on an opportunity to back the underdog. Andy has a nasty chest virus and is nowhere near fit enough to play to his full potential. This scene has been unfolding for two minutes on the televised centre court without me paying attention.

When the word 'SHIT!' comes up on my phone's screen repeatedly, I know I've made a big mistake. Considering Roddick's seeding and ability, and due to my lack of attention, we've continued betting on him while the rest of the market has reacted to a sure sign of his poor health. My carelessness has cost a large sum of money in a very small amount of time. To be more precise: in less than two minutes, we've lost around twenty thousand pounds.

That's a lot of people's yearly salary. Gone in two minutes.

'Ohh, sweet Jesus, holy fuck, you have got to be kidding me!' I gush as I read the text.

'What's up?' asks Felix. He's been equally naive and has no idea about the roller-coaster of woe I am currently riding from the core of my brain to the pit of my stomach.

'Oh. My. God,' I manage.

It gets worse as I find out how much damage has really been done, and I go from wanting to shrink into my shoes to craving a quick death via the stadium railings. Felix apologises for distracting me and I assure him the fault lies exclusively with me. My profit margins for the day are well beyond redemption. This whole goddamn week is beyond redemption!

*

I was deservedly chewed out for the blunder and lost my personal bonus that quarter. But that was nothing compared with how bad I felt. Knowing I'd just cost us twenty thousand pounds because I was tucking into a sandwich instead of concentrating on the court-side action was sickening. I felt guilty as hell for a long time after that, and it took over an hour before the sickness in my stomach went away that day.

That particular incident outlined very clearly to me the need to be alert to player fitness and keep an eye out for trainers or signs of injury. I learnt the hard way, but (taking the only positive I can from the experience) I'm glad it happened early in my trading career. I never missed a trainer after that day. Trading is a cut-throat game of numbers, percentages and observations, and if you're not quick enough you stand to lose a lot. Lesson learnt.

*

Andy Roddick never retired that day; he finished the match and was gracious in a straight-sets defeat. Despite his ailment, he went out there and tried his best to give the crowd a show. Unfortunately for Andy (and me), Pablo Cuevas was in great form and took the win. While retirement could have been an easier avenue, A-Rod saw the match out like the good sportsman he is.

However, during tournaments with scorching climates and gruelling match-ups, it is not unusual to see a player retire due to fatigue or injury. In these cases, court-siders can cash in by throwing as much money as possible onto the remaining player. The rest of the market will be oblivious to this development and a large amount of the court-sider's bets may be matched. This is free money because the court-siders know they are betting on the only horse left in the race. They've seen the player retire and are still making bets before the market is shut down. It's not an overly respectable practice because it blatantly takes advantage of less informed people. I can honestly say I never had anything to do with milking a retirement, but I know guys who have made over five grand in a couple of seconds without risking a cent.

If Andy had retired that day, my week could have been very different. The experience made me a much better trader – and I haven't had a pulled-pork sandwich since.

*

Hours later, I find myself in a fun boozer called Sandbar in Coconut Grove, Miami. I'm trying to put a decidedly shithouse week behind me and drink myself out of post-loss depression with a bunch of my mates. The whole crew are out this evening enjoying end-of-week drinks, and as usual we are getting hammered like men on a mission. Vodka, lime and sodas, beers and shots of Jäger are the main orders. The place fills in and gets rowdy. It's a typical American dive bar – plenty of booze, not many rules and heaps of fun to be had with a raucous crowd.

A few of the lads finish their night matches and turn up as reinforcements. By ten, we have a solid crew together and the stories from the week are flying. Who got to watch the best matches, the best-looking girls, the longest three-setters, the most painful and boring duels? (Plus a few obligatory jokes about who made the most gargantuan error in history.) Once we've all had a vent, the chat turns to funnier stories from the road and travels. Then we mix it up at the bar and mingle with the crowd. They're a friendly bunch, and we all do our best to chat up the local girls. Soon enough, I'm standing on a stool hollering and dancing around. I'm not wasted yet but well and truly on the way. I'm in that coherent, excitable mood that I hit when I've drunk a lot in a short time.

Two girls walk past and notice my outlandish behaviour. Somehow, this garners their attention and I yell hello at them. They come over and we hug and talk shit and get to know each other in the way drunk strangers do so well. One is blonde and the other is brunette. I like them both. Amazingly, they both seem to like me. Being forward and friendly, like most American girls, they waste no time in making out with me. Brunette first, blonde second. They then turn to each other and start making out. The boys erupt in cheers. I've got one on each arm and for the first time this week I feel like a complete winner (not to mention a total showboat at the same time). Most the guys in the bar have seen this and are taking notice.

Felix is gleefully snapping photos with his camera and trying to document as much of the action as he can. The girls suggest all three of us make out at once. I concur. What a great idea. I'm as happy as a pig in shit and all the lads are having a laugh, wondering how I managed to swing this bullshit. Then a dude walks right up to me, puts his arm around the blonde girl and extends his other hand for me to shake. I do so, wondering what the deal is, when he introduces himself.

'Hey, bro, I'm gonna have to steal this one away from you,' he says. Damn, that sucks. 'She is my girlfriend after all.' Oh . . . shit. 'But make sure you take good care of my sister, man!' What. The. Fuck? There's not even a hint of menace in his voice! I've just been making out with his sister and his girlfriend in front of everyone at the bar and he gives me credit for it by shaking my hand! I'm lucky I didn't have my head punched in.

So, I make good on his request. I have a few more drinks with the brunette. We dance, make out and talk. I suggest we go back to my place and she agrees. And that's a wrap! Sandbar: five stars! Did I say the week was beyond redemption? As I am quickly finding out, the trader lifestyle is a roller-coaster of extreme highs and lows. I am also realising I much prefer this ride to a week of mundane normality. The clay season is fast approaching, and now that I am a little wiser (albeit poorer), I can't wait to hit Europe for the summer.

7

MONTE CARLO

I'm feeling quite out of my league among a prestigious crowd at the Monte-Carlo Rolex Masters. It's a lavish event, perched on the rocky cliffs of Roquebrune-Cap-Martin, which is actually a stone's throw over the border in France. Although the tournament isn't technically held in Monte Carlo, the stands overlook some of the most cherished and expensive land in the world. I'd hate to think how much the grounds themselves are worth. Millions is probably an understatement. The vista from centre court is nothing short of spectacular. Grand European architecture meets the azure shades of the Mediterranean Sea while rocky cliffs extend high above the arena. It is something special to see. Not to mention the crowd: the rich and famous fill the stands, dressed to the nines in fashion that you only see elsewhere in magazine advertisements or *GQ* exposés. And it's trader heaven!

I've never been to a tournament with more traders. They flock to the gambling haven in droves from Italy, France, Switzerland and all around the world. The top sixty-four male tennis players in the world duke it out for the week on clay courts and we sit in the stands and trade as much of it as we can. To my knowledge, nobody has ever been kicked out of this event for trading. Monaco's image exists because of the gambling industry, and it would be quite hypocritical to evict traders from an event that openly celebrates betting. Here's where tennis runs into a quandary. Many of the event sponsors are gambling companies. Why do the ATP and WTA accept such sponsorship while the officials insist gambling threatens the integrity of the sport?

If the online gambling industry continues to thrive, then tennis may find itself faced with a paradoxical reality: relying on an industry it feels threatened by for support. It would be nice if the two could enjoy a harmonious, symbiotic relationship in the future, but I find it hard to picture with the officials' current stance and intolerance towards gamblers.

*

The Andy Roddick fiasco made me focus a lot more on my responsibilities as a trader. While I was still loving the job, I realised it wasn't all fun and games. Errors of that proportion would not be tolerated and I had to improve if I wanted to remain gainfully employed on the tour. I'd had a volatile start to the year and wasn't confident with my place as a trader until the clay season rolled around. The blunder did, however, make me a better trader. From then on, I was more alert and aware of the subtleties unfolding on court. If a player stretched his or her back, I immediately took note. If someone grabbed at a calf muscle or hamstring, I'd suspend us from taking bets and monitor his or her movements to see if a trainer was called in. I was conscious of players' physical states at all times.

But there still remained one sneaky and frustrating problem that I could not predict: fixed matches. How does one know if a player is throwing a match? Are they having a shocking day? Are they injured? Or are they really fixing a match in front of the entire crowd? As I was about to learn, thrown matches could be even more dangerous than injured players.

*

Felix and I are staying at a beachside hotel on the border of Italy and Monaco. A few of the other boys are staying 'down the road' in Nice. Lodging in the Monte Carlo just isn't an option if you value any of the money in your bank account. Our hotel is perched on a rocky cliff and overlooks a calm Mediterranean Sea. Over breakfast, we get to talk to the owners of the hotel. They are two ladies in their late thirties who can speak Italian, French, English, Spanish and German. The fact that most people in this part of the world can speak several languages leaves me feeling somewhat ignorant and linguistically incapable after my upbringing in Brisbane. That's the only problem with growing up in Australia – our neighbour-less island state has no need to entertain any language other than English. We grow up sheltered from the rest of the world and its wonderful variety of culture. At least I'll get my fair share this week.

After breakfast, we grab our gear and head into the tennis. Our commute is a breathtaking walk along the snaking coastal road into Monte Carlo. I see Arturo, Romeo, Gio, Leo and Vittorio along the way. They are accompanied by about five other Italian traders, whom I've never even seen before. A Swiss guy named Jett joins the trader train too. As we near the venue, not one but two Bugatti Veyrons roll past us, with their beastly engines purring beneath their hoods. We all nod to each other approvingly and admire the vehicles. They're the fastest and most expensive production cars on the planet. Quite fitting that I see my first one in Monaco. Seeing two at once just epitomises this place: opulent and flamboyant to the point of hedonism.

Most tournaments are quite classy events, as tennis is considered an upper-class sport. But the wealth and luxury are in overdrive here. Usually, I can do my best to blend in and feel like I belong at an event. Not here, though. As I walk through the gates, I feel underdressed, obtuse and insignificant. I'm a trader, not a brain surgeon. I watch tennis matches rather than brokering major deals and managing corporations. If I were to sit down at dinner with any of the members present at this event, I'd most likely be marginalised as a nobody with a silly hobby. They'd probably look down at me from their lofty social ranks and judge the nature of my disputably 'shady' employment.

Then I think about the amount of pressure and tension in their lives and I'm quite happy with mine. This is probably the only day of the year when they come to the tennis and enjoy themselves while watching some live sport. It's a daily occurrence for me. Let them judge my gambling endeavours all they want; at the end of the day, I'm still sitting next to them, enjoying the good life.

*

If I were to explain to the pompous people sitting next to me why I am constantly hitting buttons on my phone, they might put the pieces together and feel either annoyed that they didn't think of this whole trading thing themselves or resentful towards the nature of this enterprise. We have the information before the general public, and we purposefully act upon it for personal gain. This leaves the average Joe punters back home at a distinct disadvantage. If the legality and morality of court-siding intrigues you, there are numerous accessible debates raging across online betting forums that you can research. Court-siding is a grey area. Hence it will always be a highly contested and volatile area of discussion in the gambling world.

Now, before we go any further, I want to make my stance on this clear. We are not criminals by any means. I have met numerous traders from every corner of the globe during my time on the tennis circuit, and I can honestly say that none of them have criminal or negative intentions towards the gambling world or the wonderful sport of tennis. They are, however, entrepreneurs and capitalists making a living out of a market that most people don't realise exists. In my opinion, if a group of people have the intellect and audacity to go and commit to something so distinctive and unusual, and be successful at it, then let them have it! Yes, we do have a marked advantage over all other gamblers and yes it is an opportunistic and surreptitious way to make money. The rest of the world might be a little confused and possibly resentful but, considering the lifestyle and profit that is to be enjoyed, I'd take the job every time. I think most people would. I never felt bad about it and I never met another trader who did either. It's an entrepreneurial venture that requires commitment and risk. It's like counting cards; most people wish they could do it but few actually dedicate the time and money to make it a reality. More importantly, only a few have the gall to get out there and give it a shot. Any bet-from-home gambler who complains about court-siders is welcome to take the same initiative and try their luck in the stands with us.

The ATP, WTA and ITF, however, have different ideas regarding this somewhat mysterious and apparently 'shady' practice. As I learnt in Memphis, the officials do not like traders at their events because of their ties to gambling. There are deep concerns about corruption marring the sport. It is no secret that, in the past, tennis players, both male and female, have thrown matches. They will most probably continue to do so in the future. It is a frustrating and demoralising occurrence for any sport, especially one as popular and esteemed as tennis. Who throws these matches? I've heard plenty of rumours about dodgy characters and alleged cheats but I don't have any concrete knowledge of specific incidents outside of the general public's. However, it can be attested that these corrupt players generally sit on the periphery of the rankings and play for countries that don't support their endeavours particularly well. Sponsorship deals, while incredibly lucrative for those at the very top, can only go so far, and those who miss out sometimes look for other ways to fund their bank accounts. In 2007 Russian former top-ten player Nikolay Davydenko was at the centre of a match-fixing scandal after retiring due to injury during a match played in Poland. Betfair refused to pay $7 million worth of bets to several Russian accounts because of the irregular size and suspicious timing of the wagers. Davydenko was cleared of any wrongdoing in 2008. He's an incredibly talented player so I don't figure him for a cheat. Ekaterina Bychkova has publicly spoken about being approached by Russian gambler, Dmitry Avilov, with a proposal to throw a match. She declined but also failed to report the incident and was subsequently fined and suspended for thirty days. I've never met Dmitry and I don't want to. But there have been articles published wherein he speaks openly about his attempts to fix matches. The Russians have definitely had their share of scandals. They love their tennis, gambling and money. Many people also claim they have a powerful criminal network that thrives on corruption and forces players into difficult situations. Spain's Guillermo Olaso claimed to be one of these victims of the Russian mafia at his disciplinary hearing in 2013 (he received a five-year ban and a

$25,000 fine for violations of the Uniform Tennis Anti-Corruption Program). Russia may be in the spotlight but Italian, Dutch, Austrian, Spanish and Serbian players have all been fined and banned from the sport for corruption offences.

As far as corruption in tennis goes, I despise it and have no respect for any professional athlete who takes part in a match knowingly acting to adversely influence or decide the final outcome. The other traders all share a similar perspective, considering we are all, at heart, tennis fans . . . and the fact that a thrown match tends to fuck each and every one of us over in a big way. The governing bodies, however, do not realise this. They believe that the more money available on the gambling market, the more likely it is that a player may be enticed or convinced to throw a match. We are the gamblers, adding money to the market, and, as a result, we are (apparently) part of, if not *the*, problem. This is erroneous, because I have never once met a trader who discussed an intention, past or present, to corrupt the sport. (Not to say this has never happened. I can't testify for everyone out there – that would be naive and impossible.) However, seeing most traders' faces after a suspected thrown match is enough to convince you of their hostility to it.

As I've explained, traders watch the match's progress and try to bet on the likely winner. Thrown matches usually result in the favourite giving away a winning position and uncharacteristically playing to a level well below their standard. This can have horrific results for traders risking large sums of money. Why would a match fixer come to the scene of their crime anyway? Surely, anyone who has fixed a match would sit back in the safety of their own home or be out celebrating their corrupt 'win' on a balcony with some champagne. Let's hope it tastes bitter.

I'm not attacking the tennis authorities in any way here. I understand their viewpoint and respect it. As far as our opinions on corruption go, we're in accordance. It's just a shame there has been no agreement with or tolerance towards court-siders thus far. Communication is the best antidote and unfortunately the governing bodies have chosen not to pursue that avenue with traders. They probably think it's best to ignore us in an attempt to keep a gambling scandal involving tennis out of the media. They may have to rethink their prospective sponsors in the future if they want to maintain a cohesive image, though.

*

I ponder all of these issues as I sit on centre court during this sparkling Mediterranean afternoon. I'm trying to process the vexing spectacle I witnessed unfold on an outside court during my second match today. I'd never seen anything like it. The two players and the court will remain unnamed to avoid any speculation. I have no idea whether this was a thrown match or not, and it is not my prerogative to spark conjecture. But I am perplexed and a little shocked by the incident.

The two players were middle order, talent and ratings wise. The sun had stayed out and I was really enjoying such a relaxed yet upbeat tournament. Between points, I was watching paragliders float down from the rocky cliffs above, envying their view. I'd much rather be paragliding than working, but trading was still an agreeable consolation. There was no threat of security and all of the traders were sitting on court blatantly doing their thing. There must have been ten of us around the court. It was fun to sit there and spot new traders while they worked in the stands, like a real-life version of *Where's Wally?*. Unfortunately, the fun did not last long. The match was into the second set and we were in a good position . . . when the shit hit the fan. Although, it wasn't the explosive affair you might expect from such an idiom – it was a slow revelation that ground its way into our consciousness and left us all stunned and outraged.

The player in the lead was serving for the set. After playing a good game of tennis, his serve was easily broken. This happens often, so the shit hadn't hit the fan at that stage. But it was on a collision course. He lost the next game and suddenly the momentum had swung from the commanding position of 5–4 to the nail-biting apex of 5–6. Then, the player who appeared to be choking called for the trainer. He was given on-court treatment and the proverbial shit finally made contact with the rotor blades. It flung around the court in slow motion, taking another twenty minutes to really splatter across the stands. That's how long it took for our possibly injured choker to lose the next game and the following set 6–0.

It was all over. The traders jumped up and swore in a swathe of European cuss words. *'Vaffanculo!' 'Mierda!' 'Che cazzo?' 'C'est des conneries!'* I could see them animatedly talking to each other, arguing and debating over the outcome. Vittorio even turned and kicked his chair. He was so angry he snapped the bloody thing in half! I looked around the court in alarm, still unsure what had happened. My communication with the back end had been at a minimum during that quick set and I had yet to find out the repercussions. The following conversation ensued:

Me: Nads, what the fuck happened there?

Nads: You tell me, buddy. We just got fucked big time!

Me: Oh, no! How bad? Looks like every trader on here did too!

Nads: Pretty bad, mate – worst loss since Roddick.

Me: What? Fucking hell, I do not need that next to my name! How did it happen?

Nads: Well, we were big into 'the choker' when he was serving for it.

Me: Fair play. I suspected enough. Would have made sense at the time.

Nads: Exactly. But, just as he got broken, somebody on the market threw a truckload of cash on his competitor. By the time the trainer came out, our money was already matched and we had no way of escaping our position. We got taken to the cleaners.

Me: That sounds dodgy as hell to me. You think it was fixed?

Nads: Hard to say, mate, but it sure looks suspicious, doesn't it?

I looked around the stand again and saw traders shaking their heads as they left. We'd all been screwed out of a significant amount of cash, and it appeared someone had known something before everyone else. Could it have been one of the traders on court? I doubted it. I knew most of them and nobody looked the least bit impressed. Could it have been fixed? Possibly, but I sure like to think not. The fact of the matter is someone could have easily arranged for a bet to take place at a certain point in the match. Now, that would suggest the match was fixed, and the realisation that I may have just witnessed such corruption left a sense of revulsion in my stomach as I left the stand.

Incidents like this one are exactly why the tennis officials despise us. I can see why they want us banned from their events. From their perspective, we are a viable threat. All it would take is a few bad eggs to do great damage to the sport. But why not communicate with us and clear the air rather than blindly label us as 'rodents' and incense us to the point of mutual loathing? We could be an asset rather than a scapegoated enemy.

To combat such incidents, the governing bodies formed the Tennis Integrity Unit (TIU) in 2008. On the unit's official website, it states, 'This decisive action followed publication of a comprehensive, independent report into the risks and threats that faced tennis as a sport subject to ever-increasing attention from the gambling community.'

Interesting, then, that the governing bodies still allow gambling companies to promote themselves by sponsoring tennis events. The TIU has the power to investigate players, coaches, officials and any other would-be corruptors. They can request phone records and bank details, and interview anyone under suspicion. They also liaise with the large gambling companies to identify any suspicious betting patterns or incidents that may have taken place during matches. If they do identify a breach in the anti-corruption code, the TIU can fine players hundreds of thousands of dollars and/or ban them for life from the sport.

Good. Fuck every corrupt player out there, and anyone else involved, whether they be officials, coaches, traders or various nefarious others. The TIU is a proactive initiative from the governing bodies to stamp out corruption in the sport, and so far they have had some success. I sincerely hope they continue in their endeavours and keep tennis a clean and respectable sport. I just wish they'd come to a better understanding of traders' intentions on court and stop harassing us like we're the kingpin criminals! They could save us all a lot of time and money!

*

Like most people, I try to clear my head and forget about this crap once work finishes for the day. I'm in Monte Carlo, after all, and we are going out. It's not every day you go and hit the tables at *the* Monte Carlo Casino. After passing the strict dress standards at the entry, we grab a few drinks and take in the view. The establishment practically doubles as an art gallery, and many fine paintings adorn the walls. 'People watching' is also an entertaining option, as half the patrons have bodyguards, chauffeurs, trophy wives and fat stacks of chips to play with. We take our drinks to the roulette tables for a quick dabble, and exhaust our relatively limited funds in no time at all. I keep one of the sparkly orange chips as a memento (yes, it's only a five-euro effort), and I still have it to this day. We leave the ultra-rich in their casino and once outside realise we're standing next to the famous Formula One track.

'Hey, I recognise this hairpin corner from *Gran Turismo* on PlayStation!' shouts Felix.

We proceed to run around the track, making revving engine noises like complete dickheads, pretending to be cars. To think we were rubbing shoulders with the rich and famous a few minutes ago.

When we come to our senses and find a suitable venue (it takes some time as we don't want to sit down at a billion-dollar buffet), we enjoy an indulgent dinner. It is amazing. It has to be. There are no cheap options available. It's either an expensive restaurant or private dinner on a yacht where your personal crew serves champagne and caviar. While some of the lads have had a profitable day's trading, none of us owns so much as a private canoe. We opt for an expensive three-course-restaurant meal like the other plebs of Monaco.

*

After a busy working week, I'm rewarded with a bit of leisure time. I realise I'll be spending most of my downtime in Nice, so I switch hotels to stay with the other lads. The train ride along the Côte d'Azur is the definition of a Mediterranean scenic coastal route. As I walk out of the station, I immediately notice a change in pace and atmosphere. Monte is nice but Nice is nicer. Monte has the über-expensive casinos and egotistical celebrities, but it can keep them, as far as I'm concerned. Nice is more my speed: a party town of raucous bars and nightclubs nestled amid cosy cobblestoned alleyways and quintessential European streets, all overlooked by a lofty vantage point and girt by the sparkling aqua-blue sea.

In the new hotel, I find a brochure that advertises helicopter transfers from Nice into Monaco. It takes seven minutes and costs over a hundred euros per person. Unfortunately, that's not an option after our huge loss earlier in the week. It would have been a pretty unique transit to start off a working day, though! It blows my mind to realise that some of the spectators I shared the stand with today will no doubt have taken the chopper in to save their precious time. *C'est la vie* in the playground of Europe's rich and famous.

Saturday morning, I manage a sneaky side trip to Cannes to see what all the fuss is about. It's a debonair destination, and I enjoy wandering in and out of designer boutiques, watching the rich and famous drive their supercars, and most of all sitting in as a spectator while the old messieurs go about their traditional games of boules. Regrettably, I can't stay all day – I've got an afternoon session to trade, and I need to purchase a second-hand ticket before they're all gone.

By the time I arrive at the venue, tickets are being resold by touts for a small fortune. After some unsuccessful haggling, I cough up the ridiculous asking price and jump on the charming centre court for a final session of trading that week. Nadal is set to continue his clay warpath and secure yet another victory at this coveted event. Although I've mentioned how I tire of his grinding, defensive style of play, it's still an honour to watch the king of clay in his element. There's no denying that he is one of the all-time greats.

Work, however, is the lacklustre part of the day. After catching the train back along the coast, I meet up with my co-workers and a bunch of other traders. We enjoy an affordable pub dinner for a change, hit the beers and shots, tell stories, debate the suspicious happenings of earlier in the week and have a cracking night out that escalates into an early morning. I end up making the acquaintance of a lovely Norwegian girl and we wander back to the hotel through the pleasant streets of Nice. Life is grand on the Côte d'Azur . . . If only I didn't have to fly to Africa tomorrow.

8

THE CANCER OF TENNIS

I'm trudging down a dirt road, without a soul in sight, lost, rattled and alone after just being threatened with wrongful imprisonment. Night is fast approaching and the chirping of crickets in the long grass by the road does little to ease my nerves. I'm a long way up shit creek. My phone is my only friend. Not to mention my worst enemy. I text my current predicament to my workmates – if only to complain – but there's not much they can do for me. It's always my bloody phone that gets me into these situations. My next text says it all: 'Why the hell did we have to come and trade in Morocco?!'

*

I *could* have been enjoying an epic week of sunshine, beaches and comfortable trading in Estoril, Portugal. I could have been flirting with Corona's charming promotional girls, drinking free beers, playing tennis with my mates and sneaking in a surf of a morning. A few of the other lads had scored that one, though, so I was stuck with Africa.

After our enjoyable week on the Côte d'Azur, Felix and I flew from Monte Carlo to Casablanca, where we then took a five-hour train ride from Casablanca to Fez. At one point, a young boy entered the carriage with some naan bread and offered it to every person in there, including us. We accepted his offer and enjoyed some scraps of the delicious bread, but when we tried to reciprocate later with a bag of potato chips from the food cart it didn't quite match his generosity.

After a long, tiring day of travel, we looked forward to crashing in the comfort and solitude of our hotel. Alas, our taxi rolled straight past the luxurious hotel where the players were staying and pulled up at a very average-looking abode. We'd booked ourselves into a dive by accident! In developing countries, anything below three stars is the equivalent of a first-class shithole. The place stank. The mattresses felt like lumpy concrete covered in sheets, and the pillows were like bags of potatoes. The flashy hotel next to us was booked out. After living it up for the past week, we came plummeting back down to earth with the stench of sewage in our nostrils. It was going to be a long week, and we hadn't even seen the tournament yet.

After eating a bland breakfast of bread and pastry, and checking the order of play, we packed our gear and made our way to the tournament. There were no matches of interest being played today, and that was not going to change all week. Our taxi cost next to nothing, and we finally found something positive about Morocco – we'd spend very little cash here this week.

The grounds were miles from town. Entering them proved a unique challenge. Upon trying to walk in, we were asked for our tickets. When we explained that we didn't have any but wanted to purchase some, there was confusion. Apparently, this was an 'invitation only' event, and you had to have a personal invite from the tournament director to enter.

'Okay, so how do we get one of those?' I enquired.

We were ushered into an official booth and given stamped tickets for next to nothing. Evidently, that was all it took. We walked into the dilapidated grounds and got the lie of the land.

Fez is a major contender for the 'world's shittiest tennis tournament' award. The players seem to agree – the top seed for the tournament was ranked forty-two in the world. There were zero traders present at this event, and for good reason. Fez is on the 'no go' list for traders. There are certain tournaments you just do not go to, unless you want to run the gauntlet of third-world police integrity. Morocco, Malaysia and India are all on this list. China, Russia, Croatia and Bulgaria are not far behind. There is never a moment when you feel comfortable or relaxed while trading in these countries.

None of our crew had ever suffered anything harsher than a slap on the wrist while being booted out of a tournament. However, there was the story of Leo being arrested and detained in a Kuala Lumpur jail for nine days. I'd had my doubts about this story until I had dinner with Leo and Giovanni one night at a pub in Houston, Texas.

'So, dude, tell me: you seriously got banged up in KL?'

'Yes, don't ever go there. It's bad news. I'm never going back.'

'Yes, but this madman returned after a previous warning!' interrupted Giovanni.

Leo explained how he'd been thrown into a cell full of rough local inmates and had to literally fight his way through the week. All they had to eat was rice, which they scrapped over and scoffed with their hands. One night, he awoke to the sound of loud panting nearby. He sat up to see one of the inmates kneeling across from him with his pants down. The creep was staring straight at Leo and jerking himself off! This led to yet another awkward but necessary fight. Needless to say, Leo was more than relieved to escape from that place. He didn't quit trading, though; he was just a lot smarter in the future. Once that story spread, and we all knew the stakes, all of us traders were a little more cautious.

*

Yet, here we are, trading like fools in the simmering frying pan that is Fez. Being a relative newcomer to the game, I'm eager to impress and will trade any tournament. Felix and I split up to avoid being caught together and head off to our designated courts. It is downright awkward being here. As the only white spectator, I stick out like dogs' balls and know it's just a matter of time until somebody notices me. But I am there to do a job, and I get right to it on centre court, where massive cracks run through the shoddy clay surface.

I walk onto a concrete stand across from the umpire that's completely empty and baking hot in the open glare of the sun. I sit down for a grand total of twenty seconds then get the fuck out of there. After rounding the court, I manage to sneak into a VIP section and trade from the relative comfort of a tented area. Being a white, middle-class male from Australia means I still stand out – it does not matter where I go in this tournament. The only other spectators present are suited officials or locals in burqas and kaftans. To my surprise and relief, I survive the first two matches and we do rather well from them.

I have a break before my next match is due to start so I try to track down some food. After walking around for a few minutes and having no luck, I ask one of the event staff if they can point me in the right direction. Coincidentally, the guy is a chef and walks me to the main food tent, where a buffet is being served. *Oh, shit*, I realise, *he thinks I'm a player or a coach*. I am given my own table and full access to the feast on offer. What am I going to do: get up and leave? I fill my plate and eat like a king. *If I'm going to be eating couscous off a cell floor for the next nine days, I may as well get my fill now*, I figure. It is uncomfortable, though. Players walk by and look at me with confusion. I don't want to make conversation in case people pry about my business here, so I keep to myself and get out of there as soon as possible, making sure to thank the chef for his hospitality on the way out.

I then do the rounds of the venue. There isn't much to see. They have a few stands selling drinks and old confectionery in faded packets, a small park and a few practice courts that are in even worse shape than the match courts.

No sooner have I sat down and set up my phone to begin trading the next match than an official approaches me. With his seedy moustache and tacky suit he looks like an angry Moroccan version of Borat.

'You! Come with me now!'

He is acting like a man whose time is too valuable for this altercation. I pause my phone and say, 'What's the problem?' It's worth a try.

'Shut up and follow me,' he says.

Bluffing is not an option, apparently. We head towards the front office but on the way he stops to talk to another official. I am not going to wait around like some sacrificial lamb, so I keep walking towards the exit.

'Hey! Stop!' he shouts.

'What's the problem?' I ask again. 'I'm going to leave.'

'No, you're not,' he corrects. 'Unless you want me to get *their* attention?'

He motions towards the exit and I see five policemen with rifles over their shoulders. They lounge about, idly chatting to each other. But they would jump at any second if summoned by an official. Running is not an option either.

'Shit! This guy has got me!' I curse under my breath. It is the first time I've been properly busted in four months on the job. Another official joins us as I am walked into the front office.

'Passport,' cranky Borat demands.

I've heard that in many countries you need to have your passport on you at all times. I'd love to know how many people actually do this. I'm not one of them. I feel like telling him to fuck himself on the spot but a degree of caution is needed here. The tournament is organised and funded by King Mohammed VI of Morocco, whose wife is apparently a big tennis fan. Any official contracted to work this tournament is obviously on good terms with King Mohammed VI. It would be quite unwise to tell the King's friend to go and fuck himself.

'I don't have my passport with me,' I say.

'Give me your passport!' He slams a fist on the table rather impatiently, as if I am playing games he doesn't have time for.

'Sorry, I honestly don't have it with me.'

At this point, the other official steps in to mediate before things get out of hand. They question me as a team and settle for my driver's licence. Then they take a photo, which I'm unable to dodge. They ask for my room key from my wallet to copy down my hotel details.

'Why do you need that? That's of no relevance.'

'We must have your passport details. You have left these details with the hotel, no?'

Shit. Why is the passport so important? 'No, you don't need it. You've already got my details.'

'Passport or jail!' Borat snarls, stamping his index finger on the desk.

'Jail? I haven't done anything illegal.'

'My friend, the police outside will believe what *I* tell them to believe. So, if I tell them to arrest you, they will arrest you and throw you in jail. You are on thin ice now. I'd make a sensible decision if I was you.' The aforementioned ice shoots through my veins.

Friend, my arse!

I have no idea what the inside of a Moroccan jail looks like, but, after seeing my 'three star' hotel room, my imagination fails to render anything remotely habitable. I give them my room key. The other choice seems a little dicey for my liking. While the director is copying down my room details and calling the hotel, the other official starts talking to me.

'Why do you come here, man? This is really a stupid thing to do.' His accent is thick and undeniably French.

'It's my job,' I shrug.

'Yes. You work for gamblers. I know, I know. You make money and fly around the world like some rock star. But why come here? Go to Europe – Spain, Portugal, wherever, man – just don't do this stupid shit in Africa!'

I have to admit, the Frenchman has a point.

'This gambling is no good for the game,' he continues. 'You really are the cancer of tennis!'

'The cancer of tennis?'

'Yes. We have big concerns with integrity in this sport. You are only making things worse with your gambling.'

I have to tread lightly here – I don't want to get into some dispute about alleged match fixing that I have nothing to do with. Better to just let the topic lie. But he's questioned my integrity after what evil Borat has just threatened me with? These guys are such fucking hypocrites!

'Can I have my things back, please? I'll be leaving now if we're done here.'

The Frenchy returns my belongings and I turn to leave.

I walk out the door, eyeing the police as I approach the tournament exit. To my relief, they ignore me.

I walk around the entire complex but there is not a single taxi in sight. I have a phone number but the operators only speak Arabic. There is no way I am going back to the police or angry official for help, so I set off down the road in the direction that I assume will take me to the city. I spend the first five minutes looking back over my shoulder, wondering if anyone is going to come and apprehend me. A quick getaway would have been nice in this situation. Instead, I trundle down the dirt road unhindered, with nothing but crickets for company while the sun sets on the rocky peaks and silhouetted minarets of this breathtaking North African landscape.

*

Court-siding is not illegal in Morocco. So why was I being threatened with wrongful imprisonment in an African jail cell? Well, let's take another trip to the classroom.

Countries such as the United States, China, Spain, France and Australia are still yet to legalise in-play gambling online, and many of their respective inhabitants are completely unaware of the industry's existence. In these countries, you cannot log on to your Betfair account and trade matches while they are live. Instead, you're stuck with the old form of straight betting. Technically. The way around this is to use a server based in another country. These are easily available for purchase from numerous countries where in-play gambling is legal. This little loophole allows people to travel to countries such as the United States and

China and trade tennis matches. However, it can result in some very unsavoury reactions from security guards, officials and police if they realise what you are up to. Legally, you cannot be prosecuted because you are trading through a remote server in another country where the practice is legal. This can cause a lot of confusion with the authorities, though, and in developing countries they don't look kindly upon you straddling the legal line and rubbing it in their faces.

At some stage, a supposition was made that all traders must somehow be linked to illegal practices and corruption. We are now regarded as threats to the integrity of tennis and are vilified as a result. The officials have taken their stance and aim to convince security personnel, police and anyone else who will listen that we are the enemy and must be dealt with accordingly.

Because of this misperception, we are hated and pursued by event officials, and, in effect, by security teams. They choose to believe we are all degenerate gambling scum seeking to corrupt the sport and make an easy buck. In reality, most traders are intelligent people who use their brains to calculate odds and go to extreme lengths to be court-side at as many matches as possible. Traders are mathematicians, entrepreneurs, travellers and sports fans before anything else. Gambling barely even comes into the equation if you're following a strict model or working with algorithms. Corruption certainly does not.

So, the officials have made it one of their main concerns to have event security search the stands for any spectators who look like they might be trading. Profiling a trader isn't particularly hard – I assume they know to look for people sitting by themselves, generally male, mid-twenties to thirties, constantly using their phone or tapping some kind of device. While the Grand Slams and Masters are huge events, some of the more intimate tournaments provide little space to blend into. Especially when you're a Caucasian in China or Morocco.

That day, in the office in Fez, I saw an official folder containing photographs and details of traders who had been previously ejected from events. My profile was no doubt added to that folder, and at future tournaments I would see security teams referring to a folder while pointing me out. Once security identifies somebody they think is trading, they will walk up to that person in the stands, and the first thing you hear is usually, 'Can you come with us, please?' It's a demand rather than a question. If you don't cooperate, they call the police, and while the police cannot do much because no crime has been committed, it creates an embarrassing scene fraught with tension.

Most of the time, the police are polite and ask you not to return to the venue. Sometimes, they will issue a trespass warning to prevent your legal return. Only in very rare circumstances are you threatened or physically handled – this only happens in undeveloped countries, where overzealous security personnel know they can get away with it.

The look of pure scorn in these people's eyes is not a nice thing to see – especially when I'm just doing my job to earn a regular wage and enjoy a travelling lifestyle. Gambling seems to divide people in very strange ways: many are indifferent to the practice and don't see it as an issue; some love it; and others hate it. Personally, I find it ridiculous to have a finger pointed at me by an official who is labelling me as a 'gambler' (a word they spit with venom, as if talking about a thief or murderer). Yes, I work for a gambler. At what point do our perceptions vary so differently? I'm not Al Capone, and I don't know anybody who has any ties to illegal gambling, organised crime or anything that would raise a police officer's eyebrows. However, I do enjoy an extraordinary lifestyle, and the fact that my line of work funds it infuriates a number of people.

Thinking back to the suspicious and possibly thrown match in Monte Carlo a week earlier, I can understand why the officials took their stance. Corruption is a vile thing that should be eradicated if possible. It erodes and degrades the sport. They must see us living it up and draw conclusions about our involvement in these situations. I just wish they could see how it affected traders around the court that day and understand that we share the same perspective on this issue.

While the officials might have a somewhat jaded or exaggerated opinion of my lifestyle, at the end of the day it is still a job. Like all jobs, I have to accept responsibilities and compromises. You don't finish a week of work in Shanghai then jump on a ten-hour flight the next morning to arrive in freezing cold Moscow for fun. It's a job and it requires dedication. Sometimes, there are days on end when I feel worn down, exhausted and delirious. Then there are others when I'm literally on top of the world, on rooftop infinity pools or ski-resort lifts. The good times far outweigh the bad, and there is no way I am going to give this amazing opportunity away after one prickly situation.

*

I'm fairly sure I'm walking in the direction of the town but it was a twenty-minute cab ride here this morning and I never had my bearings in the first place. This has quickly become a dire situation. I've been in this city for one day, I barely speak a word of Arabic and the sun has already set. A lot of people would be panicking right about now. I'm comfortable in most places around the world these days. I'm also an optimist and generally assume everything will work itself out in due time. However, I must admit, there is an undeniable shard of anxiety edging its way into my mind. Nothing but garbage, rubble, stray animals and desert surrounds me. I'm lost, and my phone is running out of battery.

I wander for another fifteen minutes without seeing a single soul. The haunting sounds of the call to prayer and kawala flute drift on the breeze from a distant minaret. After a lengthy trek through the nether regions of outer Fez, I finally spot a glimmer of hope: a sealed road with some semblance of civilisation on it. I run to the road and, after a few minutes, see what I've been hoping for. A tiny red car pulls over to my flailing arms and I jump in.

'As salam a'leykum.' I show him my hotel card and he takes off with the obligatory 'Salam'.

I have next to no money left on me. But that's not an issue because – as we know – the cab ride will cost exactly that. Upon arriving at the hotel, I ask the receptionist whether anyone has called asking questions about me. She is shifty in response and looks at me like I'm some devious bastard. What has she been told?

'I gave them this number, as requested,' she replies, pointing to the entry stamp on my passport.

This is a disturbing development. The sooner I get out of here, the better. I storm into the hotel room to find Felix chilling out on his computer.

'You got booted too?' he asks.

'Yeah, mate. Pretty heavy, huh?'

'Yeah, that tournament director is a dick! Sorry I couldn't warn you – my batteries ran out before I got a chance.'

'All good. He's a major dick, isn't he? There's no way I'm going back there.'

'Nope, neither of us are. I've just been speaking to Nads. Our week here is up. We may as well split tomorrow and take our holiday a few days early.'

'Oh, that is the best news I've heard all day!' I throw Felix a high five in celebration. No more stinky rooms or need to fear tap water!

'Hell, yeah! Portugal here we come!'

Cervejas, surf and sun await. The next morning, our check-out from both the hotel and country go smoothly. By that afternoon, we are picking grilled chorizo and brie off the barbecue and sipping Portuguese beers as we watch the sun set over the Atlantic. It has been an eventful couple of days. We are out of the fire and back in the fun.

9

THE ITALIAN JOB

As I log points from a shady outside court in Madrid, I'm alert to
the threat of being dragged out by some angry security officers.
They don't mess about at Spanish tournaments, and I've heard of
mates being kicked out and even beaten by police in this country.
The discipline here is a little heavy-handed compared with most
Western European countries. I'm not exactly stoked to be in
Madrid. It's an arid, dusty, landlocked city and none of its sights
or landmarks interest me. On top of that, this tournament has a
reputation as one of the hardest to trade. The event takes place in
the new and impressive grounds of La Caja Mágica ('The Magic
Box'), where the giant steel stadium boxes glint in the sun and the
temperature rarely drops to a comfortable level.

Clay season is in full swing and my trading has been solid
since Miami. This segment of the tour is arguably the most
important for the players. There are three Masters tournaments
and two Grand Slams in the space of three months. Thousands of
rankings points are up for grabs and many pivotal matches are
played. It's definitely the most labour-intensive time of the year

for traders. This means we need to be on the ball and lying low at the same time. Making a splash on the officials' radar could be devastating at this stage.

As I try my hardest to sink into my seat on the outside practice court and trade a match that is actually happening on a different court across from me, I keep my eyes peeled and have time to reflect on this strange game we play.

*

It really is a bizarre existence, hiding from a group of people who are out to get you for something that is not illegal. They don't know me. I don't know them. But we're brought together by fate from different corners of the world to act out this stealthy pantomime while the rest of the crowd watch on and clap, totally oblivious. It's constant cat and mouse across the world. Each week, we have a new security team and tournament director to deal with, new courts and grounds to work around. It's a funny, uncanny, exciting challenge, and it makes for an amusing day of work.

However, the cardinal sin is getting another trader blacklisted through association. This is why we often only extend a head nod or wink and keep walking. If someone is watching us, we'll ignore the others. They understand. In fact, they appreciate it. At certain tournaments, where we feel safe, we'll all sit together and have a laugh. At others, it's every trader for himself, and we keep to ourselves as a sort of professional courtesy. If you get pinched, you never tell security there are other traders inside. If they ask, you laugh at the suggestion and pretend you're a lone ranger.

*

The next week in Rome, I realised being a lone trader wasn't always the safest option. I was also shocked to learn that security and police officers weren't always our biggest concern.

After escaping unscathed from Madrid, we flew to Rome to cover another clay court Masters. Here was a European city I could really enjoy my time in. Rome's sights and attractions seem almost endless when you first visit the city. What's most amazing about the place is how integrated all the historical sights are within the modern city structure. You can be walking around a corner of the CBD when suddenly, bang, there's the Colosseum in all its ancient glory. The same goes for the Pantheon, the Trevi Fountain, the Spanish Steps and the Vatican. There are countless landmarks and structures to take in during a visit to this culturally rich metropolis.

The tennis is held inside the Foro Italico sporting grounds. The venue is a product of Fascist architecture, decorated by statues and soaring umbrella pine trees. One of the courts is even built into the ground, lending a gladiatorial feel to the arena. We didn't have a sniff of trouble in the security department. Similarly to Monte Carlo, this event is a trading mecca. The Italian traders sit together in groups, visibly relaxed at their home event, and comfortably trade the week out. I'm instantly put at ease by their nonchalance and feel safe here. That is until I meet up with Mikka and hear his story.

Mikka's from Estonia and can party with the best of them. He once went out in Tallinn, Estonia, for a heavy night on the booze, only to wake up disorientated and hungover in . . . Finland! (Apparently, they'd 'commandeered' then sailed a boat over the Gulf of Finland in their revelry during the wee hours of the morning!) Mikka has an absurd accent from hanging out with English, Swedish and Australian guys. It's some mongrel breed of

Scando-cockney-Saffa that can be quite entertaining to listen to. Sometimes, he sounds South African, although in the same sentence he might pronounce something like a Londoner. Two seconds later, he's calling you 'mate' and you could swear he was Australian. But most of the time he just sounds like a Scandinavian, which is weird enough. I've only met him a few times by this stage and we really know each other through friends.

'Hey, Mikka, how you been, mate?' I ask, taking a seat next to him in the cafe.

'Eh? Fooken sheet, mate. I'm over this fooken place, I'll tell ya that much.'

'Woah, really? Why, dude? What's wrong?'

'These fooken Italians is what's wrong. I tell you, don't ever troost 'em.'

'Seriously? What happened?'

'I was walking home last night all by myself,' he begins. 'I walked through this fooken, like, some alleyway.' He gesticulates to illustrate the setting. 'And these fooken Italian punks tried to roll me!'

'What?'

'Yeah, that's what I said. There were like foive of 'em. Came up from both sides and fooken trapped me there. I was like, "What's this sheet about?" and they told me to hand over my phone. Didn't take my wallet. Didn't go through my bag. Didn't want sheet except my phone. You know what that means, right?'

'They wanted to know what you were trading with?'

'Exactly. The fookers can't handle that I'm beating them, so they're trying to steal my technology.'

'That's bullshit!' I exclaim. 'Did you belt them?' Mikka is a pretty big guy and does a lot of training; he can handle himself, and it surprised me that anyone even tried to mug him.

'Ah, nah, couldn't really. I mean I might have been able to but what the fook, eh? It's just a stupid phone. They can have it. I didn't wanna fight foive of 'em in some alleyway. Someone could have had a knife or some sheet – not worth it, eh?'

'Yeah, fair enough,' I concede. 'I just can't believe they'd do that shit! Did you recognise any of them? Like were there any traders we know there?'

'Nah, of course not. But they were put up to it by some of the other Italian guys. Everyone knows the Italians all work together.'

'Yeah, that sucks, mate.'

I try to digest all this. If other Italian traders put the muggers up to it, it's possible that guys I consider friends were responsible. Surely Arturo or Giovanni would never have anything to do with this? Could Vittorio's connections be involved? It is Rome, after all. It makes me wonder how deep these gamblers run with syndicates or whether organised-crime families such as the mafia might even be involved in some way. It's all fun and games to me, but these guys are willing to mug a fellow trader just to get the edge. They must be pretty serious (and desperate) to do such a low thing. I am disgusted and baffled. Mikka is right – who can I trust?

I keep my head down and trade the rest of the week in Rome without incident. I avoid the Italian traders – not because I am afraid of them but because I know I would say something and probably end up in a fight or at least an argument over what they allegedly did to Mikka. We have a good thing going and there is no need to cause trouble like that. Most traders have always got along well, so I just can't understand why such a disrespectful and unnecessary thing like that happened.

We never got any answers, either. Over time, the incident was forgotten, but an unspoken rift between us and some of the Italians remained from then onwards. It appeared that, for traders, room for complacency was getting smaller and smaller. The golden days were long gone and now we were all faced with the ever-tightening grip of security officers and technological advances that cut our profit margins. Greed and corruption were becoming all-too-familiar themes on the tour. My mates and I tried our best to distance ourselves from the drama and focus on the fun. Unlike the Italians, we weren't just in it for the money.

Speaking of which, it is time to board yet another plane. The two mid-year Grand Slams are fast approaching and we need to focus up. We will have to be on our A-game to take advantage of the busiest month on the tennis calendar.

10

CRAZY TOUTS
AND TAXI DRIVERS

My taxi driver beeps his horn and makes an aggressive lane change on one of the most recognisable roundabouts in the world, where car insurance is allegedly invalid – the Arc de Triomphe. I've just caught the train down from Brussels, where I traded my way through a somewhat boring and uneventful week by myself. I've been to Paris before, so I'm hardly in awe of the landmarks around me, but it is pleasant to take in the famous scenery again. I'm curious to see what Roland Garros is like, as I've heard mixed reviews from my co-workers. It will no doubt be a busy week – the Grand Slams always are.

After a short while, the taxi rolls to a stop in a typically tight Parisian side street only a few hundred metres away from the Eiffel Tower – not a bad spot to stay in for the week! I'm about to pay the driver when all hell breaks loose. A horn sounds from a white Prius behind us, followed by what I can only guess to be French profanity. My driver is nonplussed by this initial outburst and waves the other car past. It's a very tight squeeze and the other driver is nowhere near as relaxed about the situation. As he pulls up level with my driver's window, he unleashes a barrage of French insults that I can only assume to be much worse than the first, because he really hits a nerve this time. My driver shouts back in outrage and shakes his fist as the Prius speeds away. I have one foot out the door when my angry chauffeur stomps on the accelerator. I barely save my bag from becoming roadside debris and manage to slam the door closed when I realise we're in a full-on chase – this is *The Italian Job* in Paris.

The French curse words flow thick and fast from both cars, and as we pull up at a red light behind the offending driver and his passenger, my driver jumps out of our car and runs towards the Prius. This is especially not cool with me because he has left the handbrake off! As the car begins to roll backwards with me in it, the traffic light turns green. My driver realises his folly and bolts back to the taxi just in time to catch the lights – thanking me for grabbing the handbrake. Now the people in the Prius are rattled and most likely regretting their little outburst. They hit a random and illegal U-turn in the middle of a four-lane road in an effort to evade us.

It's nowhere near random or illegal enough, though – my driver has obviously clocked his fair share of hours behind the wheel in Paris. Unfortunately for them, this manoeuvre quickly leads them into gridlocked traffic stuck at another red light. Now it's really on. The driver runs up to their window shouting offences and making aggressive hand gestures. He's even had the decency to use the handbrake this time. The Prius driver gets his window up just in time to avoid a beating, but that doesn't stop my driver from punching the shield repeatedly and spitting on it in disgust – all the while surrounded by traffic and awestruck bystanders.

A moment later, he hops back in the car and calmly apologises to me. 'Sorry. I'm very sorry for you to see this. This man . . . he is so rude. I cannot describe.'

'It's cool, man,' I reply, not really knowing what else to say. I laugh a little; it can't be helped after what I've just seen.

'I will change this.' He points to the meter, which is still running.

'Oh, nah, don't worry about it, mate. My expenses will cover that. It was well and truly worth it for the entertainment.'

'Okay, *merci beaucoup*.'

'No worries, dude. Safe driving, huh?'

I wander into the lobby bemused and keen to tell the lads what I've just witnessed. Paris is shaping up to be an interesting week indeed.

*

In all honesty, the French Open is a low point on the tour for me. I don't particularly care for clay-court tennis and the style of play it encourages. I definitely don't enjoy the infamous Parisian hospitality (read lack thereof), and I straight up hate dealing with heaving crowds for twelve hours a day. From the moment you set foot outside the hotel, you have to fight the crowds in the Métro, ticket lines, food lines and bathroom lines, and it all grinds on you. The grounds themselves are attractive and the crowd is extremely supportive – I'm sure if there were half as many people present I'd quite enjoy the event. In the end, it's not really much fun for me and unfortunately Roland Garros earns a place at number four as my least favourite Grand Slam.

That's not to say we don't have our share of adventures – although it should be noted that 'an adventure' isn't always a good thing. After the first few gruelling days working on outside courts for eight to twelve hours at a time, we find ourselves heading towards the business end of the tournament. The workload becomes a little lighter, but this means more matches are being moved to the show courts. There is such a high demand from the tennis-mad general public that all sessions on show courts are sold out well in advance. That leaves only one option. Dealing with ticket touts is an unsavoury but necessary part of securing tickets to trade the entire week at Roland Garros. I do not know just how trying a process this will become, though.

*

DEALING WITH TOUTS

In case you ever find yourself in need of a sold-out ticket at the tennis, here are some quick tips for dealing with touts that may save you a lot of time and money:

1. It's all about supply and demand. Watch the scene for a minute or two and gauge the situation. Are tickets in demand or are the touts struggling? Is it a buyer's or seller's market? Make an assessment, and take advantage if you can.

2. If you want to buy a ticket for a set price, have that amount of money at the ready. Don't flash a wallet full of cash around, for bargain and safety reasons.

3. Touts are nefarious fellows by trade. They prey on opportunity and scrounge the best deals in town. They're always out to make a buck, so if you're in a good position don't let them try to get one over you. Stand fast and you'll usually get your price. Don't be afraid to walk away. The thing about touts is there is almost always another one just around the corner to

barter with. Just be careful they're not all working together as a team; you don't want to get on the wrong side of an Albanian mini-mafia.

4. Watch out for police! In some countries, scalping tickets is actually illegal. You do not want to get stung for such a silly thing. Keep an eye out for police in the area if you're making a transaction.

5. Before you hand any money over, check the ticket to be sure it is genuine – colour printers and photoshop programs can do amazing things these days.

*

It's Saturday morning and I'm out the front of Roland Garros try-ing desperately to secure a ticket to the second show court – named after Suzanne Lenglen. Five minutes ago, I watched my co-work-ers do a deal with a shady-looking tout behind a truck for a centre-court ticket. We're sorted in that department for the day, but now I'm left with the difficult task of scoring a ticket to Suzanne Len-glen. The problem is del Potro is playing Djokovic and everyone wants to see it. For once, centre court is not the main priority – people would rather watch these two tennis giants duke it out.

This makes life tough for me. Initially hesitant to approach the touts standing around in groups, I begin to fret that I'm run-ning out of options after hearing the reply, 'It's not possible, there are no more tickets left.' I get busy and (keeping an eye out for police) start hitting up any tout in sight for a ticket. The same response keeps coming back: 'We're sold out.' That's hard to believe, considering the outrageous asking price these street tick-ets have been going for. But the amount we pay for expensive tick-ets doesn't even make a mark on the potential profit we could make from a day on a Grand Slam show court, so I simply offer more cash. After some heavy negotiations with a group of North African guys, I agree to pay five hundred euros for a ticket. Yes, five hundred euros. Who in their right mind would pay that much for a fucking tennis ticket? The guys I've done the negotiations with don't have the ticket, though – their mates on the other side of the venue are the only ones with any left.

The grounds are huge and would take around twenty minutes to walk around, so they tell me to jump on the back of a scooter and we weave our way through the hectic traffic. I'm wary of this situation – I've just admitted to having five hundred euros on me and I'm being driven off to some unknown rendezvous point by an Algerian guy I don't even know. The pressure is on, though – I need to get a ticket and I need to be on court asap – so I do what I've got to do and negotiate with the new guys I'm introduced to. There's been a mix-up and somehow we've agreed on four hundred and fifty euros. Works for me. Except the guy with the ticket is cautious of police and other watchful eyes, so he asks me to follow him down the street.

We walk for a couple of hundred metres and enter a large grocery store for cover. He looks around and finds a quiet spot in the confectionery aisle to do the deal. I take the ticket and hand him a thick wad of cash. The deal is done. But wait a minute . . . 'This is a player invitational ticket!' (I'm not going to say who it belonged to, but she's a successful WTA player who has been in the top ten before and whom I happen to have a bit of a crush on . . . then again that could be about twenty different girls.) Who knows how the touts got hold of it. These tickets are meant to be handed out to players' personal invitees, whether they be friends, family or associates. It could be cancelled or even marked as lost or stolen.

'It's okay, it's okay,' he assures me. 'Don't worry, you'll have no problem with this.'

I tell him I'd better fucking well not or he'll quickly hear about it (although I'm not sure what I'll be able to do about it with his crew surrounding him).

My fears are resolved minutes later as I scan my ticket through the gate and breathe a sigh of relief – I would have been in deep shit if that much money had gone down the drain! The escapade isn't over, however. As I show my ticket to the ushers, they smile at my VIP status and escort me towards the players' box. This is not good. In fact, this is disastrous. Half the officials will be in the area, and as soon as I'm sat next to the rest of this particular player's guests, I will be revealed as a fraud.

'Oh, sorry, I've got to go to the bathroom,' I mumble and walk towards a set of stairs.

'No, sir, it's no problem. There are toilets this way,' they insist.

'Oh, okay,' I reply, only to duck into a crowd of people as the ushers turn their backs.

I weave my way into another stand, sneak past another set of ushers and find a vacant seat. Finally, I can sit down and relax! Pity I've now got eight hours of tennis requiring my undivided attention. I've run the gauntlet just to get on court and I haven't even started work for the day!

*

In other Roland Garros news, I purchased the most expensive umbrella I've ever paid for in my life. The piece of official merchandise came in at an even sixty euros! (It was raining, so at least I got to use it immediately, and have you seen those RG umbrellas? They're the business!)

The English lads pulled off one of the greatest trading manoeuvres I've ever heard of, laying Kim Clijsters in the second round at 1.01 with a risk of £400. Kim uncharacteristically lost her nerve, bombed out of her commanding position and lost the match – giving the lads a return of £40,000! Let's think about that for a minute . . . a few poor bastards were confident and greedy enough to back Kim at 1.01 for a profit of next to nothing, and lost it all! There's a yearly salary down the drain (or straight into your bank account if you're a lucky trader).

To keep us all on our toes, midweek, Dylan was literally dragged off court by four security guards and interrogated because they thought he looked suspicious. Fair play to them too, he was hitting points by tapping buttons strapped to his thighs, which he'd wired up to his phone. Realising the mistake, he tried to make good by explaining the true story – better than being arrested as a terror suspect. He gave them quite a scare when he pulled his shorts down to reveal his wired-up legs/secret trading system! Hard to believe, but it was all in the name of gambling.

*

At the end of the week, I reflect that, while Roland Garros hasn't been my favourite event on tour, it certainly hasn't been boring. It's been full of entertaining surprises that kept us all alert. The clay season has been fun but greener pastures are literally on the horizon. We are almost midway through the year, and I now feel at home on the tour. I'm looking forward to the grass tournaments and some exciting, fast-paced tennis to trade.

11

SW19

The lads and I each take a free newspaper from the promotional workers and immediately use them as blankets on the soggy grass. It's a sunny day in London but the grass never seems to dry out properly in England. There's a throng of activity around us as we line up for the world's premier tennis tournament: Wimbledon. People come from all over the country, and world, to watch the grass-court championships. The atmosphere is buzzing. London is home not only to the English royal family's collection of riches but also to the crown jewel of the tennis world.

The whole experience of Wimbledon is entirely different to any other tournament on earth, from the moment you see that mammoth line-up in the morning until the moment you walk (or are walked) out of those regal wrought-iron gates. In fact, Wimbledon is so popular you need to line up early just to have a *chance* of obtaining a grounds pass. Tickets to show-court sessions are sold out long before the tournament begins, and they go for enormous sums. It is possible to buy show-court tickets on the day but there are only a few available for those dedicated fans who camp out overnight and secure their spot at the front of the queue. However, the majority of spectators are here to take part in the spectacle and wander the grounds and outside courts. Once you get in the queue, you are given a card to acknowledge your place in the snaking line of people, which fills an entire field. Then you have a four- to five-hour wait to endure.

That doesn't bother me. I'm happy to pull out a book and lose myself in Don Winslow's *Savages* while I relax on the grass. If you get in line early enough (around 7 a.m. is a safe bet), then you will have the opportunity to purchase a grounds pass for £20 (cash only, to speed up the process). It's an incredible deal for a day at such a significant event. Unfortunately, it's the only thing about the day that will be cheap – food, drinks and merchandise range from exorbitant to extortionate. You hand over your cash knowing you have contributed to an amazing event – and played an infinitesimal part in covering the tournament's prize money. First-round singles losers at Wimbledon leave with over £15,000! Imagine turning up to a tournament knowing that the worst you can do is have a hit and walk away with over £15,000 for a couple of hours' effort. The winner, however, dwarfs this amount with a cool million, and the total prize money for the tournament tops out at just over £16,000,000. While this may be a major sweetener for the players, I like to think they strive more for the prestige and accomplishment of success at Wimbledon. It is the ultimate proving ground for any great player. As Novak Djokovic once said, 'My ambition or goal is to become number one. My dream is to win Wimbledon.'

Fair enough – it's a dreamy place. Once you've endured the lengthy line-up, purchased a grounds ticket and passed the stringent security check (we are all quite worried they might find and quiz us about our spare batteries and equipment), you are finally free to enter the gates of the legendary grounds. The first thing you see is the crowd of people milling in every direction. The ground capacity is approximately 40,000, so your personal space is likely to be invaded until you walk out the gates (actually, you've still got the pedestrians, traffic and Tube crowd to jostle with then). London is a busy city, full stop. It's also a great city full of history and tradition. Wimbledon is one of its greatest assets and maintains both these qualities with the utmost opulence. The grounds are immaculately kept, with green hedges, vines and trees decorating the landscape. The traditional colour scheme of green, purple and gold dominates the visage of the grounds and the grand centre-court building is tastefully covered in lush green vines.

All this greenery is fitting, considering Wimbledon is now the only Grand Slam tournament played on grass. I've already explained how I dislike clay tennis because of the slow, grinding style of offensive play it encourages. Grass is the opposite. Many people argue that it rewards fast servers too heavily, and I have to agree this can be a detracting factor. However, it also rewards clever, attacking stroke play and allows for much more entertaining points to unfold. When running in to volley, players can dive across the court to stop a passing shot. Grass tennis is quick, concise and explosive. It keeps the players on their toes and the spectators satisfied.

A key ingredient for all this flourishing greenery is, of course, rain. A dry day at Wimbledon is rare, and a genuine experience at the Championships isn't complete without a shower or two interrupting play. Hiding from a downpour is a great opportunity to partake in tradition and enjoy a helping of strawberries and cream or a generously garnished Pimm's. The price tag on either is enough to make the average punter scream in despair, but they are undeniably delicious.

My only visit to Wimbledon prior to this was in 2008, while I was living in London. I went with my cousin and we watched a bunch of different men's and women's matches. The highlight for me was getting onto court one in the afternoon and watching Marat Safin play Andreas Seppi. Safin had always been one of my tennis idols, with his rampant temper and hilarious antics both on and off court. Not to mention his actual skills with a racquet. He proudly holds the world record for smashed racquets in a season – eighty-seven being the number – and has also stated that he broke over a thousand in his career. Sadly, the day ended in a minor tragedy as I left my wallet on the Tube and never saw it again. While that misfortune had left a bit of a sour taste in my mouth, I still couldn't wait to return to the tournament (I'd never imagined it would one day be my workplace) and enjoy some A-grade grass tennis.

*

There are numerous entertainers, promotional workers, ushers and journalists among the crowd when you line up at Wimbledon. Chatting to them helps pass the time. While sitting on our newspapers, we are approached by a couple of reporters to do an interview for television. A few of the boys decline because they don't want their faces being broadcast to the world from a tennis venue, but Mono is happy to oblige.

'Who are you looking forward to seeing today?'

'Umm, Pete Sampras,' he says.

'Pete Sampras? He retired years ago, mate. I don't think he'll be playing this week.'

'I know that, but I'd still like to see him get out there and give it a go. Age shouldn't be a boundary.'

'Interesting. So who out of the women are you looking forward to seeing?'

'Well, I'd have to say Maria Sharapova, I guess.'

'Okay, and why's that? Do you fancy her?'

'Ah, yep.'

'Right, that will probably do us then. Thanks for your time.'

Somehow, I don't think they'll ever use that interview.

Aside from the usual crew, we have two new traders sitting in line. They have recently been recruited to work with us and will be cutting their teeth this week. Archie is a native Londoner and Tim is a fellow Australian. I've been on tour for six months now and finally feel like one of the team. I am settled in the trading lifestyle and feel comfortable and competent in my job. Meeting the new crew and gauging their reactions and personalities on their first day, it feels funny to think I am now one of the more senior members. I know the ropes and gladly share this knowledge with the new guys, aiding them in their training and transition into such a foreign occupation.

We all chat, read and people watch during the four-hour exercise that is lining up at Wimbledon. By the time we make it in, everyone has got to know each other quite well. We each purchase a grounds pass, wish one another good luck and head off to our respective courts to start the day's work. Despite my confidence and optimism, nothing has prepared me for the Wimbledon security team.

Court sixteen will be my office for the day. Nestled between the stadiums of centre court and court one, it is a medium-sized court, and the first match is to be a men's singles. I nab a great seat in the second row and proceed to trade as per usual. My phone is tucked under my knee and I make the effort to clap every so often to blend in. Almost every seat is full (apart from the one next to mine) and I feel comfortable, relaxed and happy – I am trading the world's premier tennis tournament!

I notice a red-headed guy in his thirties poke his head around the stand looking for a seat, and signal to him that I have one spare next to me. He jumps in with his tennis bag and thanks me. As play continues, he begins making comments to me about the match and how the players are performing. He is from New Zealand and it is obvious this guy knows his tennis. After six months of watching the game almost every day, I am well-educated enough to hold an engaging conversation with him. I ask whether he plays on the challenger tour or coaches, and he replies that he simply does 'some work hitting with these guys', signalling towards one of the players. Okay, he is involved with the players. I can be friendly, but not that friendly. My phone remains tucked under my knee.

'So, are you living over here in London or doing some travelling around?' he asks.

'Well, I've been travelling around Europe the past few months,' I reply truthfully, 'and now that I'm in London I might find myself some work.'

'Okay, so you're not working . . . right now?' He looks pointedly at the hand tucked under my knee. What. The. Hell? Surely I've misconstrued that question.

'Ah, no, nah, I'm just staying with some mates and will probably start looking for work soon,' I lie, feeling flustered. How does he know?

He drops the inquisition and we continue to talk about how the game is unfolding. The first set is over soon enough and he excuses himself to go check out another match.

'Nice to meet you, mate. Have a good day,' he says.

'Yeah, you too,' I reply.

It is then that I receive a text from one of the lads: 'Be careful – a few of the boys have already been booted out – so keep an eye.'

Shit. I thought this tournament was going to be a walk in the park. I almost mention the strange run-in with the Kiwi but pass it off as a coincidence. There aren't many people around who even know that court-side traders exist, let alone being able to make one on court.

I'll never know whether the Kiwi had me done or not but a few games later security approach me. A middle-aged man with short, grey hair and a goatee walks around the corner of the stand and points straight at me.

'Excuse me, mate – yes, you – come have a chat with me, please. Yep, you can stop texting and put your phone away, we're going to have a quiet chat outside.'

Shit! I didn't even see it coming. Even after my quizzical run-in, I remained on court in a confident and optimistic mood. Idiot. I vacate my seat, trying to ignore the curious and critical looks from fellow spectators, and round the corner to meet the head of Wimbledon security and two police officers.

'Hi, mate. My name is James and I'm in charge of security here. Just come around the corner with us, please. We're going to have a chat about that phone and what you've been doing today.' James is polite but firm and clearly wants to do this as discreetly as possible. At such a prestigious club, event management obviously want to steer clear of any type of scandal.

'Now, we have cameras, and we've been watching you. So you can say what you like but you are under suspicion of transmitting data and live scores from our event, which is a breach of the ticket-purchase agreement. These officers are going to search your belongings and take your details, then we're going to politely ask you to leave.'

'Right, okay then,' I reply. There is no point arguing; they know what they're doing and I have zero chance of getting out of this one.

'Hi, mate, what's your name?' asks the male police officer.

I tell him and he verifies this by checking my identification.

'Okay, my name is Sergeant Daniels. Do you have anything with you that you shouldn't?' he asks.

'No. You've got nothing to worry about and if they are requesting that I leave then I'm happy to go right now.'

That doesn't work.

'Well, under the *Terrorism Act 2006* we have the right to search and detain you if necessary. So I'm going to go through your bag here and search your things.'

'If you say so,' I reply. This is quite embarrassing; a lot of people are walking by and whispering about what I could possibly have done. Sergeant Daniels sifts through my jacket, book, water bottle, sunglasses and lunch before finding the spare batteries. It's quite hilarious the way security staff and police react when they catch a glimpse of spare batteries in a trader's bag. It's like they've found a bloody murder weapon with fingerprints on it.

'Okay, we've got spare batteries!' declares the head of security. 'You've got a few here – they would have got you through the whole day, wouldn't they?'

'Would have,' I sulk.

He writes down a list of my possessions along with all of my personal details, as per my driver's licence, which they have removed from my wallet.

'One last thing,' he says, while walking me towards the gate. 'I just need you to stop here and look up at that camera over there for me.'

'No, I don't have to do that,' I reply.

'Yes, I'm afraid you do, sir,' Sergeant Daniels steps in.

My shoulders slump in frustration and I look up at the camera. That's when I realise how they spotted me so easily. If that

CCTV camera – up on the wall about five metres high and ten metres away – can clearly zoom in on my face and take a decent photograph, then it's no wonder they could see me trading on court. I thank Sergeant Daniels and James for being gentlemen and bid them good day. They walk with me to the gates and suggest I do not return to the grounds. I look at my watch. It is barely the afternoon and I have been given my marching orders. What an epic failure that has turned out to be! So much for trading my way through the week.

I contact the other lads by text and am shocked to hear that three of the others have already been booted. This security team are on a whole different level. They are hunting us with disturbing proficiency. When I meet up with Nads down the road, he tells me he was done first game! He'd scarcely had a chance to hit any buttons when they grabbed him. What's even more amazing is that they took two elderly men out of the crowd near him and tried to kick them out for using their phones.

'No, no, leave these guys alone,' Nads cried. 'They haven't done anything wrong.' The poor gentlemen were in a state of alarm and had no idea what was going on. The Wimbledon security team sure do, though. We've been eliminated in a matter of hours and only a few of the boys remain undetected.

*

Being booted this afternoon leaves me at a loose end. Instead of leaving late at night, I am now free to roam the city of London. My hotel is in nearby Earls Court, and on the Tube I have time to reflect on my day and consider my options. I've always had a love–hate relationship with the city of London. It's probably the best city in the world in terms of transport, landmarks, culture, accessibility and excitement. As the old saying from Samuel Johnson goes,

'When a man is tired of London, he is tired of life.' There's always something to do – from restaurants, shops and tours to sightseeing and relaxing in Hyde Park. I love that side of London. But, as a born and bred Queenslander, I can't stand the fucking weather! In winter, I damn near lost my mind living there. The foul weather is generally reflected in people's moods – many carry a shitty, you're-on-your-own attitude and their behaviour can range from snobby to hostile (depending on which district you're in).

Despite my mixed feelings, I am happy to be back in the big smoke. It holds a certain air of nostalgia for me after the amazing times I spent here. I pass the afternoon wandering the West End, looking in shops and exploring Carnaby Street. The weather, for a change, is quite agreeable. But, no matter how sunny things look, I can't ignore that little nagging voice in my head saying, 'How on earth are you going to trade the week out at Wimbledon?'

*

Stock take. Court sixteen and all those courts between the two big stadiums are blacklisted. They're under CCTV surveillance and it's a suicide mission to try to trade them. We know that now. That leaves us with courts three through to fourteen: plenty of space to trade and hopefully stay out of sight . . . right?

*

The next day is overcast and cool. I wear a jacket and hat as a disguise and trade while keeping a constant eye out for security. To mix things up, I change courts after every match. It works, and I walk out those gates of my own accord that Tuesday afternoon. It's a long day, waking up before 6 a.m., working until 8 p.m. and getting back to the hotel to eat dinner an hour later. But I've survived, and I drift off to sleep a content man.

Wednesday sees a warmer day so my jacket isn't really an option. I continue to work the safer outside courts and move around the grounds after each match. I change sides after each set and try to find hidden vantage points from which to trade. At around three in the afternoon, I'm nestled into a nice little shaded area by court ten and am trading my third match for the day when a familiar voice says, 'How are things going, mate?'

I look around to discover Sergeant Daniels standing next to me. I never even saw him coming . . . again!

'Oh dear, you've got your phone out again, haven't you?'

I sigh in defeat and hold up my phone. Daniels isn't being facetious, just doing his job, so I go with the flow. 'Caught red-handed!'

'We'd better come over here for another chat then, mate.'

He walks me over to a quiet area, where James joins us. The procedure is much the same as on Monday, except for the minor detail that this time I am banned from Wimbledon for life!

'We've given you a warning and you've returned, so the club has decided that you will be banned from the grounds from this day forward. A letter will be sent to your home address and we strongly advise that you do not return again. This club has a prestige and reputation to uphold. We have very good lawyers and it would be a shame to have to take action against you in the future.'

'Fair enough,' I reply. 'I'll be on my way.'

I bid them farewell for the second and final time that week and am escorted to the gates. Banned for life from the world's premier tennis tournament! There is no way I will go back. A warning can be ignored but a direct legal order cannot. My time at Wimbledon has come to a premature close.

*

This sudden intensification in security vigilance has shocked us all. The authorities have just proven that, if they want us gone, they can do it quite easily. We need to be more alert to threats at upcoming tournaments – getting our names and faces recognised at events is not a good move for our future as traders.

While the Championships have been undeniably crowded and expensive, the level of discomfort hasn't come close to that of Roland Garros, and overall I've found it to be a much more enjoyable experience. Despite the frustrating and astonishingly competent security team, I've enjoyed my time at the tournament immensely. I am disappointed to be banned for life – Wimbledon is a special place – and, despite coming away with a great story to tell the grandchildren one day, I can't help feeling frustrated that I've had to sacrifice my privilege to attend the event because of my line of work. Banned for life from Wimbledon! I do say, old chap, what a jolly fucking shame that is.

12

GOD BLESS AMERICA

I wake up with the strange sensation that an earthquake struck last night. The building is still here, so surely not. But, if it was a dream, then it was pretty damn vivid. I remember being literally shaken awake. Except there wasn't anybody there, just my bed vibrating like crazy for no apparent reason. I sat up and tried to shrug off a deep slumber but fell right back asleep again.

'Did we have an earthquake?' I ask Archie now, in his bed across the room. But he's slept through the whole thing and doesn't have the faintest idea. A quick trawl of Google reveals that LA did indeed experience a 3-point earthquake early in the a.m.! What a fitting welcome to the San Andreas region of west-coast America.

The new lads have cut their teeth in the toughest tournament of them all and are ready to be unleashed on the tour. I say unleashed because they are like a pair of wild animals (in a good way). I've never met blokes with a greater appetite for booze, women, banter and random acts of debauchery. I've got to know them quickly, and within no time their shenanigans on nights out have become tales of trading lore. As we crossed the Atlantic to trade the American leg of the tour, it became apparent how wild the road was going to be with these new recruits on board.

I'd flown to California a week earlier than the others to enjoy some surf in my favourite US city, San Diego. When I arrived at LAX to pick Archie up, I was greeted with a ridiculous scene. The kid stumbled through arrivals with a handful of black bin bags all piled up on top of each other. They contained the entire contents of what *had* been in his suitcase. He was dropping clothes, toiletries and books left, right and centre, trying desperately to juggle a load of luggage that one could have mistaken for trash. He looked like a bloody garbage man!

'Good to see ya, pal. What the hell is going on here?' I enquired, taking a few bags off his hands and helping him towards the car park.

'All right, mate. Long story: I was late for my flight so they wouldn't let me check any luggage onto the plane. There was no way I could miss it because I'd most likely get fired, so I resorted to desperate measures. When I asked the hostess if I could pile my clothes into bin bags and drag them on as hand luggage, she stared at me and said, "Nobody has ever done that before." Ha ha! Well they have now!'

'You're a lunatic!'

'Yeah, but I'm here, ain't I? And I've still got my job.'

'What about your suitcase?'

'Left it at the airport. Hopefully it didn't cause a bomb scare or anything.'

'You clown! Good work though, pal. I'm glad your resourcefulness got you here; it should be a good week.'

And it was. As I quickly discovered, Archie Heckingbottom-Smith the third is one in a million. I have no hesitation in saying he's one of the most interesting, intriguing and engaging people I have ever met. He's got a quick sense of humour, which, when paired with an expansive repertoire of quotes from movies and television shows and a consummate love for sixties music, makes for epic banter around the bar. Unfortunately, he's an unpredictable drunk. After six or seven pints, he hits a fork in the road. Depending on his mood, he can either fire on all cylinders or crash and burn. You either get epic-banter-pick-up-artist-comedian Archie or you're left with narcoleptic-bar-napping-sideways-drunk Archie. Both are entertaining in their own right.

In London, he played piano in a cover band that didn't cover many piano songs – so he spent most of his stage time leaning against his piano drinking pints. He's been an extra in a number of advertisements, TV shows and movies. He shares my love for literature and writing, and reads more than anyone I've ever met. For four years, he successfully lived off online poker winnings and did whatever he pleased in-between tournaments. He even participated in a poker tournament on a cruise ship in the Bahamas and bought himself a ridiculously expensive watch with the winnings. He's the type of guy who will win $15,000 and have nothing to show for it by the week's end. Aside from being an admitted 'degenerate gambler', he's also a relentless booze hound who will shamelessly chat up any woman you point him in the direction of. He makes rash, bold, illogical decisions, and they inexplicably pay off more often than not.

Getting to know Archie, I realised he probably has a similar personality to those dysfunctional rock stars who stumble through life somehow making it better for everyone around them while barely holding their own shit together. He's messy, sporadic, disorganised and dependent. But I love him regardless and we get along like brothers. Not surprisingly, he's a major source of entertainment and a key contributor when it comes to epic stories from the road.

Archie's most infamous story (and my personal favourite) took place the week before he arrived in California. He was trading his second tournament on the tour, in Washington DC with Felix. He'd worked a busy week and put in some long hours, so when Friday rolled around he jumped on an opportunity to explore the local nightlife. Felix had to work the Friday-night session, so Archie went out on a solo mission. His goal? To get drunk, hit the bars, chat to some locals and, with any luck, meet an adventurous girl to go home with.

He had no problem achieving the first part. A few beers at the hotel between showering, charging phone batteries and checking the next day's work schedule were the standard modus operandi. Then he called a cab and asked the driver to take him to a bar. Archie has never had a problem starting conversations with random people. While the idea of heading out alone in a foreign country might be daunting to some people, it doesn't faze him one bit. The only annoying part was he had to take his passport out with him because they don't accept foreign driver's licences in the States. Knowing that he'd get excessively drunk, this was a risk. However, it was one he was willing to take, and so here he was – drunk in a Washington dive bar trying to pick up some local girls.

Having a distinguished London accent and incredibly sociable manner helps a lot in such situations, and before long Archie found himself chatting away with a bunch of locals at the bar. Intrigued by the friendly Englishman, they asked a range of questions and drank numerous rounds together. This then led to shots. Shots are Archie's Achilles heel. He can drink beer all night but if you bring out the straight alcohol he will be a raging, opinionated, slurring, dishevelled mess in no time. Tequila? Sure, why not. A few minutes later, he was arguing with everyone at the bar about Barack Obama and ridiculing American politics – a slippery slope at the best of times. The rest is recalled in a series of sporadic freeze frames. There was dancing. More shots. Then he got kicked out. The second bar was even dingier. His shoes got ruined. He met a girl. Then he was back at her hotel room getting busy. Then . . . Well, then it got weird.

After a sustained period of blackout, our boy experienced one of those horrible, jolting moments of clarity. Through the blinding tequila haze, he found a second to shake his head and come to . . . in the middle of a hotel stairwell, pissing all over the wall. His piss (which was probably seventy per cent beer and thirty per cent tequila) was cascading down the concrete stairs while he swayed against the wall in a disgraceful state. Naked. That's right, butt naked. Completely nude. Urinating all over the place in his birthday suit. Oh dear, he thought, as this moment of relative sobriety hit him. He had been in the girl's hotel room, he remembered that much. But what was the room number?

He stumbled back into the bright hotel hallway and stared at a jumble of doors that he did not recognise. This was bad. Under the harsh fluorescent lights, his predicament began to set in. Was it 204 or 206? It had to be one of those close by – he couldn't have got far with his clothes off. But which room was it? 210? He had to be a hundred per cent certain before he knocked on somebody's door at whatever hour it was in the early a.m. Hovering with his knuckles over door after door, Archie came to the horrible realisation that he honestly had no idea. It was a pure guess, and he could not risk standing in someone's doorway absolutely starkers at this hour of the morning. He'd get beaten up, arrested or worse. So what to do? What the fuck does one do in this situation?

In a panic, he ran back to the familiar stairwell and made his way down to the ground floor. Luckily, the stairwell led straight out to the car park, so he didn't have to negotiate a receptionist or lobby. But now he was outside, in the dark, butt naked in a strange city with no wallet, phone or passport. It was a nightmare come true. The headlights of a car peeked over the horizon, so he ran and hid behind a dumpster. It was behind this big bin that Archie found his salvation: two black aprons. They must have been thrown out by the hotel's hospitality staff. He wasted no time in tying one on the front and one on the back. Now, with his makeshift outfit, at least he had some chance of avoiding immediate arrest.

With his pasty white arse barely covered by the apron, he crept across the parking lot and tried to get his bearings by the roadside. It was a main road and luckily the drunkard recognised one of the billboards. He had been here before. His hotel was about a mile away. So Archie made a bolt for it – a lost white boy running down a main road in the lightening DC dawn, with two discarded aprons he'd found in a bin the only thing stopping him from being butt naked. Cars beeped their horns and people yelled from their windows. He ran as fast as he could the entire way and somehow avoided police, drug dealers, thugs and any real human interaction. He stumbled through the hotel lobby around 5 a.m. and banged on the door of Felix's room.

Poor Felix got quite a shock when he opened the door.

'What. The. Fuck?' was his response.

'Mate, you won't believe this. What a fucking nightmare!' Archie proceeded to explain the predicament he'd just got himself into. Felix shook his head in bemused disbelief – they'd only just met a week before and this guy was rocking up at five in the morning with nothing but aprons for clothes, having lost his wallet, room key, work phone and passport! The run had almost sobered Archie up by this stage, and he had the presence of mind to snap a quick photo and document the moment. I've seen it and, lo and behold, there is the lad with nothing but a skimpy black apron to cover him up. Lunatic!

Archie awoke several hours later to the mortifying realisation that his belongings were all lost. He was due to hop on an international flight that afternoon. He was in deep shit. Two weeks into the job and he was facing almost certain dismissal.

In typical Archie form, everything worked out just fine. The girl he'd been fooling around with before blindly staggering off for a slash in the stairwell was kind and honest enough to return all of his belongings. He was overjoyed to see her in the lobby after she'd tracked his room key back to the hotel. There she stood with his entire documented life and chances of keeping his job in her hands. Thanks go out to that lovely lady for her act of kindness and for giving my favourite story from the road a happy ending. Tequila and aprons – you've been warned!

*

Archie and I trade the Californian tourneys without any drama, apart from that isolated earthquake, which Archie had slept through in blissful ignorance anyway. It is a solid month of sun, beaches, bars, good food, live music (we manage to see Rage Against the Machine perform their last ever show to date in LA) and security-free trading. Well, there is one undercover scout present at these events, but he is so inept that we never feel any danger. I trade one set from my pocket while standing next to him for a laugh. I am so relaxed I even have the nerve to take a photograph of the ignorant scout while he searches the stands with his binoculars.

It is what trading should be like. The tournaments are held at impressive university campuses such as UCLA and Stanford, or at ritzy venues such as La Costa Spa Resort in San Diego County. After our month of Californian bliss, Archie takes off to trade some tournaments over on the east coast and I fly to Texas to rendezvous with Tim.

*

Upon arrival, I learn that Dallas is in the middle of a major heat wave. Cali was hot but this is just ridiculous! They have gone almost a hundred days in a row without the mercury dipping below one hundred degrees! I arrive at the hotel to find Tim six beers down and blasting music. He has just purchased a new suitcase and a fresh wardrobe of clothes. He's been on the job for two weeks and an airline has already managed to lose his luggage. I dread the day he and Archie work together. Organising a piss-up in a brewery is probably the *only* thing they could manage between them.

Tim Fitzgerald is also one in a million. I guess the job attracts a certain type of person. Fitzy, aka Bin Bin, is a rare unit indeed. His gruff Aussie accent, long hair and penchant for beanies and flat-brim caps ensures he stands out in any crowd. He's a natural comedian and can entertain a whole bar full of people with comedic rants of crude observational humour. The subject of his searing observations is, more often than not, himself. As an exhibitionist, he's never shy about throwing his birthday suit on (or is that off?) after a few froths.

Fitzy's main ambition in life is to own a racehorse named My Face. Why? Well, apart from being a lover of horse racing and gambling, Fitzy just can't wait for the day when he hears a whole crowd of punters shouting . . . well, I'm sure you can figure that one out. That's the type of humour Tim loves, and when he's not entertaining with jokes he will be watching sport and talking odds.

Despite his lost luggage, the lad is all fired up and ready to trade. He loves his new job, and who can blame him? However, after California, Dallas presents quite a shock. They have a real grudge against traders here. Fitzy and I are oblivious to this fact so we go in with our guards down. Play does not start until 5 p.m., which gives us plenty of time to go to a bar for lunch and drink beer. It's happy hour at the bar, except the beer prices are so ridiculously cheap we don't even notice when the hour is over. Lunch there is also a bargain so we enjoy a feast and chat with our outgoing waitress, who is friendly enough to leave me her number on a napkin. We manage to down about six pints before heading off and arrive at the tennis moderately inebriated.

This does nothing for my covert trading techniques. During my second match, I realise I am being watched. The stands back up against each other because of the way the courts are set up. I take a glance over my shoulder to see a security guard in the stand behind me. He's been peering over my shoulder, trying to see what's on my phone screen. I pause my phone and slip it into my pocket while he's not looking. Then I hear his walkie-talkie crackle: 'What's going on down there? Is he still texting?'

It is time to leave. I jump up at the next change and head for the gate. The security guard follows me and, when he asks me to 'Stop right there, sir', I pick up the pace. A big fat guard appears at the exit and tries to block my path. I keep walking and he steps across to try to stop me. This is the United States, not Spain; I know he doesn't have the right to physically restrain me or hold me here against my will. As the big boy tries to grab me, I drop my shoulder and barge straight through him.

'Don't fucking touch me!' makes my attitude pretty clear. As soon as I'm out the gate, it's a quick jog to the taxi rank and I'm out of there. That was a close call, but I'm on their radar now and it's only Monday.

Back at the hotel, I ask the concierge about things to do in Dallas. He tells me there are a few bars not far from here but they won't be open tonight. He also tells me he'll happily drive us in the complimentary shuttle bus to and from any local destination we would like to visit and mentions the existence of a wakeboarding park just down the road. There's also the famous Cowboys Stadium, which holds over a hundred thousand people and offers regular tours and NFL clashes. This is shaping up to be an epic week, regardless of the security threats.

Speaking of which, Fitzy walks through the hotel doors and rolls his eyes at me – he's been booted. After my exodus, it appears security have upped the ante, as they were straight onto Fitzy before he had a chance to bolt. He has been given a trespass order by the police and cannot legally return to the venue for a year. I don't like my chances tomorrow. As the bars are all closed on Monday night, we opt for a few quiet beers at the hotel and plan what should be an exciting week ahead.

On the Tuesday, I wake up feeling fresh and jog out the hotel doors with the intention of doing some serious exercise. I've forgotten we are currently staying in a state whose climate imitates that famous kitchen appliance called an oven almost every day of the year. The tar under my feet feels sticky, as if it's only a few degrees away from melting. Exercise? Fuck that. I'm going back to the air conditioning. Now I understand why play doesn't commence until late this afternoon. You couldn't pay me to sit in the crowd in this heat. As for *playing* three sets of tennis? I'd rather trade Fez again!

Later that afternoon, once the oppressive heat has subsided and the sun has dipped into the horizon, I purchase my ticket, sneak through the grounds and start trading the Tuesday match-ups. I notice only two other traders in the crowd. One is a Russian girl whom I've spoken to once or twice and the other is a French-man. I stay well away from both of them because I know I'm a tar-get. It doesn't take security long. Towards the end of the first match, I hear a creepy whisper come from the stand behind me: 'Get out . . . now!' I turn around to see an angry security guard boring his eyes into mine.

'Sorry, are you talking to me?'

'So, stop texting and leave now.'

'Well, I can't, mate. For one, I'm not texting and two, they're in the middle of a game. You can't just get up and walk out on a small court like this! It distracts the players and is very poor form.'

He realises I have a point. I figure I may as well keep trading until the change. This does not please him. But he's on the other side of the fence, so there's not much he can do apart from trying to order me to 'Stop texting! Now!' – which I ignore with a smirk on my face.

As a court-sider, I've always hated deuce. Fucking deuce can turn a quick day into a nightmare. It can go back and forward for-ever. I've traded twenty-minute games in my time because of relentless deuce swings. I've also traded sets that only went for twenty minutes, so you can see why I hate deuce. But this is the most memorable and most hated deuce of them all for me. It comes at the most inopportune and awkward time imaginable.

I'm sitting there ignoring the cranky security guard, who is complaining to his superiors into the walkie-talkie, 'He's *still* tex-ting,' and the players decide they want to have an all-out battle-royal shitfight for the next six or seven minutes. They scrap back and forward, struggling to find momentum and take consecutive points. I'm trading every point and I can't wait to get off court

and get this over and done with. Across the court, I see two security guards watching me. Then a third. Then a fourth. Then an
official joins. They even summon an event photographer to take
snaps of me with her big zoom lens. I pretend to itch my face
with an extended middle finger. Meanwhile, the score is bouncing back and forth as evenly and almost as quickly as the ball.
This is torture! It's four all, deuce in the second set. There isn't a
more pivotal point in a match! The worst part is I know I won't be
able to trade the rest and we will miss out on a great opportunity
to cash in.

When I'm finally given a chance to bail, a security guard of
honour greets me outside the stand. There are six of them. They
have lined the pavement that leads to the exit and are all glaring at
me like I'm Adolf Hitler. Arseholes. They don't even know what
this is about. Even if they do understand the situation, what reason
do they have to be so mad at me? I see the photographer snapping
away and wave to her. She shies away and looks embarrassed . . .
How does she think *I* feel? As I approach the exit gate, I am
stopped by a uniformed police officer. He's covered in tattoos and
has that deep Texan drawl down to a fine art. Another squad car
arrives and two more officers step out to surround me.

'All this for me?' I joke. 'You guys must have me confused with
an actual criminal.'

With all the commotion, the rent-a-cops decide they want to
join in the fun. People stare at me as I'm interrogated by three
policemen and six security personnel. It's embarrassing and a little insane. I've been updating live scores, not murdering puppies
while streaking! Officer redneck takes my details and issues me
with the same trespass warning he gave Fitzy. They ask whether I
know any other traders, particularly one by the name of Tim, and
try to coerce me into ratting on anyone else inside who is still

trading. Although I don't know the Russian girl or French guy very well, there is no way I'd ever rat them out to the authorities for going about their business. They might be competitors but they're not enemies. In the end, I'm banned from the ground for a calendar year. Looks like I won't be trading Dallas this year or next year! As we finish up with the formalities, officer redneck asks the head of security, 'So whaa'd he doo?'

I look at them and laugh. 'They don't even know,' I reply. The six security guards all stand there trying to look tough instead of ignorant. None of them say a word. An official obviously told them to kick me out and they followed orders without question. I look to the cop and smile. 'See? I'm good to go, right?'

He seems confused. He's probably wondering why he just issued a trespass order at somebody else's request without doing his own police work first. 'Yeah, we're all done here, sonny. You can leave now.'

'Thank you. Oh, and gentlemen?' The security crew all look up. 'Good luck finding Tim back in there. He's shaved his head. Happy hunting!'

'Aw, we'll git 'im. Don't yeew worry, boy!' one of them shouts. They turn to each other, invigorated by this challenge.

I walk away laughing to myself, wondering how long the goose chase will last, and hail a cab. Looks like work is over for the week – it's beer o'clock!

*

Two hours later, our complimentary shuttle bus is dropping us outside a bar. It is time to meet the Dallas locals. For some unknown reason, Texan girls seem to go mental for Australian guys. I'm not sure what they think they know about us, but they are welcome to keep on thinking it.

'Dude, check it out.' Fitzy nudges me. 'You can literally see the news of our arrival spreading around the bar!'

He's not kidding. People are pointing at us and turning to their friends to spread the word. A girl walks up to us and says, 'Hey, are you guys really from Australia?'

'Yeah, we are. We're here for the tennis,' I reply.

'Oh, wow. So you guys are tennis players?'

This is always the conclusion people draw when you tell them you're in town for the tennis. I usually correct them straight away – I hate the idea of lying to get into someone's good graces. But we're drunk and Tim says, 'Yeah, we're the best bloody doubles team you've ever seen!' There's enough laughter in his voice to suggest he's joking but the girls hear what they want to hear and now we are surrounded by eager 'fans' who want to buy us drinks.

One of the girls used to live in Sydney and starts chatting to us about her memories of Australia. She's around thirty but has a Hugh Hefner-style sugar daddy with her who looks to be well into his sixties. He asks what we're drinking. We try to decline politely but he insists.

'Don't worry, he's rich!' the girl gushes. 'You should see his car!'

'Yeah, honey, take the boys out and show them the car. Here are the keys.'

I notice a Mercedes symbol on the key. But it's not until we walk out to the parking lot with drinks in hand (yeah, security are a lot more relaxed here than at the tennis) that I realise he is the owner of an SLS AMG. It's the most expensive and powerful car Mercedes-Benz makes, and the most expensive car anyone's ever handed me the keys to. Roger Federer happens to be the face of the brand and I've read that he is also a proud owner of one of these fine automobiles. Fitzy and I swing the gullwing doors open and jump into the plush leather bucket seats with drinks in hand.

I hit the ignition button and fire the engine up. It roars to life and purrs beautifully . . . until I slam my foot down on the accelerator and redline it. Now it's screaming like a jet engine. Tim grins at me from the passenger seat with pure, childlike joy in his eyes. It's a beast, and, while I'm pretty sure I'll never own one, I relish the opportunity to pretend for a couple of minutes.

Back in the bar, we're dragged into a round of whiskey shots. There are a whole group of people asking us questions and buying us drinks. Texans are definitely some of the friendliest people I've ever met. They're all about having a good time, too. One girl bails me up and starts chatting at the bar, only to be interrupted by another girl, who presents me with an ultimatum. 'So, who will it be then? Her or me?'

I'm speechless. This type of thing doesn't happen in real life. That's the problem with my life, though – it's not a normal, real person's life. I shudder to think how I'll ever fit into a real job or career one day. But I'm quickly distracted from these thoughts and dragged into yet another round of shots. We drink, dance, tell jokes, laugh and make out with local Texan girls. It's a great night, and an early morning by the time our faithful shuttle-bus driver comes to pick us up. Now that's service! On the way home, we rejoice over the fact that tomorrow offers wakeboarding and warm, sunny weather, *sans* work. It is going to be an amazing week.

The problem is it's too good to be true. A few hours later, I'm startled out of my slumber by the piercing tone of my phone ringing. It's Nads. We've both been booted, so we're dead weight in Dallas. He's booking us on a flight to New York . . . today! Shitballs! At least in New York, we can trade the qualifiers in the US Open. I have a list of girls' phone numbers and was looking forward to hitting the wakeboard park. Too bad. Looks like it's time to pack our bags yet again. Life could be worse, though – we're off to the Big Apple!

13

NEW YORK, NEW YORK

It's my first time. In all my travels, I've never even come close to visiting the Big Apple. Of all the amazing cities on earth I've seen – London, Paris, Rome, Istanbul, Athens, Moscow and the rest – I have yet to add arguably the most prolific and prodigious of them to my list.

New York is the epitome of a thriving metropolis. Everywhere you look, something is happening. People are filming TV shows, commercials, movies, you name it. Onlookers are filming the filming. Actors, musicians and all types of celebrities pass you by on the street. There are urban legends of alligators in the sewers below (the steam actually rises up through the manhole covers like a scene from *Ninja Turtles* or *Ghostbusters*) but your attention is usually fixed on the soaring skyscrapers overhead. This glinting jungle of monstrous structures is the crown jewel in America's claim as the leading capitalist superpower of our world. It is a symbol of her twenty-first-century mission to lead capitalism, corporate growth and finance to new heights. From the Financial District of Wall Street to the World Trade Center site and the

UN headquarters, New York boasts the biggest and the best. The thing is, nobody is exempt from this seemingly elite area. Anyone can tread the streets and take in their fill of New York. As a result, all walks of life converge in this vast and dynamic city. The multi-cultural melting pot bubbles away at an all-time high in Manhattan, where you can hear Russian to your left, Spanish to your right, English blaring from car stereos, and whatever it is you call that strange language that the locals speak.

New Yorkers are the most flamboyant, loudmouthed and individualistic people on earth. They are opinionated and will always voice their two cents for the world to hear. Their actions speak even louder, though, with dancing, singing, busking, skateboarding and all sorts of entertainment lining the streets. Everywhere you look, your senses are assaulted. It's busy, robust, colourful and diverse. There is simply no place on earth like New York.

*

As Fitzy and I jump in an unlicensed taxi at JFK Airport, we soak up a bunch of local knowledge from our loud, overweight and somewhat ignorant cab driver. He's lived in Queens all his life, knows New York inside out and sports a thick Yankee accent. Apparently, he used to be an acquaintance of John Gotti's, the Teflon Don. Fitzy and I look at each other and roll our eyes as he says this. It's very hard to picture this man being affiliated with the late head of the Gambino crime family. When we give him the address of our hotel in Brooklyn, he warns us to be careful during our stay.

'It's a pretty rough neighbourhood out there. Lot a ghetto people about so you guys just keep your wits about you when ya walkin' the street, okay?'

We nod in agreement. We have no idea what to expect during our fist visit to this big city.

'And look out for the Puerto Ricans too. Those fuckin' Puerto Ricans are dangerous.'

We continue nodding. This oddly racist lecture gets stranger by the minute. He tells us where to go out, which sights are worth seeing and which places to avoid. From what we can gather, he lives with his mother and spends most of his time on the couch, watching television and eating pizza. He's an interesting character, a clichéd New Yorker, and the perfect taxi driver to introduce us to the local mindset and attitude.

The view from our hotel room is impressive. The Williamsburg, Manhattan and Brooklyn bridges all extend over the East River to the glinting, staggered horizon of Manhattan as it shines in a pink haze of sunset. I instantly recognise the Empire State Building. The photogenic Chrysler Building also stands out among the gargantuan towers in the skyline. As I soak in this horizon, I see Gotham City, the scene of King Kong's final stand, Patrick Bateman's killing grounds and Godzilla's mosh pit. I see the metropolis where aliens rained down hellfire in *War of the Worlds* and *Independence Day*. I've seen this landscape in the past, present, future and even in alternate realities. It's been depicted to me on TV and cinema screens all of my life. I've known it ever since I was a child – even *Sesame Street* is set here! It's the most recognisable and influential city in the world, and I've finally got a chance to walk its streets and soak up the vibrant energy that ten million inhabitants create on a daily basis.

I've almost forgotten – I'm here for work! It's September and we're about to enter a Grand Slam week, so there's no time to be squandered exploring and sightseeing. We'll be working long hours to trade every point possible, and staying focused on the tennis is our primary task. Consequently, the first of New York's famous attributes I'm introduced to is the Subway. I'm not impressed. Compared with European metro systems, I find it ugly, dilapidated and shambolic. The tracks are littered with rubbish and rats. For one of the most populated and industrious cities in the world, New York is somewhat let down by its famous Subway. It serves its purpose, though, and gets us to Flushing Meadows, the home of the fourth and final Grand Slam event of the year – the US Open.

It is interesting to think we're here to gamble on a major sporting event where the general public will spectate and barrack ferociously but never seem to get too caught up in the betting side of the sport. The United States has always had a strange relationship with gambling and for the moment remains well behind the United Kingdom in terms of online betting and leniency in gambling laws. Sports such as basketball, baseball and grid iron have never been popular with the online gambling market. You can trade these sports using Betfair but only if you're in a country where it is legal. As a result, Americans have very little to do with online gambling. In fact, I've never once met or heard of a trader who hails from the States. Can you imagine the amount of money that would be traded online during big NBA matches if the general public of America were willing and able to bet in play? But, because the Betfair market consists predominantly of European and British punters, the online trading focus has remained on sports with a large following in the United Kingdom and Europe, soccer and tennis being the major drawcards. While soccer has a larger fan base, it simply can't produce constant bountiful trading opportunities, and this leaves the great sport of tennis at the top of the trading world.

So, when we enter the grounds of Flushing Meadows's famous tennis centre, we're quietly confident that nobody around us has the faintest idea what we're up to. Security guards, police and spectators are more concerned about terrorists (the tournament does take place in early September, after all) than obscure professional gamblers.

Despite the crowds, the line-up to get in is a simple exercise compared with that of Wimbledon or even Roland Garros. The grounds are huge, and the weather is surprisingly hot and muggy in New York at this time of the year. There's a massive crowd present, and a buzz of excitement is in the air. We are all stoked to have the added crowd cover and instantly settle into a relaxed state to trade these big matches. The show courts are immense (Arthur Ashe centre court is the largest tennis stadium on the planet), and the crowd produces an electric atmosphere for each match. The players rise to the occasion, and I walk out the gates telling friends, 'I've just watched the best match of tennis I've ever seen in my life!' on two separate occasions that week.

The trading atmosphere is equally intense. This year has seen a number of new players enter the game. Looking around on court, I can count up to twenty traders present just in one stand. In Rome, it became clear that some traders were struggling and being left behind. With such fierce competition on the tour, the focus has shifted to speed and technology. Traders are making significant investments and going to incredibly resourceful lengths to make sure they have the best possible Wi-Fi connection and systems to log points with. It's at the Grand Slam events that these big competitors really come to the fore and make their presence known on the market.

A good phone is essential – it needs to have a compatible and accessible operating system and allow traders to install their trading software confidently before they hit the court. The English lads have recently purchased special-agent-like kits with tiny little flesh-coloured earpieces and beige wires to hook up a microphone underneath their shirt. They sit in the crowd chewing gum and slyly chatting to their back end on Skype while people around them are none the wiser. This is the clearest means of communication but it can limit speed, as their back end then has to input the bet manually.

Some guys install a program for their phone and click as each point comes through. Once a button is clicked, it sends information through to a server, where an automated bet is processed according to the mathematical model. This is our method, and, while it's very simple, it's hard to say what's the best. It's not as quick as having a mini-computer to gamble with directly in the stands, as other guys do. However, these days, sitting on court with Betfair open on a laptop commonly results in these traders being dragged out of the stadium quick smart.

Other traders use remote devices that connect to their matrix or program via Bluetooth. I know a few guys who've used Nintendo Wii controllers in their pockets. They sit on court with their hands by their side and tap the button through their pants each time a point is decided. Some traders use car remotes and others even program digital cameras to send the signal through each time they press a particular button – blending in like your everyday punter or tourist, relaxing in the crowd.

Wi-Fi connection is a very important facet of the game, and most traders will purchase SIM cards local to the area to ensure the best coverage and connection. I've heard of some guys sneaking onto the tournament's Wi-Fi by obtaining a press pass and using access codes or even paying people for them. Getting a solid Wi-Fi connection is always the first priority at an event, but it becomes paramount at the US Open, where the dense population and huge crowds can affect the network coverage and often cause drops or delays in signals. This is not a problem you want to be plagued with during a pivotal match.

To combat these difficulties, we sometimes use Mi-Fi devices and create a local private network to boost our phone's connection. Conveniently, in the United States, Verizon released a 4G version of this little tool, which offered a marked speed advantage over the outdated 3G models. One of the English traders, Dylan, went around to stores in New York and pretty much bribed Verizon employees to set him up with a number of false accounts just so he could get access to these 4G Mi-Fis. Seeing as nobody else had them, he traded the rest of the tournament with a distinct advantage over the competition. I wish he'd let us in on that secret a littler earlier in the week!

Another fickle phone issue is battery life. As we often work ten- to twelve-hour days, we need a number of phone and Mi-Fi batteries to last us through. This is fine if we get a chance to change them between sets or matches, but if our battery dies midpoint we stand to lose a lot of precious time during crucial moments in a match. We may get caught out in a bad position and it could cost us. One of the funniest things I see on court this week is two of my Swedish friends sitting their Mi-Fi unit on a bag of ice to prevent the battery from overheating and dying on them suddenly. Traders really are a resourceful bunch.

With so much money at stake, the technological edge becomes an obsession. By this stage, you might be wondering just how much money we're talking about. If a person can purchase a flight, hotel, weekly ticket package and still stand to make a healthy profit, then how much are they winning? Well, as a benchmark, during the 2012 US Open final, where Andy Murray defeated Novak Djokovic for his first Grand Slam title, over £65 million was matched on the Betfair market. You only need to share in a tiny fraction of that to understand the profit potential.

All this technology is key to winning but it's hard to explain why you've brought it with you if you're questioned at the tennis. I receive many an odd look from fellow spectators while dropping spare batteries on the ground or fiddling around with the suspicious-looking Mi-Fi device in my bag. One dude stares at me as I walk through Arthur Ashe Stadium and I can't understand why until I look down and see my Mi-Fi unit with its red light flashing through my carry bag. He must think I'm a terrorist or something! I take off in the opposite direction because I don't want to be reported to the police. It must make me look even more suspicious, but I don't want to cop any heat. Giving the real explanation will still result in me being kicked out of the grounds and banned.

*

Sitting on court, trying not to go insane in the middle of a sixty-hour week, I realise I have been trading on the tour for over eight months! I am settled in my role as a trader and have grown accustomed to a fantastic lifestyle. By my rough calculations, I must have traded somewhere between six and seven hundred tennis matches so far this year! No wonder I feel comfortable with the phone in my hands these days.

After spending so much time on court, you become very familiar not only with the buttons on your phone but also with the players' quirks and habits. It can be quite amusing to watch. Many of them display superstition through routine and behaviour. They can be pedantic about the smallest details on court. Sometimes, they'll tell their coach to go away because they feel they're being distracted by his or her presence. Sometimes, they'll complain about noise in the crowd or flashing lights affecting their concentration. I've seen players become animated and agitated with the crowd on numerous occasions. And vice versa for that matter. Failed ball-tosses and double-digit bounces on serve get tedious to watch for spectators, and many players seem to drag their serve out on the big points to try and build a mental advantage. Some players have annoying habits (like cheering when their opponent loses a point), while others employ negative tactics (like waving their racquet about to distract their opponent during serve). There are a million little things that can affect a game but sometimes these quirks border on the obsessive-compulsive side.

For instance, Rafael Nadal has to have his water bottles sitting in the perfect position before resuming play. He'll hover the bottle meticulously an inch or so off the ground until he has it lined up in just the right spot. Then he'll stride off to the back of the court (making sure he always crosses each line with his right foot first) and go through his serving routine. The serve itself has a whole ritual, which, last time I checked, consists of picking the legs of his shorts, left then right, then the shoulders of his T-shirt, left then right, bouncing the ball while wiping sweat from his eyebrows, then putting his hair behind his ears, then the famous wedgie pick before switching the ball to the other hand for a few more bounces and finally serving. He's a prime example, but he's definitely not the only one who does it. Many of the male and female players have their own superstitions and routines they follow to keep them calm and focused. Sharapova's a stickler for it. She avoids stepping on the lines whenever on court. I go insane watching her sometimes. She's stunning, but she's so methodical and repetitive it's almost robotic. Which is not hot, but it does win tennis matches. Before each serve she stares directly at the spot she wants to hit, trying to envision the action and willing it to happen. Djokovic does a hilarious impersonation of her pre-serve hair-flicking, racquet-string-picking routine. Having said that, even he's got the time-consuming excessive ball-bouncing habit. A lot of the girls slap themselves on the thigh to pep up before serving. Dominika Cibulková even sniffs the balls (behave) before serving because she likes the smell of them! When players win a point on serve they often demand the ball boy or girl throw the same ball back to them so they can use it on the next point. They even refuse to take balls from one corner if they don't feel like it. Wouldn't want to fuck up the feng shui now would we? It's all about maintaining rhythm, focus and a positive mindset - recreating good form and performance. For a trader it can be amusing, fascinating or (after long enough on tour), soul-crushingly tedious.

As traders, we too have routines and patterns we fall into on tour. We need to be engrossed and relaxed to do our job properly. Just like the players, we are required to perform and we have our ups and downs. To get ourselves into a rhythm for the week and feel comfortable on court every day, we become creatures of habit and keep things simple. We might grow fond of a particular food stall or seat in the stand, which we keep returning to (year after year in some cases). We might all meet in the same cafe or park after work each day. Or we might eat breakfast at the same restaurant to kick off every morning. One thing we all love to do is share stories of massive wins, painful mistakes and other interesting occurrences that light up our day. It gets boring on court on our own, so we all enjoy a chance to share some banter. I know I whinge a lot about being bored, and I know I'm in no position to complain. But imagine watching tennis all day, six days a week for a year! I shake my head sometimes when I realise how often I take live tennis for granted compared to the average, excited, paying fan. They'll be giving a standing ovation to a great match while

I'm already jogging out of the stadium, ringing my mates to catch up for a feed and a beer.

As I sit on court seven towards the end of the week, I notice an amusing dialogue take place between Leo and Romeo. Nobody else in the thousands of people around me have a clue. But, as I've taken note that Leo is sitting in the stand, my attention flicks in his direction when I see him signalling across the court. It takes me a second but then I see Romeo around fifty metres away, sitting on court six in the stand opposite us. He's holding up seven fingers and has an exultant smile pasted across his face. He must have just won seven grand on that last match. I'm jealous. Lucky bastard! Leo is obviously jealous too. The two are good friends and Leo flicks him the bird dismissively. Romeo points in his direction as if to ask 'And you?'. In response, Leo stands up in the middle of the crowd, bends over and makes a pointing motion back and forth at his arse. Looks like he hasn't had quite the same amount of luck. 'I've just been fucked!' seems to be the message. I chuckle to myself in the stand and wonder what the other spectators around us must be thinking.

While we all love to share good meals, funny stories and interesting tennis facts, the most predictable and recurrent habit of any trader is to explore each new destination's sights and nightlife. My sixty-hour work week hasn't afforded much time for the above leisure activities. But that's the beauty of Grand Slams – they go for two weeks – the second of which is much less work intensive and a lot more fun.

*

'Okay, so we've got duck à l'orange, poached shrimp, grilled baby chicken, roasted lamb shanks and our special for tonight is the swordfish with chorizo,' says our waiter. We're in Dressler, a chic restaurant with a great range of meals and booze, situated under the Williamsburg Bridge. Our waiter has just recited the menu from the top of his head and also highlights some of the starter and dessert options if we're inclined. The service industry in America really goes above and beyond that of many other countries. Waiting staff hustle to give you the best possible service, and this is where you see the tipping system really work effectively. We have a few beers, enjoy an amazing dinner (with a cheeky dessert), pay our bill, tip our waiter for his efforts and step out into the street feeling like a million bucks.

The hard work is behind us and fun is on the horizon. Week two has been quite enjoyable and in my spare time I've managed to visit Wall Street, the World Trade Center site, the Natural History Museum, Times Square and the Statue of Liberty. That old rumour about the whispering gallery in Grand Central Station turns out to be true: on the lower floor there is a domed area where you can whisper into one corner of the room and another person can clearly hear it at the opposite side. I've enjoyed the remarkable view from the top of the Empire State Building, and ridden a bike around the enormous and revitalising grounds of Central Park (we even saw a few tennis players taking a jog through the grounds for their daily exercise).

It's been an amazing few weeks, I reflect, as we walk into a convenience store to buy some 'road beers' for the walk towards the Williamsburg bar district. I buy a few Tecates (they're a Mexican beer in a red can, so it looks like you're drinking a Coke if the cops pass by), and we stroll on down the road. We've had a successful tournament and it's time to celebrate. Life is looking pretty incredible right about now. I've got two weeks off and flights booked to Mexico and Cuba, where I'll be meeting an Argentinian friend of mine who does some part-time modelling when she's not working as a marine biologist. A week from now, I'll be snorkelling with whale sharks, learning to kite surf, enjoying all-inclusive cocktails, buffets and entertainment, and following in the wake of Fidel Castro and Che Guevara across the Caribbean. There's nothing I'd change right now. New York has been good to me, but the road always beckons.

14

BANGKOK MADNESS

I come to in a bundle of cosy white linen, wishing my head felt as soft and fluffy. It's pounding like a sledgehammer. I'm in Bangkok, I remember. I say 'come to' because it's not just waking up; it's that hazy, disorientating process you go through when you're in a new location and your brain is fighting off a lack of sleep and an inundation of alcohol. Yeah, I'm still drunk. It's 11.45 a.m. Oh shit! I jump up in bed, realising I start work at noon. It's Monday morning and I need to be down at the tennis to kick off the week at the PTT Thailand Open. This means getting to the venue, collecting tickets and finding a suitable, discreet spot to trade from, all in the space of fifteen minutes. Then I look across to see an empty bed next to me. Mono didn't come home last night. Ultimately, I assume this is good news for him, but it is Bangkok and he could either be lost, dead, kidnapped or on his way home after getting laid. I'm hoping it's the latter.

The venue is close, I know that much. So I run to the bathroom for a power shower then make contact with the back end. Nads is online, and I'm hoping he's in a good mood so he's less likely to flip his shit at us for running late.

Me: NADS! HOLY FUCK I'M STILL SHITFACED! I HAVE NO IDEA WHERE MONO IS! HE'S NOT BACK AT THE HOTEL!

Nads: Oh dear god.

Me: I'm going to head down now and try to get shit sorted, hopefully get on court in time for play.

Nads: Godspeed, I'll try calling Mono.

I run down to the lobby and enquire about transportation to the tennis venue. A courtesy golf cart rolls into the drive and invites me on. This is a new one! I'm enjoying the ride when, about a minute later, we pull up outside the venue. Oh. Now I feel like a dick – I could easily have walked! No time to complain, though. I thank the driver and run off to the ticket booth. The language barrier is a small issue but our order form has the necessary details and after a few minutes I'm in possession of our tickets for the week.

Still no sign of Mono, though. I relay this to Nads, who is slightly bothered, but I'm sensing more of a feeling of pride and amusement from him. Nads loves Thailand and has been egging us on with various suggestions and tips; I'm sure he expected nothing less this morning. My phone rings. Mono is alive and at the venue.

'Where the fuck are you, dude?' I ask.

'Um, j-just out the front of some, oh, I don't know, mate. I'm near some stairs,' he replies. His voice is unsteady and indicative of self-imposed suffering.

I laugh. It's been a big night for the lad. I look up and see him standing in the middle of the walkway wearing the same clothes he had on last night. He looks bedraggled. I laugh again. Welcome to Bangkok, Mono! As I approach, I notice the stains of booze on his shirt and the black bags under his eyes, and I can't help but laugh some more at the state of him.

'Hey, mate!' I yell. 'Ready to trade some tennis?'

'Pfft, fooken hell, mate. I'm in no state for this. Ha ha, shit! What the fuck happened last night?'

'Don't ask me, bro. I was about to ask you!'

'Oh well, we'd better get going. We're late already.'

Our tickets are in the fancy-pants area. This is not good because, for once, we don't want to be in the fancy-pants area, out in the open, close to the action, where people can spot us and recognise us or figure us out. It's hard to explain this to the friendly Thai ushers who want to escort us down to the gold seats. Fuck that, we're hiding up the back in the dark! After a quick game of charades, we manage to slip by the ushers and sneak into some inconspicuous seats with a lofty vantage point. To our utter joy, the venue is indoors, air conditioned and fitted with cushioned, cinema-style seats. Score! As a sweetener, we will be able to sit together all day because the courts are both viewable from our vantage point. Today might not be so bad after all. We let Nads know we're ready to roll and start trading.

I'm not usually a fan of indoor tournaments – I'd rather be outside enjoying the sunshine and breeze rather than air conditioning and fluorescent light. But this one is a godsend. When you're hungover to the point where you are trying to piece together the past twelve hours of your life, the luxuries of air conditioning and cushioned seats are like an early Christmas. The best part is almost every fast-food chain imaginable is open for business on the ground floor. At Thai prices! (Read dirt-cheap.)

As we settle in for the morning, I realise there is a lot of local talent present at the event. It's good to see some of the Thai players getting in as wildcards. Their names are incredibly hard to figure out, though. Names such as Udomchoke and Kumkhum are quite amusing, while longer ones such as Lertpitaksinchai or Wachira-manowong are downright impossible to pronounce for the average Westerner. Interestingly enough, the MC of this event is an Australian expat who has somehow found his niche in announcing Thai tennis events. In his professional manner, he alternates from announcing things in mind-bending, tongue-twisting Thai to speaking in Australian-accented English from sentence to sentence. It's nothing short of hilarious to listen to, and quite a unique talent, I must admit.

Between each break, the local Thai fan club break into song and dance, cheering their country on. They have drums, shakers, gongs and various other delightfully loud instruments. They make quite the racket for a hungover head to cope with, but they've got character and I quite like listening to them cheer their players on with 'Thailand, Thailand', rattle, rattle, bang, bang. Repeat. It's surprisingly catchy.

During one of these breaks, Mono describes his eventful morning to me. He woke up in bed with a local Thai girl by the name of Pornthip. He knows this because he has a piece of paper with her name and email address on it. He then realised he was going to be late for work and scrambled out onto the street to hail a taxi. Once he'd explained the destination to the driver (around forty-five minutes away), he did his best from the back seat to stress how important it was he arrive there in the next twenty minutes.

'See my watch? It's 11.40 a.m. now, right? If I don't get there before 12.00 p.m., I'm done!'

'Done?' The taxi driver shot him a panicked look of concern through the rear-view mirror. He'd taken 'done' a little too literally.

'Done,' confirmed Mono with a stony nod, taking complete advantage of the misunderstanding. The man's face widened in shock and he stepped on the accelerator. Apparently, the next twenty minutes were spent speeding past traffic in makeshift slip lanes and refuse bays, beeping the horn and weaving through the throng of glinting mobiles that litter Bangkok's highways. Mono tipped the man well for his efforts and bolted into the venue to meet me. He wasn't really going to die but he sure felt like it at the time.

Back at the tennis, things are going smoothly. It appears we won't have any issues with security this week – so far they are non-existent. We've also spotted a few traders in the crowd; Mikka, Romeo, Leo and a few of the English guys are all present. This is good news as we now have extra drinking buddies for the week.

'Seriously, dude, what the fuck happened last night? I can't remember much at all,' I say during the second set.

Mono relays the story of last night – taking particular joy in retelling moments I have no recollection of whatsoever.

It is like *The Hangover*. Mono and I catch a cab into the centre of town to meet up with Archie, whose holiday just happens to coincide with our work schedule: a recipe for mayhem. We eat street-cooked egg noodle on the infamous Khao San Road and head up to Archie's hotel for some Chang beers and a few rounds of pool to get us warmed up. Then we head down to the street party and have a few mixers. Khao San is a circus. It's the type of place I hate; a tourist trap that has spun out of control, populated by the whole range of seasoned travellers to ignorant and innocent first-timers. The locals who frequent the place just want money. They're loud, aggressive and incessant. But they manage to talk us into going to a ping-pong show. It's our first time in Thailand, so it has to be done, I guess. It's kind of like a rite of passage.

We jump in the tuktuk with our driver, who is happy to stop off at 7–11 while we grab some road beers. It turns out to be quite a journey. We're in traffic for around twenty minutes, hurtling down side streets and dark alleys at intense speeds in our little cart. We're yelling and screaming for dramatic effect, singing along to the radio and passing beers to our driver, who gladly pops them open with his teeth and hands them back. We tip him with a couple of beers and find ourselves out the front of the seedy establishment that is home to one of Bangkok's infamous ping-pong shows.

The next hour is grim. We get drinks and take our seats. A strip show follows and quickly deteriorates into hilarious yet sad acts of human debauchery. We laugh and shout in shock and fascination. We clap when prompted to and joke with fellow audience members about the depravity of it all but, by the time it finishes, we're all slightly sickened and ashamed by the whole charade. We're also hammered drunk on Thai whisky and fortunately it's time to get back in the tuktuk. We've all had enough of the seedy Thai underbelly and avoid the swathe of prostitutes, ladyboys and panhandlers on the Khao San Road, opting for the old-fashioned entertainment of drinking in a bar. We find one with a live band and order a bottle of the dreaded but dearly loved Sangsom whisky. If you've never had it, be warned – that stuff sends you bat-shit crazy. If you have, then you know what I mean. I don't know what they put in it but the results are never boring.

Life is as cheap as it gets in Thailand, so the three of us attack the bottle with vigour. Next thing we know, we're dancing on stage with the band and jumping on top of the tables, doing handstands and sculling drinks. Archie has to stop me from diving head first into a pool to catch a goldfish. The owners aren't particularly happy about this and we eventually get kicked out. Fair play, we're shitfaced by this stage. So onto the street it is.

This is where my memory evades me. Mono explains how we end up dancing on the street with girls, trying on all sorts of different hats and sunglasses from street vendors and drinking whatever we can purchase off the roadside shops. It appears I was destined to get wet anyway. The sky has opened in the past hour and dumped torrents of rain from the heavens. The streets are knee deep with gushing currents of filthy water. We wade down the street with our shoes off and our jeans rolled up.

Out of nowhere, we bump into Arturo – the Godfather! Bangkok is one of his favourite destinations and he's been coming here for years. He loves the nightlife and laughs at our random run-in. Mono and Arty start chatting up some girls and disappear. Archie also disappears into the ether and I manage to hail an apparently amphibious taxi (which I pay way too much for, being the drunken, oblivious *farang* that I am), and hit the pillow blackout drunk.

Mono tells me all this during the first match. We laugh our arses off in the stand and it barely feels like we're at work.

Archie makes an unexpected appearance and stumbles into our aisle. He looks rather dishevelled for a man on holiday.

'What the hell happened to you last night? I looked everywhere for ya!'

'I have some advice for you,' Archie declares. "Do not *ever* smoke opium!'

'Umm, okay. What the fuck, dude? Are you serious?!'

'Yeah mate, I got a bit carried away last night. That bloody Sangsom. Tequila. Fish bowls. And then the opium pipe came out. I thought it was just hookah or shisha or something."

'You're a maniac! Heroin is made from opium, dude.'

'Well that doesn't surprise me – I spent half the fucking night passed out in some filthy back alley of the Khao San road! Woke up around 5 a.m. to a local Thai woman covering me with cardboard to keep me warm.'

Mono hands me his phone and asks me to trade his match while he goes to the toilet. Archie's not helping – he's hungover and on holiday. It's not easy trying to cover two matches at once, let alone being quick and accurate on points. I've never practised it and before Mono is even out of the aisle he hears me curse under my breath.

Me: Sorry, Nads, I fucked up there. Trading Mono's match for him too.

Nads: Umm, righto, so where's Mono?

Me: He's taking a shit, and getting McDonald's.

Nads: Of course he is!

So begins a ridiculous week of 'work' in one of the most colourful and crazy cities in the world. We get back to the hotel a few hours later, ready to catch up on some much-needed sleep. But first I find my camera. Now it is literally like the end of *The Hangover*. Mono and I lose our minds as we flick through a collection of outrageous photos of us wearing fake, fluorescent Ray-Bans and dancing on tables, doing handstands on the dance floor, singing karaoke on stage, drinking Sangsom straight from the bottle, fending off ladyboys, buying buckets of cocktails, necking beers in the back of the tuktuk and partying with girls on the street. Gotta love Bangkok!

15

REPRIEVE

My morning jog takes me through some peaceful woodland, alongside a trickling stream and under one of the largest stone arch bridges in the world. The Adolphe Bridge is an impressive landmark and proud monument of Luxembourg. My laboured breath billows out in front of me like a grey shroud in the frigid air. The only question on my mind is 'What the hell happened to my endless summer?'. It's two degrees Celsius out here and my thermals are barely doing the job. After ten months of uninter-rupted sunshine and warm weather, my body is in shock. My suit-case isn't kitted out to deal with these conditions either – I didn't consider single-digit temperatures while packing at the start of the year.

Summer is fast approaching back in Australia, and, as the year draws to an end, I can't wait to get home. My travel bug has been quelled for the time being. Ten months of constant flights, make-shift meals, laundromats, fluctuating time zones, work schedules and climates has run me down and worn me out. I am stuffed! It's been an unremitting slog, and I haven't given myself a spare moment to recover or recharge. The matches and memories all pile up and blend into a mix of endless rallies and all-night benders.

During the past months, I've improved as a trader. Mistakes and mix-ups are far behind me. I rarely make errors these days. My co-workers have become great mates, and I know everyone on tour. I've become accustomed to this fantastic lifestyle and have every intention of staying on next year. The crew are happy with my performance and it seems my spot on tour will be available for my return next year. I'm a privileged member of the trading elite and I'm quite happy to keep it that way. This is the life for me. But before I turn all my attention to the following year, there are still points to be traded until the final boarding call. The last few weeks go by in a blur, and, while they may feel quick for me, they still continue to provide a menagerie of bizarre challenges and scenarios to negotiate.

The Luxembourg Open is held in a quaint, barn-like building out in the countryside. It's back to indoor tournaments for the rest of the year, which is a welcome relief in these temperatures. Fitzy and I keep a low profile and cover all the matches without a single sketchy moment. We're doing well on the trading front, but there is some troubling news travelling along the grapevine. Sitting in the stand chatting to Giovanni and Dylan at the start of the week, we discuss rumours of a multimillion-dollar contract that may drastically affect traders next year. Apparently, the official live scores will be input into a computer system by the umpire's hand, reducing the delay window that gives court-siders an edge over the rest of the market. As if that's not a big enough problem, this exclusive and lucrative contract will almost guarantee an increase in security measures and a crackdown on traders in general. If you paid millions of dollars for 'exclusive' rights to live scores, would you want other people beating you to it? It seems this deal will create a monopoly for the live-score market and a big setback for traders around the world. At the moment, it is only a rumour, so there's no point getting too stressed out. It does offer some food for thought, though, and leaves me wondering how long this industry will continue to flourish while hiding in plain sight on the court-side.

On the bright side, Giovanni offers me a job for next year, if I ever decide to stop working with my syndicate. It's nice to have options but I'm stoked with my current situation so I doubt there will be any need for a change.

*

After Luxembourg, I'm graced with a week off. But where does one go in Europe at this time of the year? Snow hasn't fallen in the mountains yet, and my favourite sun-soaked summer party towns have all shut down. I've already visited most countries in this part of the world, except for . . . Ireland. Off to the Emerald Isle it is then!

For a week with very little preparation, and zero expectation, I have an incredible time. My work phone doesn't come into contact with my hand for seven days; instead, it is replaced by pints of rich, creamy Guinness. I join a tour bus for the week so I can see the entire country in my short time frame and party with a crew of youthful, like-minded travellers. We stay in an establishment called The Randy Leprechaun, kiss the Blarney Stone, change euros to pounds to explore the intense walled neighbourhoods of Northern Ireland's Derry, down copious amounts of booze, party every night, visit the mysterious Giant's Causeway and the magnificent Cliffs of Moher, and perfect the art of pouring Guinness at the official factory in Dublin.

Admittedly, the weather is heinous and the temperature is well below my liking, but we use the dreary climate as an excuse to see the inside of as many drinking establishments as possible. Most of my co-travellers are students and expats, working hard between trips to fund more excursions to new destinations. They express disbelief and wonder at my privileged line of work. To think I was in their shoes only a year ago. More than anything, I think they're envious of my next destination – by the seaside in Spain. It's one of the only areas of Europe that's yet to be choked by the cold fingers of winter, and I can't wait to get back into the sun.

*

It's crazy to think a two-and-a-half-hour flight can land you in a country with a different language, culture and climate. Valencia is about twenty degrees warmer than Dublin and there's not a drop of rain on the horizon. Felix and I have a comfortable apartment only a few minutes' walk from the tennis. The venue itself is amazing. The Valencia Open 500 is situated in the Ciudad de las Artes y las Ciencias, 'City of the Arts and Sciences'. This particular area of Valencia is quite famous for its attractions and events. Architecturally, it is one of the most distinctive and impressive places I've ever seen. The buildings are constructed of huge glass panels, white concrete and steel supports. They look like a collection of alien spacecraft, creating a futuristic scene that could pass as the backdrop for a sci-fi film. Centre court is set up inside a towering blue structure known as L'Agora and provides a cathedral-like amphitheatre in which to enjoy the action.

I haven't been here since 2008, when we stopped in before heading to the famous tomato-throwing festival, La Tomatina. Last time I was here, we were chased out of the area by security guards for swimming in the vast water features that surround the striking buildings. To be fair, it was stinking hot and we'd consumed our fair share of sangria.

Things have changed a little, and, while I am here on business this time, I'm still drawing the attention of the unforgiving security team. The Spanish tournaments have a rep for heavy security, and Valencia has no problem living up to it. Felix is the first to go – dragged out on the Thursday. I do my best to blend into the crowd and feel like I have a chance by Friday afternoon.

During my lunchtime break, I receive the biggest shock of the week when a rogue gust of wind blusters into the building. I'm walking out the door as this huge burst comes through. Chairs, tables, rubbish and umbrellas all topple over and are swept away. Just as I step across the threshold of the building, the glass door next to me explodes from the pressure! We're talking about a thick glass panel a metre wide by three metres high. Shattered glass goes flying in all directions and the majority of it cascades to the floor like a thawing waterfall in the spring melt. One of the tiny shards hits me in the eye and I'm frozen in a moment of panic. This could have terrible repercussions. Luckily for me, I'm able to keep my eye closed until I can stumble downstairs to the bathroom and wash it out. That was a close call. Thankfully, nobody appears to be injured and the tournament carries on.

As normality returns, I take a seat behind the baseline and prepare for my third match of the day. An attractive local girl taps me on the shoulder and starts talking to me in rapid Spanish. I try my hardest to keep up but the Valencian tongue is too quick and varied for me. For a second, I think I might have picked up . . . then I realise the hand signals towards my phone are her way of telling me I'm about to get dragged out of there by the scruff of my neck. Damn it, she works for the WTA!

My week is over. There's no way I'm going to be allowed back in the venue. An eager security guard pushes me around and forcefully ejects me from the building, growling Spanish profanities in my ear and making it very clear that he'd like to punch my head in if he were given the chance. Forget about the trespass issue, I'm not going back and risking a beating to trade a few matches. But, with both of us banned from the grounds, we are left with semis begging to be traded on Saturday and no chance of getting in.

We stand to make a good profit from these matches, though, so how can we do it? The boys on the back end are all busy and nobody can get a live feed on the internet anyway (if necessary we trade from TV or internet feeds, it's just never as profitable). Felix is due to fly out, so the onus falls upon my shoulders to employ some ingenuity for the team. After much deliberation and searching, I find myself enjoying a solitary evening in a tapas bar, *cerveza* in one hand, phone in the other, trading off the TV from my bar stool. The delay isn't too bad because the match is being telecast on a local sports station. In the end, we make a solid profit, even though I'm not court-side. It's a strange 'day at the office' but later that night I am out with Mikka and Dylan, enjoying the Valencian nightlife and turning a tidy profit at the casino. Mission accomplished in the south of Spain.

*

My final stop is the Paris Masters. Forgive me for not subscribing to the general romantic consensus, but I dislike Paris in general, and especially around this time of year. There's dog shit all over the pavement, the weather is grim and the overpopulated streets are a-bustle with selfish people too busy to look where they're going. Okay, I'll admit that Paris does have some amazing architecture, and there is no denying its status as a top tourist destination, but it's just not enough to overcome my distaste for the place during the miserable European winter. Maybe I'm just getting picky.

The tournament is held in Bercy's 'indoorground' venue. It's a massive complex and provides good cover from the watchful eyes of security personnel and undercover police who are known to frequent the stands. Roger Federer hits 'demigod' mode and demolishes the field with relative ease, providing some entertaining viewing as I count down my final matches of the year.

I must admit, the crowd atmosphere here entertains me. Bongo drums, chants and the encouraging cry of '*Allez*' ring around the venue incessantly. Different countries have different chants and, over the year, I've come to know them well. Every place has its own version of 'Come on!' or 'Let's go!', and it doesn't take long to learn it once you arrive in a new country: '*Allez*' for the French, '*Vamos*' for the Spaniards, '*Forza*' or '*Vai*' for the Italians, '*Hajde*' in Serbian, '*JiĐ Yoú*' in Chinese (interestingly enough, it translates to 'add fuel'), '*Davai*' for the Russians, '*Auf geht's*' in German, '*Yalla*' in Arabic, and so on. It's invigorating to see a player win an epic point and turn to the crowd for inspiration and energy. Nothing sparks the spectators up more than a rampant, performing pro asking for their approval and support. The French fans are more than happy to oblige in Bercy. Beware their wrath though. They are fanatical but brutal, and I've seen them furiously boo and whistle bad sports (foreigners and locals alike) at the slightest opportunity.

On our final night in Paris, a group of us get together and enjoy a restaurant meal, raising our glasses to a phenomenal year on tour. It really is a joy to be part of this extraordinary group of people, and it's been a year I'll never forget.

*

The next day, I'm sitting at a bar in Dubai Airport with Fitzy and a motley crew, waiting for my flight home to Australia. This is only a stopover, so I won't be seeing the sights of Dubai today. I have a few friends who live here and was lucky enough to explore the city a few years ago. It's an oasis of glinting metal reaching for the sky in an effort to escape the dusty desert landscape below. There's no chance of it snowing in the searing temperatures here . . . but that hasn't stopped them from building the world's premier indoor skiing field. Dubai's shopping centres boast ice-skating rinks, aquariums and enough retail therapy to quell the most avid shopper's addiction. Dubai's famous six-star Burj Al Arab hotel is where Federer and Agassi had their much-documented exhibition hit on a lofty helipad overlooking the city. It was designed to promote the tournament held here early each calendar year. I missed it this time around but maybe I'll get to trade it next year. I'm getting ahead of myself, though, for now it's time to get home and relax.

My flight is thirteen hours, or something like that – it's long, I know that much. All these long-haul flights and airport terminals, hotel check-ins and check-outs, immigration clearances, passport stamps, delays and baggage collections have worn me out. We got unexpectedly drunk on our flight from Paris to Dubai. Fitzy and I ordered so many beers from the hostesses we ended up with a massive pile of crushed tinnies on our fold-out trays. A South African hostess freaked out when she passed by and noticed the mess.

'Did you two drink all these? You'll get us fired if anyone hears about this!'

What better way to celebrate such an unbelievable year? The revelry is carried on during our stopover and we manage to collect a few hangers-on, who join us for drinks in the bar. There's another Australian guy who hails from Byron Bay and works for the world-famous travelling circus Cirque du Soleil, an American who specialises in breeding racing camels in the desert of Dubai (his talents in horse racing transferred into this bizarre industry and a rewarding new career in the UAE), and a Nigerian business-man who's on his way to Europe to broker a new deal. They're all intriguing people with great stories to share, but, above all else, they're determined to hear about this unique job Fitzy and I have mentioned.

As I explain the secret world of court-side trading, they all look on with amazement and intrigue. I realise I now know what I'm talking about when people ask me what I do for a living. Eleven months ago, I needed the facts spoonfed to me by Jethro to even understand why we were on court; now I'm a proficient authority in the field. My explanation raises eyebrows, questions and glasses. I'll 'cheers' to that. Sometimes, we take it all for granted, and it takes special occasions like this to step back and appreciate what a wonderful life we live.

*

As my flight departs and the tennis year draws to a close, I finally have time to kick back and relax, twenty-three countries, thirty-five tennis tournaments, a bunch of frequent-flyer miles and way too many games of tennis later. It will be strange staying in one place longer than a week or two. But it will also be a welcome relief. I've been away so long, coming home is a holiday in its own right. To be honest, I can't wait – I'm exhausted and run down from almost eleven months on the road. I'll have a few weeks to visit family and friends, to catch up on what I've missed during the year and to share all of the amazing experiences I've amassed on tour. It's been such a hectic year that I haven't had time to pause and take stock of my existence. Now is a great chance to reflect on what has been the most exciting, transient and incredible time of my life thus far.

I'm looking forward to the festive season with my family and friends, staying put for a change, relaxing by the beach and getting a surfboard back under my feet. The best part is I'm locked in to do it all again next year. There will be new locations to explore, tournaments to survive and matches to trade. The tennis tour will continue and the road will go on. . . In fact, forget staying put, I'm already planning a holiday to Sri Lanka for New Year's Eve. Bring on 2012!

16

HIGH STAKES ON THE SUBCONTINENT

'You're under arrest' is a sentence you never want to hear, especially in a developing country. Unfortunately for me, it's exactly what I've just been told by a man of authority who has my wrist in a vice-like grip. Happy New Year to you too! The police in India carry bamboo sticks to beat people if necessary. Not to mention the guns. Human rights aren't a huge priority in a place where over a billion people struggle for survival each day. I haven't done anything illegal and I know it. However, as the menacing official is all too keen to point out, the police in Chennai will believe his side of the story. He seems hell-bent on painting a bad one. They take me to an office under the tennis stadium, block the door with an armed guard and grind me for information.

'You're a long way from home, my friend.' Surprisingly, he speaks with a thick South African accent. 'Now you need to make some smart decisions or you may never get back there. This isn't a nice place to get into trouble, and once you're behind bars in this country you may never get out. It's very easy for you to get "lost" in the prison system.'

He's bluffing, the smug prick. But, fuck me, it's one hell of a bluff to call. I go for the middle ground. 'I'm happy to cooperate with you but you're taking liberties here and I don't appreciate it.'

This does not appease him. 'Listen to me, mate,' he leans in and growls. 'You're not getting the picture. We'll drag you into the back alley and beat the shit out of you right now if you don't give us exactly what we ask.'

Silence hangs in the air while I digest this threat. 'Wow' is all I can manage. I'm a schoolteacher, not a career criminal; I've never heard that one before. How has it come to this?

Only a few days ago, I was in Sri Lanka, attending the wedding of one of my closest friends. We welcomed in the New Year with champagne at a raging beach party, photographed leopards, elephants and crocodiles on safari and sipped cocktails by the poolside of a five-star resort. Now I'm being held against my will by armed guards and threatened with a jail sentence!

'Okay, I'm going to take my phone call now,' I decide.

'No,' he replies, snatching my phone – the very instrument that got me into this fiasco – off the table and out of my reach. 'The rules have changed. You don't get a phone call any more.'

Motherfucker! This has been going on for an hour and I'm beginning to feel the pinch. It's not every day you're threatened with police corruption in an impoverished country. This is playing out like an interrogation scene from a movie. I thought this type of 'bad cop' game was only reserved for the scum of the earth. While I've tried to play it cool until now, things are getting quite daunting. So, do I give up my syndicate's information or do I risk a beating and potential imprisonment in an Indian jail cell? As you can see, this is *not* an average day at the office. But, as I've come to learn, there's no such thing in my line of work.

*

I'd been excited to trade the Indian tournament. I'd even *requested* to be sent there because my friend's wedding in Sri Lanka tied in so well with the schedule. I was well aware of the threats that such a place presented, but, with my usual optimistic expectations, I simply assumed I'd get away with it. A lot of my friends had been to India and loved it. They'd travelled to remote places and enjoyed those enriching and inspirational cultural experiences one can only attain by traversing developing nations.

Sri Lanka had dished up this type of emancipation to me in many ways. I'd let off fireworks on the beach for kids to watch, and set up my slackline by the pool and taught people how to tightrope walk. I'd been privileged enough to see a leopard tackle a mongoose in the jungle, shared some of the richest food I've ever eaten in my life and learnt about the crippling civil war that had lasted over twenty-five years and ostracised this beautiful country from the world. The old name for Sri Lanka – Ceylon – was derived from the word serendipity; a wonderful and fitting homage to this island nation, in my opinion.

At the wedding, the bride's father asked me where my next port of call would be on the tennis tour.

'I'm off to Chennai,' I answered.

'Ah, from the paradise to the shithole!' he replied with a laugh. Everyone around us joined in – it seemed all the Sri Lankans shared this opinion. For such a gentle and easy-going group of people, I found it surprising to hear such negativity. It wasn't until two days later when my taxi veered out into the thronging traffic of Chennai that I understood.

India is a huge country, in every way. Most people know it has the second-largest population on earth – at 1.1 billion people – but it's not until you get there that you really begin to *comprehend* this behemoth proportion. Picture cars, motor rickshaws, pedestrians, bicycles, scooters, taxis, buses, people and animals of all types all over the road, all making as much noise as possible, all trying to get to their destination as quickly as possible. It is the definition of mayhem. Blaring horns and shouts ring through the sweltering heat as the sun beats down on the dense jungle of dirty concrete and glinting, bumper to bumper steel. And it goes on and on and on. It never stops!

My initial experience in this land didn't really remind me of those romantic notions I'd read about in Gregory David Roberts's *Shantaram*. Speaking of which, Doug the cockney trader had told me of a comparable adventure he'd survived out in India during the nineties. He'd followed the hippy trail through beach towns such as Goa and fallen into the labyrinth of opioid obsession that so many travellers succumb to. He recalled how he'd fled the place in a desperate moment of clarity and flown back to the United Kingdom just to straighten out . . . only to fly back again to rescue a friend who had fallen deeper into that consuming well of oblivion.

Kingfisher beers would be the strongest substance I'd partake of during my time in India, and I felt like I needed one after my shock introduction to the place. I grew up with parkland, greenery and beaches all around me. I'm used to hearing birds chirp in the mornings and water trickle or crash in its natural state nearby. This urban maze offered quite the opposite. The filthy grit of dust, rubbish and concrete gave me the same feeling you get from listening to fingernails screech down a chalkboard. It was a sobering thought to realise I was looking at the future of our world if overpopulation continues. It sure ain't pretty.

The hotel is, though – it's a shiny new building that gleams among the inner-city debris that typifies the urban sprawl of Chennai. I meet Archie there, and, being a fellow optimist, he is also excited to give this new country a chance and explore the sights. We go for a wander around the streets to get our bearings and discuss the week ahead. Barefoot children run by and the occasional beggar asks for spare change. We're comfortable walking the streets here. The area appears to be a regular, diverse neighbourhood of inner-city Chennai. We agree that security is a serious concern for both of us in this country but we also agree to push it to the back of our minds and focus on the positives of our first visit to India.

The cuisine is similar to (and almost as delicious as) the Sri Lankan fare. Being a little wary of catching 'Delhi belly', we err on the side of caution and stick to an upper-class restaurant for dinner. While this option is a lot more expensive, we are rewarded with a veritable feast for the senses. Tandoori chicken, onion bhajis, garlic naan, mint yoghurt, basmati rice, spicy sambal and a delightful array of other Indian treats are all enjoyed. The hectic streets are a world away as we enjoy beers by the poolside of a rooftop restaurant that happens to be hosting the tennis players of this week's tournament. We notice a few pass by but opt to keep to ourselves, and retire to our hotel down the road for an early night and a fresh start to the week.

The next day, we are greeted with typical muggy Indian conditions as we make our way to the tournament. Tuktuks or rickshaws are the major mode of transport in this part of the world. We jump on the back of one and are at the venue in no time. I take a video of the traffic along the way – I can't help myself. It is a heaving mass of gridlocked congestion that somehow flows through the blaring horns, dust and exhaust fumes.

Upon entering the grounds, my apprehension ensures I take it easy to begin with. I wander the venue, keeping my eye out for potential threats, get the lie of the land and find my way to an outside court where Janko Tipsarević is playing a practice match against Milos Raonic. As this match-up unfolds, I realise it is almost a guaranteed precursor to the final. They are the two top seeds for the tournament and certainly the two most talented players here. Milos is bombing down enormous kicker serves that are bouncing up to Janko's shoulder height. While Janko might be the better all-round player, I figure he'll have great difficulty breaking Milos's serve, especially returning the ball on his backhand at that height. I put a chunk of money on Milos to win the tournament . . . eager to see whether my homework will pay off at the end of the week.

By then, it is time to get among the action. I make my way over to the large, concrete centre court and find a spot to trade from. I'm deflated to realise it is a nightmare court for traders. There are no blind spots, every seat is wide open to prying eyes and I'm the only Caucasian in the place. I try to ignore these ominous factors and concentrate on my first match for the day.

About an hour in, I receive a worrying text from Archie.

Archie: Mate, just survived a pickle. Be careful of a big South African guy who is the head of security. He's one mean bastard.

Me: Shit, that's not good. But you got out of it?

Archie: Just. Told him I was a county cricket player over here to play some matches and wanted to check out the tennis.

Me: Ha ha, he bought that?

Archie: I told him I was texting my girlfriend, and luckily I had just been texting a bird from back home. He saw the messages and let me go after that. Beware, though, pal. He's onto it.

This is troubling news but at least I know I have a chance of talking my way out of it if things get heavy. The conversation leaves me felling a little conspicuous on court. I am the only white guy in the crowd and I'm sitting by myself. The worst part is a security camera at the top of the media booth seems to be directed at me. I can't quite see well enough but I could swear it's zooming in on me. I dismiss these thoughts as demons of paranoia, figments of my isolated imagination. I am so wrong. The longer I pursue my career in tennis trading, the more I learn that sometimes it just pays to be paranoid and act on instinct.

It's not long into the second match when a heavy hand comes down on my right shoulder and I hear a thick South African voice behind me say, 'Stop what you're doing right now and come with me.'

I spin around in surprise and counter with the standard, 'Sorry, what's going on?'

I'm met by the silhouette of a large man who means business. His face darkens and I realise this is a bad situation. I'm caught red-handed – who knows how long they've been watching or even standing behind me?

'Don't give me any of that bullshit, mate. I know exactly what you're up to and it's not going to work out well for you here. Now come with me – you're under arrest!' he says, grabbing my wrist and yanking the phone from my hand before I even have a chance to react.

The other spectators all look around in shock and begin whispering among themselves. Once again, I've become the embarrassed and vilified talking point of the crowd. Their gossiping is the least of my worries, though. As I'm dragged to the exit, I see an armed-police officer join us. He has the standard-issue *lathis* (bamboo beating sticks) and AK-47s slung over his shoulder. This is no ordinary eviction. This is heavy.

My protests and pleas are ignored as I'm hauled under the stadium into a guarded room for interrogation. My stomach plunges as the door slams shut behind me. Left alone with these two shady individuals I realise just how nasty this situation could turn. The Saffa is around six foot four. He probably weighs twice as much as me. He's a big, black, bald man with a menacing leer. His police guard isn't as big, but he's armed and standing by the only exit of this concrete room.

Stay cool, you'll be right, I tell myself. Despite my efforts, I can feel my heart rate rise from the adrenalin. On any other occasion, I would love that feeling.

'Look, guys, I—'

'Sit down,' the big Saffa demands.

I sigh and take a seat across from his desk.

'The police officer here is going to search your personal belongings,' he explains. 'You'd be wise to cooperate – it's not like you have any other options.'

I watch as my bag is emptied onto the desk in front of me. A spare phone and bunch of batteries are among the pile of personal belongings photographed as evidence.

'Do you want a bottle of water?' the Saffa asks me.

'No thanks,' I reply.

'Take a bottle. You're going to need it.' He places it on the desk in front of me, next to my phone. 'Now, you're going to explain to me how this phone of yours works, how you're gambling and who you're doing it for. This can be as easy or as difficult as you like. But I promise, you will not leave this room until you've given me what I want.'

My heart really starts to hammer. It's never come down to this before. There's no way I'm turning my syndicate in after all they've done for me. There's also no way I'm going to jail. But what other options do I have?

I've only ever seen this type of scenario unfold on the television screen. This is a full-blown interrogation, straight out of *Law*

& Order. They grill me with questions, trying to find cracks in my story and make me slip up. The examination is fast and unrelenting. They repeat their questions and try to make me second-guess myself. I can feel my nerves rising and my mouth starting to go dry. That bastard was right – I'd love a sip of water right about now. But I'll be damned if I show him any sign of weakness or guilt by taking one. The bottle remains on the table.

My ordeal lasts for over an hour. During this time, I grapple with my predicament. Is my job really worth this kind of pressure? I love trading but I'd give it up in a second if I had to choose between this lifestyle or an Indian jail cell. Captured drug dealers get put through this kind of horror. I definitely don't need it. Guys who run drugs are lowlife scumbags trying to get rich by ruining other people's lives – I find it hard to draw parallels.

My job doesn't hurt anyone. It's given me so much, and offers so much in the future if I can just survive this test. They want phone numbers, names, email addresses and personal details of anyone I'm involved with. They're willing to make very big threats to get them.

'This is wrong,' I insist. 'I haven't done anything illegal and you know it.'

'Fine, have it your way,' the South African replies. 'Some of these cops can get very nasty and I'm going to let them take it from here. If they decide to lock you up and throw away the key, nobody back home will ever hear shit. Good luck.' He stands and utters a few quick words of Hindi to the armed policeman.

'Wait!' I interrupt. Both men stop at the door. 'Okay . . . I'll answer the questions.'

In the end, I give them a collection of vague facts and fabricated lies. It's a huge bluff and a bet that I cannot afford to lose.

'You'd better be telling the fucking truth, mate,' the Saffa says.

'Because I'm going to call this number you've given me and check that this guy is really your manager. If you're lying to me – and I'm only going to give you one chance here – you're fucked.'

I want to take a hard gulp and bury my face in my palms. I want to grab that bottle of water and down about half of it to cure my cotton mouth. I want to shake this neurotic prick and tell him it's just not that big a deal, and ask him why he enjoys causing me such grief. I do none of the above. Instead, I look him in the eye and say, 'Okay, go ahead.'

It's a colossal gamble. Most traders would stay well away from that bet. While the odds aren't horrible, the stakes are astronomical. I've given him Jethro's number. Jethro retired from trading a few months ago, and divulging his phone number will not disturb his livelihood. He's probably unwinding at a local pub back in Australia after a regular day of work. I just hope he picks up the phone and plays along with my story. It's the longest wait of my life.

Luckily, my mentor and old mate knows the perils of trading. He convinces my interrogators they have the full story and I'm finally released. As we walk out the door, the big interrogator radios his security team and tells them to stand down.

'You see? I'm not fucking around here, mate. We had guys ready to intercept you if you tried to make a break for it. It's a good thing you were straight with us. I'm going to let you go because you've conducted yourself like a gentleman. But you leave India now, and you don't ever come back to this country and gamble again. Are we clear?'

Crystal. You couldn't blackmail me into going back on court in Chennai.

I shake my head in disbelief as I'm released into a dark back-street, dazed and surrounded by begging children. The worst part is I practically expected – nay, waited – for it to happen. I was just doing my job; but it's clear now that my job is not worth the consequences faced in developing countries. I jump into the back of a spluttering rickshaw. That was not pleasant. It's not nice to be treated or spoken to that way and it infuriates me. That guy would have ruined my life . . . but why? If I was a murderer, thief or rapist, I could understand his hatred. But he knew what I was doing and he still wanted my blood. I guess I underestimated just how strict the anti-gambling enforcement is in India.

I'm in a hurry to get back to the hotel now, and for good reason. The previous year in Chennai, a Czech trader, and friend of mine, had his hotel room raided by officials, who confiscated his laptop and other electronic devices for their investigation – an 'investigation' that exposed four-fifths of fuck all, because he was just a regular trader like me. There is no way I am going to spend a night in the same hotel after security have just rifled through my wallet and copied down my personal details and hotel information. I pay the rickshaw driver and bolt up to my room. Archie is sitting on his bed watching a movie when I storm in, still pumped with adrenalin, and insist that we get the fuck out of this place right now. We pack our bags, book another hotel, check out of the one we are in and jump in a taxi. An hour later, we're kicking back in a different hotel. At least this way, my nightmares will remain just that tonight.

*

The next day, we sold our leftover tickets and steered clear of the venue. The remainder of the week was spent in the gym with the occasional sightseeing venture around Chennai. We visited Buddhist temples, wandered through a number of crowded street markets, enjoyed southern Indian food and even made it down to the beach – a beach I was deeply disappointed with. Litter was strewn all over the place. Stalls and shops let their rubbish and products mar the natural landscape, and the water was a murky, unnatural brown that signalled rife pollution in the area. I was disillusioned with humanity and capitalism. Here was a country rich in history, culture and natural resources. Yet all the burgeoning young generation wanted to do was join the consumer culture of materialistic wealth and self-prosperity. In the land where Buddhism originated, it was sad to see such ideals fall by the wayside in favour of a petty and superficial lifestyle. But who was I to talk? My sojourn to this part of the world had almost cost me everything. All to trade two tennis matches. Was making a quick buck from a tennis match worth dying in a filthy jail cell? I had some serious thinking to do about my future on the tour.

As the week drew to a close, I realised it was not going to be a good one in my books. My experiences in India had not exactly gone swimmingly. I found the place to be a decrepit shithole, and it's rare for me to dislike a new country. There's no doubt that my run-in at the tennis soured my opinion. I know it is a jaded and unfair view, which is why I also know that, one day, I'll return to India to explore its more natural and beautiful regions – hopefully on happier terms.

17

DEBAUCHERY IN VAN DIEMEN'S LAND

It's Sunday, and I'm on a plane with a hangover, yet again. The lady next to me has never been on a plane before. She's understandably tense.

'Don't worry,' I tell her as we descend into Hobart, 'I've been on about two hundred and I'm still here.' She stares in amazement as the landing gear clunks down. 'See?' I smile. I'm happy because I'm back in my home country after the ordeal of India. As a bonus, I will be working with the two most hilarious, nefarious and downright entertaining individuals I've ever had the pleasure of meeting. The rapscallions have assembled: Fitzy, Archie and I will all work together for the first time. We're sharing a gigantic apartment room in the centre of Hobart's trendy Salamanca district.

Much to my disappointment, they're both in a dull mood when I arrive. Fitzy has broken ribs after falling from the lofty heights of Jethro's shoulders at a music festival last week. So he's munching down opoid painkillers and can't even fart without cringing in pain. That's the least of his worries, though; thanks to the oxycodone, there's no movement in the bowel region whatsoever and Tim is proud to report that he hasn't done a poo in over four days. Looks like we're having a quiet one this evening, so I crash out and wake up fresh the next day, ready for work.

To our complete and utter disgust, Archie and I are recognised, approached, thrown out and banned in record time. That's two first-day kick-outs in two weeks. Disastrous! If this strike rate keeps up, I will be looking for a new career very soon. Not cool at all. To add insult, the head of security here didn't even know what he was doing. He was stuttering and ultimately reciting a script that must have been given to him by the officials. I tried to talk my way out of it but he had another security officer in tow. He was a real ballbreaker, a strong-looking guy with a shaved head and a constant glare in his eye. He was trying to go through all of my belongings, snapping photographs of me while I proclaimed my innocence, and insisted that I had to be trading because through his binoculars he 'could see the tendons in my hand moving after each point'.

It is clear what is going on here – the powers that be have obviously decided to launch a new offensive on court-side gamblers this year. I am ejected from the venue and issued with a trespass warning. They make it clear that legal action will be taken if I dare to return. Amazingly, Fitzy (the most recognisable of all of us) survives the first day.

*

We had our suspicions that this year might see an escalation in security issues, and now they have been confirmed. It used to be that we could get the boot and keep coming back in to trade the week out. Only if we really pissed off the officials and received a second strike would a trespass order be issued. Now, we're being turfed out on the first day and threatened with severe consequences if we return.

Scouts have even been hired to sit on court and look for us! They watch until they are certain they've identified a trader, then alert security. If you're spotted on court with a phone, you're a suspect. If you're searched and have spare batteries on you, it's game over. The authorities want us gone and they are well on their way to making it a reality. Many of the small-time traders are simply starting to give up.

Things have turned sour and we fear the golden days are over. It's only the second week of the year and, after being in contact with the other traders, I've discovered that everyone has been kicked out of the concurrent tennis events in progress around the world right now. To put it in perspective, last year, only one of our crew had trouble during the first month. Now, everyone is feeling the pressure. It's an ominous and alarming change.

*

While Fitzy is still at the tennis, Archie and I go back to the hotel and spread cheeky rumours about him to the hotel receptionist. Her name is Celeste and she blushes when we tell her Fitzy is keen on her. Once we see that she's interested, we run with it. We've set Bin Bin up for a date and he hasn't even finished his second match for the day! When he returns to the hotel that evening, we tell him about our little matchmaking effort, and he's amused.

'Thanks a lot, you clowns! I'm just going to call reception now and see what the reaction is,' he says.

During the brief but friendly phone call, he gets her number, and afterwards begins to text her privately. This is all going according to plan. He looks her up on Facebook while I'm hovering over his shoulder and asks, 'Should I just add her as a friend or is that creepy?'

'Too late!' I shout with glee, stabbing the 'Add' button on his Ipad. What's done is done. Furthermore, she accepts his request in the space of seconds and they're chatting away. It's late, so we all crash out, but our mission has been accomplished and it sounds like Fitzy has a date lined up for tomorrow night.

Considering the picture messages he shows us on his phone the next morning, it looks like he is in for quite a week. Even more amazingly, the cripple has *still* not done a poo. It's been five days now and, as Fitzy explains, 'It feels like I'm going to have a fucking baby! I'm actually scared for when it finally arrives; it may be the end of me!'

When the poo baby finally does enter the world around mid-morning, Fitzy spends a good twenty minutes in labour on the porcelain throne. Being the sharing guy that he is, he even has the decency and thoughtfulness to take a photo on his phone and upload it to Facebook. That's something I (and about five hundred other people) could have done without seeing. His phone's photo gallery must be full of filth after the past twenty-four hours, (apparently he took a few snaps of his old fella for Celeste too!) So Fitzy heads off to the tennis feeling about ten pounds lighter and, against the odds, gets through another day. Archie and I feel like complete and utter failures. We spend the day checking out the city of Hobart and play a few games of tennis at a local court.

When Tim arrives back at the hotel, things get interesting. He calls down to reception and the conversation goes something like this . . .

'Meet at 9.02 in room 406? Yeah, that's cool with me. No worries. I'll see you then.'

Archie and I stare in anticipation. Fitzy looks at us and laughs.

'Well, this is happening! She's got a key for one of the spare rooms and wants me to meet her there as soon as she knocks off work at 9 p.m.'

Amazing. Good on him. The kid deserves a reward for flying the flag on our behalf and evading security for the past few days. So he meets up with our receptionist and (despite the broken ribs) strikes up quite the holiday fling. Apparently she has an impressive array of sex toys and is not afraid to use them. I'll spare the dirty details but from Fitzy's graphic recounts she sounds like quite a nymphomaniac! This takes the hospitality industry to a whole new level.

The weather goes to shit on Wednesday, so Tim wears a hoodie to work. This comes in handy when the security crew finally approach him and try to take a photograph. He puts his sunglasses on, pulls the hood over his head and pushes through them before stumbling out half-blind and running from the venue. Strike three – we're all out. There's no chance of Tim returning after creating a scene like that.

Now that the team has properly assembled, it's time to party with one of my good mates who happens to live in Hobart. I met Mongrel while snowboarding in Canada a few years ago, and it's a great opportunity to see him thriving in his home town. He runs a tasteful and successful seafood cafe and bar on the water's edge and lives in a cosy beachfront shack on the next bay over. Swimming, diving, kayaking, fishing and wakeboarding are all at arm's reach on a daily basis. It's great to see your friends do well in life and we all enjoy a barbecue and some Boag's beers on the balcony as we watch the sun set over the Tasman Sea that afternoon in Mongrel's little corner of paradise.

Upon returning to the hotel, we realise that Fitzy's new squeeze has become a little too friendly and let herself into our room while we were away. As the receptionist, she has access to all the keys. Apparently, she was hungry and helped herself to a bowl of leftover green curry that Archie cooked for lunch. The psycho warning signs are there but we're happy to share curry and we let it slide.

The next day is one of leisure. The three of us lounge around Hobart's inner-city parks, practise a little slacklining and enjoy a bit of downtime in the picturesque city. There is greenery and wildlife everywhere, and the atmosphere is tranquil. If you've never been to Tassie, I highly recommend it. While it may not be the most 'happening' place on earth, it is serene and undeniably beautiful – a protected gem in Australia's south.

We've been told that Thursday night is the big night in town. The pub directly across the road from us does five-dollar steins. Yes. Five. Dollar. Steins! Mongrel and his mates come down to join us and pretty soon we're sinking copious amounts of beer while shooting pool and the proverbial shit. Celeste comes down to join us, with a girlfriend in tow. Apparently, this girlfriend is well and truly up for a threesome with her and Fitzy. Happy times for Bin Bin! Soon enough, he's making out with both of them at the bar and looks set for a great night. Thing is, his confidence is at an all-time high, so when a pretty girl walks past and strikes up a conversation he just can't help but bite. Uh-oh. He's mid-conversation with this girl when the other two members of the potential *ménage à trois* return from the bathroom. Celeste goes ballistic and storms out of the room with her friend. The pretty girl is disconcerted by this uproar and flees the scene. Tim's gone from hero to zero in a matter of seconds. He runs outside to patch things up and we continue to sink steins.

By this stage, we've downed four or five and are well on our way. I start chatting to a girl, who invites me to the nightclub across the road. I accept and tell her I will be there shortly. I step outside to try to round up the troops and see Tim making out with the two girls again.

'Don't you wish you were that guy?' a local asks me.

I laugh and ask Fitzy where the rest of the crew have gone. Apparently, they're inside doing shots. Shit, I'd better partake. After a few Jägerbombs, we're all feeling club ready, and Archie and I decide to head back to the hotel to get changed. We walk outside and Tim is nowhere to be seen. Good for Tim! There's only one place he and the girls could be, though, which is awkward because we need to get changed or we won't be allowed in the club. We assume they haven't been gone long and leg it to room 214. Bouncing around in the elevator with a few litres of beer and shots of Jäger in us, Archie and I jump out of the lift and run to the room. The door is ajar so I burst in with the salutation, 'How's the group sex, fuckers?'

Archie flicks on the light behind me, and to our confusion and amusement we are greeted by the distressed shouts of three senior women all sat up in bed in their nightgowns. They even have those weird old-fashioned nightcaps on! I've never even seen a person wear one until that night. In my drunken state, they provide quite the spectacle.

'What?' the poor old ladies all cry in unison.

'Oh, dear me,' I manage, as the fluoro light finally flicks into action and illuminates the room properly. 'This isn't room 214 is it?'

'No, it's 314!' they all yell at me. Oh . . . I see what's happened here.

'Right, well, your door was unlocked. And this is quite awkward, so we're going to go now. Very sorry to disturb you, have a good night!' And with that Archie and I flick off the light, slam the door behind us and burst out laughing as we run down the hall.

This time, we make sure to hit 2 in the elevator and surge into 214 to see . . . nothing. An empty, silent room. Interesting. And convenient for us. We get changed and head back across the road to round up the other local lads before going clubbing.

Major problem: the pub now has security on the door, and the bouncer who greets us is none other than the angry security guard with the shaved head who kicked us all out of the tennis earlier in the week! A smug grin crosses his face as we reach the front of the line, and we don't even bother taking our IDs out. We spin around on our heels and head straight for the nightclub. Luckily, it is a two-minute walk across the road.

Once inside, we grab some shots and I bump into the girl I was chatting to earlier. Archie stumbles off somewhere and I go for a dance. An hour later, my new-found friend returns to the hotel with me. She's very amused to find Archie passed out on his bed with the remote control still in his hand. He's dead to the world – just what I was hoping for.

I wake up in the morning, next to my Taswegian friend, and find both the lads in their respective beds across the room. As I make a trip to the bathroom, I notice a bundle of stools piled up against our hotel door from the inside.

'What's going on with this makeshift fortress?' I ask the boys.

'Umm, yeah, that was to stop psycho bitch from busting in here at 5 a.m. and murdering the lot of us,' Fitzy mumbles from under the covers.

'Right, of course,' I reply. 'What the hell happened, Fitzy?'

'Well, she got all jealous and clingy again, which is not a good thing if you're trying to tee up a threesome. We started arguing and she really pissed me off, so we got into a barney . . . again, and I just bailed and came back here. Then I remembered how she got in here the other day by programming a key at reception, so I devised a makeshift barricade and finally got some shut-eye!'

The Hobart sun rises on a disgruntled psychopathic nymphomaniac receptionist, an unforgiving security guard, a perplexed local girl whom I've just put in a taxi, and a bunch of hungover mates reeling from epic stein intake. We've certainly made our mark on this city, and it is time to move on. Just across the Bass Strait, Melbourne calls with more fun in store at my favourite tournament of them all – the Australian Open. Luckily, another receptionist is manning the desk as we check out. We hail a taxi and Fitzy sums up the collective feeling while loading his bag.

'Well, it's been a sick week. Thanks, Hobart. Now let's get the fuck out of here!'

'Hey, you can't complain,' Archie chides. 'At least you got it on with the hotel receptionist – none of the other lads have ever managed that feat on tour!'

'Yeah, you're right,' Fitzy concedes. 'She sure put the ho' in Hobart.'

'Romantic, Fitzy, you filthy animal,' I say.

A few minutes later, in the taxi, I receive a picture message that makes my eyes water upon opening it.

'What the fuck Fitzy, you sick bastard?! It is way too early in the morning to be sending dick pics!'

'Whaddya mean?' Fitzy is oblivious. I show him the photo and a look of horror creeps over his face while he pats his jeans pockets down.

'Ohh, fuck. I've lost my phone. Some prick has my phone!'

Archie and I cackle in amazement at this cruel twist of fate.

The person who found his phone can't exactly be described as a Good Samaritan. Half of Fitzy's contacts received the same picture message that day . . . and if you think I was appalled just imagine how his poor mother felt!

18

BACK IN THE GAME

In Vancouver International Airport terminal, I exchange my remaining Canadian dollars for euros. The lady at the counter hasn't got euro coins, so I ask for American change instead. This works out perfectly as I've now got money for lunch during my stopover in Seattle, before I board my flight to Reykjavík, Iceland. From Reykjavík, I'll fly to my final(ish) destination: London. I know, it's a messy itinerary but it saves a lot of money. I got what I paid for.

I haven't traded in three months, so I'm hardly loaded. After sneaking through a quiet Australian Open I figured a few months of snowboarding in Whistler would be a great way to remove my all-too-familiar face from the tour (and hopefully from the minds of the officials). The majority of trading mistakes I've made on court could be attributed to daydreams about shredding powder, so it was a therapeutic hiatus. I've spent the last few months hucking off cliffs, heli-boarding with mates, and even taking a cheeky side trip to party at California's Coachella music festival. Now that I've quelled my never-ending thirst for fresh snow and crisp mountain life, it's back to the airport terminals. The passport is almost full these days. I have so many stamps from different countries, I receive suspicious looks from immigration officers and have a story ready to explain why I travel so much and how I support my lifestyle. By this stage I have so many entry and exit stamps for the United States, Canada and Mexico that I must look like Pablo Escobar's understudy just begging to be busted. I get slammed at customs in Vancouver and have to endure an hour of questioning before squeezing through in time to make my flight.

When I finally board my plane to Seattle, the dude next to me stows a pretty impressive video camera as part of his luggage. There are many amazing people in our world, and travelling for two years straight provides me with a great opportunity to meet some of them. For me, that's one of the best things about travel – you meet amazing and intriguing people who can always teach you something new or tell you about previously unheard of places. I respect these people and soak up everything they have to offer, because they're a rare and wise breed. Something gives me the feeling this bearded man in his mid-forties next to me is one of those people.

'You film for a living?' I ask him.

'Yeah, I work freelance and shoot wildlife footage everywhere from Canada to New Zealand, and Argentina to Norway,' he says.

I'm blown away. It's not often I meet somebody with a cooler job than me. His name is Jim, and he's based in San Diego, California, so he can surf when he's home. We share stories from around the world and he tells me about his wife and kids.

'You got a girlfriend?' he asks me.

'Unfortunately not, mate. I just met an incredible girl from Colorado but now I'm off to Europe to work for the summer. A relationship just isn't a realistic option with my itinerary.'

'Don't stress, pal, you'll get there eventually. There's no rush, take it from me. Travel while you're young and free and make the most of your youth. Once you get married and have kids, you're locked in and you'll regret not making the most of opportunities when you had them.'

'I hear that. I've already got married mates back home telling me the same thing. But I guess it doesn't matter who you are, the grass always seems greener, doesn't it?'

As fun as partying around the world has been, I have to admit the single life is feeling awfully hollow lately. I've been fortunate enough to forge friendships with girls from Canada, America, Austria, Russia, Sweden, Italy and many other countries, all of whom I keep in regular contact with. This gift is a catch-22, though. I get to meet some of the most amazing and attractive women around the world, only to have to say goodbye to them a few days later. I have many daydreams in the tennis stands, with my vacant stare directed at the court and my thumb moving on autopilot while my mind is thousands of miles away with a girl from the other side of the world.

I'm grateful for the opportunity to have met such amazing people during my travels, though, and I try to keep in touch with everyone I've met along the way. While the road hasn't allowed me to settle down with any of these girls, it is the reason I met them in the first place. Although these stories always keep the lads back home entertained, I have to admit I often find myself envying their stability and commitment to a settled lifestyle. It can get lonely on the road, and the comfort of ongoing intimacy and a meaningful relationship is just another thing I have to look forward to once I retire from trading.

'I've always looked at trading as a short-term career for those reasons,' I say to Jim. 'But wildlife photography or filming? That's something special, man! I envy your job because it educates people about our beautiful world and the creatures that inhabit it. It's constructive and positive.'

There are times when I have mental battles with my job and current existence. Not because I'm the 'bad guy' gambler that the authorities try to label me as, but for much more encompassing reasons. My job exists essentially to generate profit. I know – most jobs on earth do these days. But with mine it is so black and white I would have to be incredibly ignorant to disregard it. My score updates fund the bank accounts of a few people. Period. In the end, after all the flights, taxis, hotels, nights out and tennis matches covered, I'm churning out cold, hard cash that goes straight into the bank. I have a problem with it because, in essence, this job exists to feed vices: greed and selfishness. They are two things I neither respect nor wish to base my life around. I chose this job because of the lifestyle it entails. I get to do what I want, almost all of the time, while travelling the world on an expense account. Most people would define this as a perfect life. I tend to agree. However, I am beginning to see the enormity of my carbon footprint on this earth, and the novelty of travelling to places wears off the second time around.

My major gripe with this job is that I'm not helping anyone or doing anything constructive. It is a redundant and frustrating job in that sense. Hence, it cannot be a career. What it is, however, is a great opportunity. I will endeavour to enjoy myself as much as possible while I am still young and free and try to ignore that niggling little voice called conscience inside my head. A career and responsibility can wait for the time being. At least, when that time comes, I won't have any regrets.

So what do I respect? Buddhist-like ideals of zero desire for material wealth and living through minimalist, natural means.

I'm doing this job not only because I love to travel but because I need to save money. I don't want to be a millionaire but unfortunately humans have enslaved themselves to a system where you need money to survive. I've blown so much of it feeding my addiction to travelling in the past few years that this job seemed like the most sensible option for setting myself up for the future. Setting myself up in a beachside town in Australia, where I can surf every day and relax away from the hustle and bustle of the city. But for now I'll try to stomach the taste of irony and enjoy what the road throws my way.

My Californian friend bids me farewell and good luck as we arrive in Seattle. I wish him the same, but I know he doesn't need it – he's got life figured out. The remaining flights are much less enlightening, as my fellow passengers tend not to speak English. I opt for the companionship of snowboarding DVDs and watch a few movies, while considering my place in the world and my chances back on the tour . . .

*

I arrive in Munich, Germany, in great spirits and ready for my first European tournament of 2012. It's a wonderful city, populated by cheerful people who make amazing food and renowned beer. The home of Oktoberfest will always bring back fond memories for me. The hotel is lush: four stars (a modest judgement in my opinion), with great facilities and an incredible breakfast buffet. It's also within walking distance of the tennis. I'm by myself for the week, but after three months of living in a Whistler share house it's a welcome retreat. The BMW Open is nestled amid quaint, leafy countryside. It's a clay tournament and there are some great names attending, including Germany's favourite son, Tommy Haas, finding some of his old form in an amazing comeback year. I'm a bit worried, though, that security may stop me from watching him play.

I survive the first day without any problems. The grounds are small, and not ideal for trading, but I endure and remain optimistic for the week ahead. As I'm waiting for tickets on the second day, I see two traders called Torsten and Pete having a chat. I join them and catch up on some gossip from the past few months. Pete is one of the originals, a family man who lives in Germany and now only works at the European tournaments for ease of travel. He's a jovial guy, and why shouldn't he be? He's lived a fun life. Torsten is a stylish Swede and ex-table-tennis pro with a penchant for fine clothing and an obsession with the ins and outs of trading. He's not dressed to the nines today, though. Instead, he sports a training outfit that makes him look like a player or coach. He even has a tennis bag slung over his shoulder to try to blend in.

To my amusement, a local child asks for an autograph while we're talking. He obliges with a cheeky grin. Tomorrow, he'll probably be wearing a suit, to make him as opaque as possible to the watchful security radar. Tor employs one of the software gurus from the infamous website 'The Pirate Bay' to do a lot of his tech work, and uses some of the most inventive methods on tour. He's a clever guy and draws on every resource available to be successful at what he does. Both Torsten and Pete are wary of security but hopeful we can outfox them this week. 'Keep an eye out for trouble,' they warn me, and we part ways to avoid being seen together.

Day two is also cool; I spend most of it in a leather chair in the BMW bar, overlooking court three. I also venture over to court four, where I relax in a Corona sling chair and enjoy the spring sunshine. I've missed warm weather and vitamin D over the past few months and my body is welcoming it back on this sunny May day. My time spent on centre court is limited, and I leave still optimistic that the world is not ending, like most traders would have me believe. A dinner of Bavarian fare and beer follows, accompanied by some reading and a movie back in my hotel room. I've slipped back into the stress-free trader lifestyle and I'm enjoying it.

Until the stress returns, that is. I'm sitting on centre court, trading the first match of the day in surprising humidity, when across the court I see an official talking animatedly to the head security guard. I've got my sunglasses on, so I watch from the corner of my eye while I trade the match. He has a folder with him. *The* folder. I might be paranoid but it's likely he's showing the guard photos of me from previous events. He points at me just as I look up from the game point. That seals it. I'm out of here. Luckily, half the crowd are moving in and out of the stand now too. I pause my phone, jump out of my seat and weave towards the exit. Damn it! I'm too slow – he's already there. The head security guard is a large man dressed in a smart grey suit. I put my head down and stroll on but he puts his hand out to block my path and demands, 'ID!'

'Excuse me?' I reply with false shock on my face.

'Identification, you show me,' he clarifies. He struggles with English. Good for me.

'Sorry, what? No. What is this all about? I'm leaving,' I bombard him, trying to confuse the man with my foreign tongue as I push forward. He grabs my arm. I stare in mock offence at his grip on my bicep and shoot him a look that says 'You're out of order and you know it'.

He hesitates. Perfect.

'I'm leaving,' I repeat, and shrug his hand off me before heading towards the exit. He follows me to the gate and even walks down the street after me. I hustle down a set of stairs into the subway station and then run to the exit that takes me up to the other side of the road. I've avoided any real confrontation . . . for today.

There are only a few days left of the tournament and I would very much like to start back on a positive note. I go in the next day because I've not been banned from the grounds yet. Escaping without them taking your ID or being able to talk to you properly is vital to your longevity at an event. When I return, however, I spend half my time trading from television feeds in the food court, while the other half is spent standing on the periphery of centre court, out of sight of the officials. It's a dubious and vexing way to trade, but it works and I survive the week. I'm back in the game!

*

After work on Saturday, I meet up with Tor for dinner and some sightseeing around the city's vibrant centre. We walk through the Englischer Garten – English Garden – a large park in the city centre, and take photos from a bridge as keen surfers ride the famous river wave in the Eisbach. If I had a wetsuit with me, I'd be down there asking to borrow someone's board! We wander the streets, watch the landmark Rathaus-Glockenspiel do its thing in the heart of town and have dinner at a traditional German cafe just down the road. Over a few Paulaner beers, Tor opens up and divulges some interesting news to me.

'You know Vittorio threatened one of the officials over in South America at the start of the year?'

'What? No, I had no idea. What's he thinking? That will only cause problems for us.'

'I know. He told the guy, "Look, I'm from Naples, so I know people who you don't want to meet. You'd better be careful how

196

you talk to me. It's very easy for me to discover your name and details." The crazy bastard.'

'Well, no wonder they're cracking down on us like we're all criminal swine,' I groan. Sure, it was probably fun for Vittorio to mess with the official and give some shit back while he was getting booted, but no good can come of such stupidity.

'Yeah, he's caused a shitstorm,' agrees Tor.

'But it's kind of a blessing in disguise, you know? We're doing well now. With all of these security problems, a lot of guys have been pushed out of the game.' In typical Swedish form, his English is near perfect. 'Each time another trader goes bankrupt, the market opens up a little for us. If we can keep going and stay out of trouble, then we stand to make a lot of money.'

'So are you guys working every week now?' I ask.

'No, see that's the thing – we only go to tournaments where we think it will be safe. It's not worth the risk of getting our photo taken and being recognised from then on.'

He's right. It's a game of balance, taking the right amount of risk for viable return.

'That's where you guys get fucked over, man. You go to tournaments every week, and they know who you are now. Even after three months away, they still recognise you.'

He's right again. Our eagerness to trade every tournament could ultimately be our undoing. There's no doubt they have my details and photograph in that folder and are looking for me on court these days. I'm a marked man, as are many of my co-workers.

'That's why I always run,' he continues. 'In Copenhagen recently, I was chased off court after about half an hour. I saw those guys coming for me from the entrance so I ran to a fire exit and busted out of the stadium. It set off a fucking alarm and then

I really had their attention! The whole security team were chasing me and I had to jump the fence. Those crazy bastards jumped it too, though, and it took half an hour of running down backstreets and hiding in someone's garage to finally shake them.'

'Jesus, that's full on!' I remark. 'They're really out to get us these days, aren't they?'

'Yeah, but they didn't get my details or a photo that day, so it was worth it.'

'And you had no problems this week?'

'No, I had problems yesterday. The supervisor was watching me, so I got up and left. He followed me all the way out, and I could tell this because it was afternoon and I could see his shadow from the corner of my eye. It started coming closer and closer, so I picked up my pace and made it to the exit. After about fifty metres, I turned around and saw him speaking to security and pointing in my direction. That's why I wasn't there today. My partner went in and had no problems – they have no idea who he is.'

'So he's never been kicked out before then?' I ask.

'Once. In Sweden.'

'What? You guys got booted in your own backyard?'

'Yeah, the Swedish tournaments are very hard to survive now. The head of security came and kicked me out personally. Before I could go, he sat me down in a room for a long chat. He was pissed to learn that Swedish guys were trading. He was like, "Fuck, man, I can't believe this. I know there are English and Italian guys doing this but Swedes too?" It was pretty funny but he banned me in the end.'

'Bummer, man. You don't want to get done on your own turf.'

'Well, I wasn't going to be defeated that easily, so I returned the next day wearing a full-blown disguise: boring clothes that a middle-aged man might wear and a grey wig with a moustache. It worked . . . kind of. After a few hours, the security team approached me and said I looked suspicious.'

'Did they know it was *you?*'

'The head of security gave me the same chat as the day before, except he had no idea he was talking to the same guy! So I didn't get busted for trespassing. To this day, I doubt that security guy has any idea he was talking to the same person he'd banned the day before!'

'That's fucking brilliant, Torsten!' I laughed with approval. 'You guys really do get away with some funny shit. Are you still trading with those Nintendo Wii controllers connected to your phone by Wi-Fi?'

'No, not any more. We change our technology almost every week. We have to keep improving to stay competitive. You know Yves?'

I nodded. He was a good guy, very intelligent, and possibly the best left on tour.

'He's helped us out a lot. He's got an IT background and does a lot of testing to constantly improve his technology. I've watched him in his hotel room doing the tests, and he'll set up ten different phones linked to ten different Betfair accounts. He hits them all at the same time and notes which one is quickest for placing a bet. But he does this over and over, tweaking and adjusting things to get the very best result possible. He spends hours working on it. His technology is at the top now, and I think he's the quickest and makes the most money out of everybody so far this year.'

'And he's never been kicked out,' I add.

'They'll never get him. He's just a normal guy who minds his own business and stays out of trouble. He always takes his girl with him and they remain incognito. It's a good thing, too, because he works hard for this profit and he deserves it. That's the thing they don't realise about us; this is our job! We put a lot of time, money and effort into this job, but the officials don't realise it. They think we're just stealing money and trying to destroy tennis. It's nothing like that, is it?'

I agree with him and we order another round of beers. Wanting to live on the tennis tour takes dedication, commitment and acumen. Traders spend hours on end studying, testing and improving their systems. I just wish the officials could accept that and understand us instead of turning a deaf ear and focusing on the negatives.

*

Two weeks later, I'm bailed up in Madrid, and the negatives are flying thick and fast at me along with spit from an outraged official's quivering lip. I'm back in the game and back in the shit.

'You are lazy. You are stupid. I don't believe this disgusting thing you do. This is criminal and you will go to jail for it.'

'It's not illegal,' I reply calmly.

'It is illegal!' the official shrieks.

'If it was illegal, I wouldn't do it. I'm not a criminal.'

'What you are doing is illegal and you will end up in jail for it. It might not be today, but in a year or maybe even in a few weeks from now you will go to jail for this.'

I sigh and retire from the argument. I'm in no mood after what's just happened. Mono and I were grabbing lunch during a break when we bumped into a fraught-looking Felix.

'What's going on, bud?' I said to him as we sat down near a juice bar.

He shook his head at me, eyes wide.

'Oh shit, what's up?' I stood up in alarm.

'They're after me. Go! Get away from me now.'

Mono and I nodded and walked away. It was too late, though, and as we rounded the corner we came face to face with an angry official and his entourage of sneering thugs. They didn't even care about Felix any more.

'Show me your ID!' the official demanded, as his team blocked our path.

'Sorry, but why are you asking me for ID? Do you mind explaining what's going on here?'

Mono and I both knew the score but there are two reasons you always reply like that:

1.   You always stand a chance of bluffing your way out.
2.   It's just plain rude for someone to address you like that and we want the officials to extend the simplest of decencies and justify themselves before barking orders at us.

It wasn't the greatest play, though, and escalated into an ultimatum.

'Either show me your ID now or we will hold you for the police.'

We both knew the Spanish Police would be a lot more trouble than the security team. The police had beaten a friend of ours last year on a night out in Barcelona, so we were forewarned. Doesn't mean we did the smart thing, though, does it?

'No!' we answered in defiance, pissing our interrogator off to great effect.

A ruckus ensued. The guards grabbed us and threw us into all sorts of tricky security-guard holds before dragging us across La Caja Mágica in front of hundreds of shocked spectators. They did their best to manhandle us, trying to trip us up as they dragged us towards the office. Umpires and players walked out of the VIP area and threw quizzical looks in our direction. It was not cool. Then they did the full-body pat-down and search. What a fucking joke. Try shaking yourself free from a security crew and lecturing them by saying they have no right to touch you or your belongings. It ends in you either getting beaten to a pulp or just giving up.

I choose the latter. Mono and I are put in separate corners of the room while our belongings are laid out in front of us as if we were terror suspects or drug lords. I've been snowboarding for three months – so I'm wearing a hoodie and a flat-brim cap, jeans and high-top sneakers. Mono is rolling his standard monotone style in a black jacket with black shades and black jeans. I admit it; we look like a couple of punks. But we're no drug lords.

'*Mucho batterias*,' one guard observes.

Mono and I roll our eyes at each other as if to say 'Well done, Sherlock, you've found the magic clue'.

One overzealous guard pushes it too far with me and I just have to push him back. 'Get your fucking hands off me!' I erupt, to my own dismay. It could turn out to be a very bad move.

Two of them grab me and throw me back against the glass wall. '*Tranquillo, amigo, tranquillo*,' they warn me.

'*Si, si, tranquillo. Tu tranquillo!*' I tell them.

The detectives arrive and, after flashing their badges, take over. They copy all of our details down from our identification cards and take photos of our belongings. Then they take mugshot photos and make us wait while they have discussions with the officials. Mono and I look at each other. What the fuck? What is there to talk about? I've had cops involved once or twice before but this is going one step further. As we watch the officials through the window, we realise they are practically begging to have us arrested.

Thankfully, the police officers present that day are honest and decent cops. If they were corrupt or jaded officers, it might have been a very different story. But they are buying none of it and deny the wishes of the officials, saying, 'We're not doing that because we can't do that – these men have not broken any law.'

I'm dumbfounded by the officials' actions, though. They've accused us of being immoral then tried to coerce the police officers into falsely imprisoning us. The moral to the story is . . . well, I'm not sure there is any morality to it whatsoever. The officials throw their hands up in frustration, and Mono and I sigh at each other with relief.

It isn't over, though. We are then walked into a room and sat down at a desk with the officers. They hand me a pen and place a very official-looking document with a coat of arms that looks like a court order in front of me. Am I being sued? Fined? Put on trial? I try to read it but my Spanish is nowhere near good enough. I shake my head, no.

¿Qué es esto? I ask them.

There is a moment of translation as we wait nervously, and they say, 'It's a notice to say that you are banned from these grounds and will not return.'

I breathe yet another sigh of relief and scribble away. Even after all that rigmarole, they can only issue a trespass order against us. Two minutes later, Mono and I are standing outside the grounds waiting for a taxi and trying to shake the nerves out of our systems.

'Well, that was a fucking ordeal!' Mono laughs. 'As you can see, things are a little more intense these days. Welcome back to the tour, mate!'

19

SHOWDOWN AT THE CHAMPIONSHIPS

I step off the plane and stroll through Heathrow Airport. It's sunny in London for once and I throw my Prada shades on to block out the piercing rays that shine into the terminal. Typical trader attire, I think. How these two years have changed me. A mate of mine often says 'You become your environment', and I can't help but laugh in agreement today. When I started this job, I was a surf bum rolling board shorts, thongs and T-shirts everywhere. Now, as I head to the luggage carousel, I'm sporting a leather jacket with designer jeans and an expensive shirt. I'm even wearing Gucci cologne and Armani underwear, to boot. No wonder they spot me in the crowd – I'm a fully converted trader.

Of course, I'm here for Wimbledon. This is the big one. There are four Grand Slams, but just one is recognised by the players and crowd as 'the Championships'. It's the pinnacle event on the tennis calendar and only the most talented and in-form players will win it. This will be my third Wimbledon. Am I happy to be here, though? No, most definitely not. I am, after all, banned for life. However, my hands are tied in this issue. If I want to keep my job, I need to *do* my job. I've been surviving a few tournaments lately but it's been testing work. It's come to the point where I feel like some type of covert operative at times.

The weeks leading up to this Grand Slam have been tense. A fortnight ago in Halle, Germany, I found myself in the players' hotel sneaking back and forth across balconies and hallways, trying to find a clear view of the courts below. I ended up on the top-floor penthouse, which was housing none other than Roger Federer and his family for the week, and decided it was probably more of a security risk to stay there than to be on court. I eventually opted to trade from a quaint cafe that overlooked the outside court. Security was tense at this event, and Mono had already been given his marching orders, so I knew I had to be careful. The vantage point was perfect, though. Security didn't notice me and I had a full view of the court and scoreboard for the whole match. I sat back, enjoyed some Bavarian beer and a bratwurst, read the paper between points and leisurely traded a couple of matches, with my phone on my lap, in complete safety and comfort. Later in the week, with the cover of the crowd on centre court, Mono and I braved the stands. It went well for the majority of the time, but then a particular umpire with a disdain for traders spotted us.

'Fuck. He's seen us, hasn't he?' said Mono.

'Umm, I'm not sure,' I replied, trying to remain optimistic but quickly making up my mind when the umpire glared up in our direction.

'Oh shit,' we said together.

'Yeah, it's time to go,' I decided, as the umpire pulled out his radio to call security.

We didn't give them the chance to catch us, jumping up that second, leaving our seats and pushing through the crowd. I looked back just before exiting the stadium and saw a glare of absolute scorn on the umpire's face. I smiled at him, then bolted down the stairs and dissolved into the crowd outside.

A few days later, the same umpire walked straight past me in 's-Hertogenbosch, in the Netherlands (yes, it takes out the 'most ridiculous' name on tour – even the Dutch prefer to call it Den Bosch, 'the Forest', and in English we call it the Bosch). The Bosch is a mundane place. It offers none of the excitement that those other Dutch cities such as Amsterdam and Utrecht are famous for. Surrounded by farms and woodland, it's a serene and refined tournament. The sponsors – UNICEF – put on a great spread for all to enjoy and do a fantastic job of making it a successful grass tournament.

It was Monday morning and I was doing my rounds, scoping out the grounds and trying to discover the most low-key courts where I could trade under the radar. So much for that! As I wandered around a corner, I heard an unpleasant guttural hacking sound right behind me, followed by a venomous spit. Spinning on my heels, I saw the same umpire from last week striding away from me, shaking his head in disgust. What perception could he possibly have to harbour such hatred? He was on his radio again, so I didn't have time to find out. I legged it to another court and laid low.

The Bosch turned out to be quite the challenge indeed. Mono got the boot from a rather hostile security supervisor early in the week, and I was left to run the gauntlet on my own. A friend of mine named Billy, who happened to be backpacking around the Netherlands at the time, had come and stayed with us, sleeping on a makeshift bed of cushions on our hotel floor for a few nights.

That was cool with me because it meant he could come and sit on court and drink beers while keeping me company. This helped me avoid detection and got me towards the end of the week without incident.

The only problem was that, once Billy left, I was in the stands on my own again. The heat picked up from then on. The officials' building was directly across from the stand, and they could sit in their office observing me while liaising with security. I was determined to survive the week. I was sick of being treated like a second-rate human and a criminal because these people had chosen to subscribe to a misinformed perception. I wore a nondescript black cap, a dark sports jacket, a pair of jeans and some shades. I'd switch my outfit up as often as practical, and, as an extra precaution, I started trading with my hand in my jacket pocket at all times, only taking my phone out to check the score at the most essential moments. I developed a little technique where I could pretend to have a cough and at the same time look down while sliding my phone out of the pocket just far enough to confirm the right score. It worked. They watched me and watched me, but nobody ever did anything because they had no proof or reason.

On the last day, I was tested with an incredibly tight situation. I had to trade a long tiebreak under the watchful eye of about four officials and a TIU officer without checking my phone once. If I'd fucked up, it could have been disastrous, but I managed to keep it together and left the tournament victorious.

Interestingly enough, I did see a familiar face on centre court in the Bosch. It was none other than the red-headed Kiwi who may or may not have ratted me out at Wimbledon last year. I saw him further down the stand, sitting near the players' area, and made sure I stayed well out of his sight. It was a reminder that, next week, I'd face the ultimate challenge and would have to be at the peak of my undercover trading ability if I was to stand any chance of surviving Wimbledon.

*

Even after the escalation in security problems and the crackdown on traders at tournaments around the world this year, Wimbledon's security team is second to none. The Grand Slam crowd will provide some cover, but there will be CCTV cameras all over the grounds with facial-recognition technology to single us out. True to their word, the officials posted a formal letter to my Australian address after last year's ejection, banning me from the grounds for life. There is no doubt they have my photo and details on record. The club will have their elite security team working the grounds all day every day, and there are countless police available at their disposal to apprehend traders and troublemakers alike.

So, as I walk through England's busiest and most important airport, there is an undeniable sense of foreboding welling up inside me. Is this job really worth getting in trouble with the law for? I am a qualified schoolteacher, and a criminal conviction would be enough to void my registration. During my first year on tour, I cruised through the circuit without stressing too much on the security issues. I took it all as a bit of a joke – an added element of the job that kept it peculiar and lively. Tennis kick-outs had been a source of entertaining stories to share over beers. But things have changed after Chennai. It isn't all fun and games any more. It is serious. They've threatened me with prison and physical violence. In Madrid, the officials pushed as hard as possible to get me thrown in a cell. I escaped both incidents by a gnat's knob, but how many lives does a trader get? There is now a real threat of criminal action if I get caught.

This time, I know I am pushing it, and I'm not happy. The honeymoon period is well and truly over with this job. I am still having fun, but I am also missing the surf back home and want to catch up with my mates from Whistler, who have continued snowboarding and living the dream, without the unnecessary threat of legal action.

As I collect my baggage from the carousel and head towards the underground terminal, I realise my love for the job is being tested. I want to see the year out and enjoy the many opportunities I'll be afforded if I stay on the road, but am I willing to risk my future for this job? While my clothing may suggest I've converted into a fully fledged trader, I'm not sure how much longer I can stay in this increasingly demanding industry. Wimbledon will be the ultimate test.

*

Regardless of my concerns, it is uplifting and exciting to be back with all of the lads. London is a great place to socialise and mingle. There are numerous quality restaurants (we spend our first night at a restaurant called Dans Le Noir – 'In the Black' – where you eat your mystery meal in enveloping inky darkness, served by blind waiters, and only discover what was on the menu *after* you've paid the bill). There are trendy nightclubs, bars of all different sizes and crowds, and fluctuating attractions such as the Notting Hill Carnival, Borough Markets, art galleries and museums, and West End shows. It is a city that thrives on diversity and never fails to entertain.

I haven't seen some of the lads for months, so it's nice to share a few pints and catch up on stories. There are tales of kick-outs at dodgy events, new methods being employed to evade security and warnings of which scouts have been spotted sitting in the crowd lately. Once we figure out there's a scout at an event, we all do our best to warn the others by sending a description of them and their outfit around to everybody else. Knowledge is power, innit? (As a Londoner might say.) Knowing what a scout looks like might still not be enough this week. There is a whole team of professionals devoted to identifying and ejecting us. The challenge has been laid down, and we're here to tackle it head on. I'm just hoping I don't have to call my lawyer this week.

*

So, here we are: the Championships. I'm nervous, worried and tense. But, at the same time, I've resigned myself to the fact that I will be trading this tournament, and I am determined to give it my best shot. I now know what we're up against here and I'm ready for the challenge. If worst comes to worst, then what better tournament to be kicked out of? While I'm not overly excited about my predicament, I'm quite thrilled to be back among these coveted grounds and their courts. It's such a wonderful atmosphere and a spectacle that it never gets old. No matter how this week pans out, I feel quite privileged to be able to say I've attended three Wimbledons.

As an additional precaution, we've got two new lads on board the trader train: Sandy and Freddy G. They're both funny guys from the United Kingdom who've been keen to jump on the tour for years. A few fresh faces will hopefully ensure a couple of us survive the gauntlet we're about to step into.

We go through the rigmarole of lining up and securing tickets, and eventually make our way into the grounds, half-expecting them to stop us at the gates. They don't. That's hurdle number one out of the way – best we split up to avoid any multiple ejections. We wish each other good luck and disperse for the day. It's time to get my game face on. The Bosch primed me for this challenge and I'm ready to trade in stealth mode. The black cap, dark sports jacket and sunglasses are all on. There's no way facial-recognition cameras are going to pick me up, and there's no way anyone can see my phone while I keep it in my jacket pocket at all times. Additionally, I'm moving position every couple of games: standing up for twenty minutes, then sitting on the other side of the court for ten. This goes on for the entire day. I spot a few of the English traders and offer them only the slyest of nods so as not to give either of us up. I see a number of security members and officials throughout the day. Each time they pass by, I try to take a deep breath and look inconspicuous. None of them give me so much as a second glance. Before I know it, the sun is setting on a calm London day. I've survived, and so have my co-workers.

The only negative about surviving is you get home around 9 or 10 p.m., fall into bed and wake up at the crack of dawn to do it all again. I hardly have a chance to celebrate my survival before I'm back in the mix, doing my finest impersonation of a secret agent once again. It's all serves, volleys and scores ticking over for the next few hours. I'm starting to relax and feel like I might just stand a chance here this week. After all, it's been a year and I've had a lot of practice trading in a surreptitious manner since I was last here. So I settle in for a five-setter and enjoy the tennis.

*

Good tennis is beautiful. I'm sure any sports fan would agree with that. When two skilled and motivated players are pitted against each other in front of a supportive crowd and the stakes are high, you're almost guaranteed a spectacle. If both players are in form and matching each other, struggling for the advantage, the rallies unfold like a mesmerising dance. Tennis requires a rare balance of grace and power that not many sports can showcase. Each match is a battle, and the crowd goes through this tug of war for dominance, offering its support and encouragement. Each point is a carefully constructed undertaking. Like a game of chess, the players move about the court, securing a stronghold from which to defend or attack – rallying from the baseline, volleying at the net or unleashing an all-court onslaught to wear their opponents down and run them ragged.

It is a game of strategy and resilience – mental strength plays a bigger role in this sport than any spectator would ever guess. The beauty of it is neither player can ever cover all their territory at once. No position is infallible, no premeditation is guaranteed. So players do the closest thing they can to guarantee victory: they back themselves, reading the play and moving in anticipation, turning defence into attack, and, after years of practicing shots and building court awareness, they give it everything they can.

There is no bigger motivation for a player than Wimbledon, and no finer venue to showcase these battles of will and skill. Grass tennis lends itself to the quicker, more aggressive shots and styles of play. The serve-volley, ace and slice all come into their element. As I've said, on grass courts, players can dive and literally throw their bodies on the line in desperation to make a shot. The action is fast, intense and exhilarating. I love it!

It's a pleasure to watch, and, fortunately, it's my job to watch it. More importantly, it's my job to *read* it, to understand what's happening on court and to premeditate the run of play as it's unfolding in the players' heads. The quicker I am, the more we profit. I've been doing this for eighteen months now and I'm confident, quick and concise. I can trade without moving a muscle, apart from my thumb. I can now sit on court with a deadpan expression (the traders' equivalent of a poker face) and log points without looking at my screen once during a game. I don't, though – I want to blend in. To do that, I need to clap and cheer, to get involved and play the role of an avid fan. I've had enough practice at this to throw most scouts off me if they're watching in the crowd. And, because this is Wimbledon, I don't need to pretend; I'm loving every second. Let's face it, I *am* a fan.

Evidently, all the practice in the world won't save me from Wimbledon security, though. It's midway through the fourth set and I've just spotted the spotter out of the corner of my eye. It's James, the same guy who personally turfed me out last year. I reach down and snatch my bag before swinging out into the crowd. It's time for the cat-and-mouse game described at the start of this book to unfold. I give him the slip, hide in the toilet block and relocate to a new court. But James is relentless and I'm chased off that court too. A minute later, while weaving my way through naive spectators, a large man in a suit blocks my path and I hear those all-too-familiar words, 'Excuse me, sir. Stop right there, please!' The gig is up.

Now the big question is, will they take legal action?

'Mate, you look mighty familiar to me. You were here last year, weren't you?' says James. And then he answers himself before I even have a chance to reply. 'Yes, yes, you were. And you got sent a letter too!'

Uh-oh. This is the scenario I've been dreading for the past few days. 'Well, I wouldn't know about any letter,' I explain. 'I haven't been back to my home address since we last met, so I never received a letter from Wimbledon.'

'Ah, I see,' he concedes. 'Isn't that convenient?'

I shrug my shoulders – there's no way I'm providing them with any cannon fodder. The police arrive to oversee my ejection. There are three of them, and one liaises with the security team while two question me, take my details and search my belongings.

This all happens right beside court ten with countless onlookers walking by.

'Oh dear, looks like that chap's in a bit of trouble!' I hear one bloke say to his wife. This is the height of embarrassment as far as tennis boots go.

The police ask numerous questions and try to press for details of my co-workers. When I decline to answer, they do not persist. This is a civilised and professional investigation, nothing like Chennai.

'So, how much do you earn then?' asks one of the officers. I can tell by her tone that this question is not part of the interview and simply a matter of curiosity.

I wink at her and shake my head. 'It's a secret,' I whisper.

The officers look at each other and smirk. They know why I'm being ejected and they're not sure whether to regard me as a wealthy entrepreneur or an uppity punk.

I'm feeling okay about this whole situation so far. There's no animosity from any of the security or police. It is a fine line I'm treading, though. I know that cooperation here is key. One of my friends was chased down the road, arrested and handcuffed last year for trying to push his way out the gates instead of obliging.

James joins our conversation and explains to the police that I was here last year. 'Now, apparently he didn't receive the letter we sent out, banning him from the event. So we're going to make sure he receives one today in the presence of our club lawyer. That will settle the issue for good,' he declares.

We wait for the lawyer to arrive while spectators pass by and ogle me in the custody of three police. 'I wonder what he's done!' is the general remark.

An official lawyer of the All England Lawn Tennis and Croquet Club (AELTC) arrives with a signed trespass order and presents me with it. There are police witnesses and I'm given my ultimatum: if I return, they will take legal action. I've officially been served with a trespass order in the eyes of the law; I'm banned from Wimbledon for life. Again. There will be no further excuses if I'm caught in the grounds in future. It looks like I've seen my last game of tennis at the Championships.

I make up my mind right there and then that I'll never return as a trader. I tell James this as he escorts me to the gate with the police.

'I'm glad to hear it, mate. You seem like one of the decent guys. I know you're just doing your job here but so am I and I can't have you breaching or ignoring our rules. We've given you a second chance but there won't be a third. Don't make us have to take action against you.'

'That won't be necessary, James. This is the last you'll see of me. Thanks for being a gentleman about it all.'

We shake hands and part with some level of mutual respect. I'm elated to get off so easily. Once again, I've escaped any major consequence. It could have been a lot worse and I'm thankful the only lawyer I had to talk to was the one serving me papers. At the same time, I'm disappointed. My job has cost me the privilege of watching tennis here for a lifetime. Maybe I'll come back here many years down the track, once my face has been forgotten. I'd like to be able to visit Wimbledon with my children or family if the chance ever arises in the future. But even then I'll technically be breaking the law.

In many ways, this tournament signals the beginning of the end for my trading career. Being banned from tournaments for life is nothing to laugh at. If I am blacklisted from too many tournaments in the future, then I'll be no use on the tour at all. With all of this security pressure, there is no doubt my job is starting to lose its appeal. The good times are now being out-weighed by the nerve-wracking ones and the fun is fading from our beloved occupation.

*

The next day, I escape the clutter of London for the more peace-ful countryside of England's South West. I have family and friends who live in Bristol, so I'm going to spend my spare time catching up with them, exploring Bath, shopping, sipping ciders and relax-ing away from the hustle and bustle. Although I've only worked two days, I feel burnt out and exhausted from the pressure of dodging security crews the past few weeks. As I stare out the window at the greenery while my train whisks me westwards, I wonder how much longer this tumultuous ride can last.

20

MISSION IMPOSSIBLE

My cab is hurtling down Interstate 40 in the damp darkness of pre-dawn, delivering me to my fourth airport in three days. My taxi driver's a tad crazy – she's disappointed I'm leaving town without sampling some of her home-made moonshine. Even I think it's a little early in the morning for that. Two days ago, I flew from Cincinnati to Greensboro, connecting through Charlotte. Today, I'm flying from Greensboro to New Haven, connecting through Philadelphia. Why? Got the boot, didn't I? Again. It's the week before the US Open, and these sleepy little tournaments are on top of their security issues – not surprisingly, as there's little else for them to do. Faced with a week to kill in Winston-Salem's pouring rain and the realisation that North Carolina is one of the more boring places on earth, I feared I might go insane. Hence the 4.30 a.m. wake-up call and early flight to Connecticut was not entirely opposed as an escape route.

I touch down in New Haven, drop my bags at the hotel and head straight to the tennis . . . only to take a thorough booting within my first hour of trading. Fuckers! There's nothing I can do. This week is mission impossible. I didn't even walk on court and they got me. They are so on top of it. Each time I'm ejected these days, the police will approach me and address me by name. There's no talking my way out of it or giving them phony details. They've identified me from the photos in the dreaded folder and they've got me covered before I even know it. All they have to do is look for me. I'm trying to trade tennis *and* keep an eye out for any security threats. How can I hope to survive?

As I'm escorted out of the grounds on a golf cart, I ask the police what there is to do in New Haven now that I have a bit of spare time on my hands.

'Be careful!' is the answer from the sergeant. I laugh but he's serious. 'This town has about as many shootings and murders as Detroit and Oakland, buddy, so watch yourself. The only reason we don't have more murders is that we've got amazing medics who save a lot of lives at the hospitals in town.'

'Hmm, okay, thanks for the heads up.' I had no idea.

'No worries. We'll call you a cab if you like, pal. You've been much politer than that snotty little guy we kicked out earlier.'

'Oh shit, you kicked one of the other boys out? Who was it?' I'm intrigued.

'None of your business. Don't you worry. He was an Italian or something.'

'Oh really. Was it Arty?' They shake their heads, refusing to play ball.

'Romeo?'

There is a sideways look shared between the police. I laugh.

'Damn, you guys got Romeo too? So he was being difficult then?'

'Oh yeah, he was a fucken asshole that guy. We sure didn't offer to call him a taxi.'

Ten minutes later, in the taxi, I'm astounded to see a drug deal happen right in front of my eyes, in public, in broad daylight. A van pulls up on a one-way street and a wad of cash is thrown into the van's window in exchange for a re-up. The slinger runs off down the street with his package and disappears into a back alley in a matter of seconds.

'This here used to be a two-way street back in the day,' my taxi driver explains. 'But they had it cut down to one so the police could block people off running drugs.'

Not this time, though. I can't believe the differences in society here in New Haven. Tennis tournaments are generally held in high-status towns or famous resort locations. The local population is usually well off and sophisticated. New Haven isn't exactly a cesspit; it's just a blindingly contrasted place. It is the home of Yale University and the headquarters of the charitable Knights of Columbus. The town centre is a cosmopolitan hub, full of chic restaurants and fine hotels (indeed, we're staying in one). But this neighbourhood between the city centre and the tennis is like something out of HBO's *The Wire*. Growing up in a conservative Australian suburb, I'm not used to walking through ghettos or projects, dodging drug dealers, panhandlers, junkies and actually being worried for my safety. My taxi delivers me to my hotel bullet free, and I decide I'll stick to this side of town from now on.

In the hotel room, I remark to Archie how neat the bed is. You see, Felix *was* trading this tournament until he got the boot. He and I swapped places once we realised we were both dead weight. We booked flights and switched locations in an effort to trade the week out. The bed has just been freshly changed. For good reason, too. Archie divulges a secret to me. They had a big night out as soon as they arrived, and he got himself typically plastered. He took a girl home and then blacked out as per usual.

When he came to, in the big-spoon position, the girl was gone. He had got up for a glass of water in the middle of the night and jumped back into Felix's bed by accident! Felix was equally drunk and oblivious to his current small-spoon status. The worst was yet to come though. An hour later Archie awoke to the appalling realisation that he'd just pissed himself! He stumbled out of Felix's soiled bed, still blind drunk, wondering where his girl had gone, and passed out in his own bed for a change. The next morning, Felix accused Archie of spilling beer in his bed. He took the allegation on the chin – he just didn't have the heart to tell Felix the awful truth. I laughed in disbelief, and thanked Archie for having the bed refitted. To this day, I don't think Felix has a clue what really happened.

The next day, I attempt to trade matches from the live internet feed on my computer while Archie returns to the tennis to resell our remaining tickets. He manages to get rid of a few but also makes the poor decision to walk home afterwards. On the way back, he gets thoroughly lost and finds himself wandering through the heart of the hood like a complete misfit.

'Yo! What da fuck is whitey doin' up in the projects with his fuckin' tennis hat on?' was the most memorable quote he recounted to me after his sketchy detour.

By the time Sunday rolls around, we have seen the sights of New Haven and are ready to train it down to New York. The train turns out to be an interesting little ride. We're drinking beer to avoid our hangovers from the night before. Archie offers the girl across from us one and she joins the party. She gives us free tickets to a club opening that Jay-Z will be appearing at during the week. She also wants to keep drinking and offers to buy us a round of shots at Grand Central Station once we arrive. Half an hour later, we're shotting whiskey at midday and Archie's new-found friend is catching the metro back to Queens with us. We check into the hotel and I take my leave. Archie makes use of the room the instant he checks in and christens our new digs while I catch up with a few of the other lads. You never know your luck in the big city. The kid is a prodigy.

*

We are keeping the road alive – just. However, the sketchy 'off-court' efforts – trading from hidden vantage points – are getting out of hand. Security crew are all over the stands and the scouts have been scanning the crowd for us constantly. Our only option has been to retreat to safer territory. This often results in a compromised view, so we can't trade as quickly or as confidently. At what stage do we lose our 'court-side' advantage?

I crack up laughing at the US Open one day after spotting Archie trading from the balcony of a bar. His position is so ridiculously awkward he can only see half the court. It is resourceful but desperate thinking. No other traders are game to go on court and he has still managed to find a viewing platform. Only a few weeks later, Archie finds himself running around the corridors of the St Petersburg indoor tournament, trying to find a good area to trade from, when he stumbles out of a door onto the rafters of the building! He is looking down onto the court from a spot usually reserved for photographers with special passes. Jackpot. Or is it? If any of the Russian security guards catch him up there, it is going to be nasty.

Plan B is being implemented far too often. Windows, rooftops, cafes, bars and balconies are being used as ulterior viewing areas. It's a farce compared to the golden days – two years prior Felix and Jethro survived an entire circuit without a single incident – now we're being chased across the globe like Frank Abagnale Jr.

I've even suggested using binoculars for some courts! It's getting beyond desperate and there is no reprieve in sight. The States have been a battlefield, which is a real worry, as we've always felt comfortable trading US tournaments. If things are this tough in friendly, English-speaking, developed America, how the hell are we going to survive Asia?

21

THE ORIENT EXPRESS

It was a tough truth to swallow and I'd grappled with it for a few weeks before finally admitting to myself that the road was not going to last much longer. Despite the dim-looking future, I was committed to milking this lifestyle while it existed. I had been in contact with a number of other traders, and heard the same story over and over: 'We're quitting. It's not worth it these days. The security issues make it impossible. It's all over.'

I began to notice the absence of traders, particularly at the smaller events, which were now becoming near impossible to survive. Leo, Giovanni, Romeo and Mikka all dropped off the tour. Even Arturo stopped showing his recognisable face at tournaments – opting to send in an apprentice instead. The Swedish guys who had initially welcomed the security pinch now seemed to be feeling it too. After a while, they also fell victim to the onslaught. The trader population was plummeting like a fat kid on a see-saw, and nobody seemed immune to the crackdown.

I spoke to one of the Mexican lads who worked for a European data-outsourcing company. His job had been to input scores so the company could sell them on to third parties. Essentially, he was not a trader, but the basis of his job was still the same. We'd kept in touch throughout the year but I'd also noticed his absence at recent events. It turned out his company had struck a deal with the governing bodies. They were not allowed to trade the ATP and WTA events because of an exclusive contract; however, they were covering other ITF events around the globe. It looked like the entire industry was being shaped around corporate contracts, and the big companies were trying to shut traders out once and for all. We were being strong-armed by their foot soldiers and had no solution to their blitzkrieg. This was no crackdown – it was an extermination.

*

My first work stop in the East is a place I've never even heard of before: Guangzhou, China. I feel ignorant for not knowing of its existence before arriving in town. After all, it is home to over twelve million people! It's the third-largest city in China and one of the fastest-growing metropolises and transport hubs in the world.

Trading in China is scary. The language barrier is like no other on earth. Most nationalities can speak a little English – enough for an ignorant Westerner to get by. Not China. If a Chinese person can say 'hello', they're stoked with themselves. For us to reciprocate is equally hard. The Chinese writing system has over forty thousand characters. The average person recognises between five and seven thousand of these, to get by in daily life. It takes many years before a Chinese youth can hope to read the newspaper – there are just *that* many characters to learn before a person becomes proficient in reading. On a number of occasions, I have to copy the Chinese characters of my hotel or a bar I want to visit onto a piece of paper to show to my taxi driver. I have no idea what I am writing – it is sheer blind faith! I'm certain I haven't got the stroke order correct either, but it seems legible, so it can't be too messy! It's a strange feeling to write symbols down that mean absolutely nothing to you.

As if the Chinese alphabet doesn't present enough of a challenge, the pronunciation of letters is entirely different. The Chinese use tone (pitch of voice) to distinguish words, whereas we use it to convey emotion. There are sounds in their language that don't even exist in English and vice versa. It's a vastly different world and I feel like nothing short of an alien.

Because learning the language is out of the question, the general method of communication is . . . charades. Pointing, signalling and gesticulating all become standard procedure. It is hilarious but also draining and frustrating. The communication barrier could not be wider.

To make things even more daunting, the Chinese have a very different diet to most cultures around the world. Western Chinese takeaway is a far cry from traditional Chinese food. Sure, you may occasionally see sweet and sour pork, and a range of dumplings and noodles, but the menu goes much deeper than that. Half the time, you don't even know what you've ordered. You rarely ever find out, either, because the dishes are so unusual. Delicacies include bird's nest soup, sea cucumber, intestine, ox tail, duck's tongue, frogs, turtles, colon, pig's heart, ears, feet (no part of the animal goes to waste here) and even caterpillars! I know for a fact that I'm eating fried goose intestine one evening, but there's no telling how many domestic pets I will consume without realising it during my stay.

So Felix and I arrive in bustling Guangzhou without a clue. We find a rare and, as a result, expensive English-speaking taxi driver to deliver us to our hotel and jump online to get our bearings. Holy crap. The 'internet' here is like watching an edited aeroplane version of an R-rated movie. It's only half there! Facebook, Twitter, YouTube, Betfair and countless other websites are all blocked. You can't even load these pages. The great firewall of China is impenetrable! (Unless, of course, you have access via a remote server.)

It's a shock to learn how censored and manipulated this country really is. As we flip through the TV channels in search of something we can vaguely understand, we notice a news item detailing the ongoing conflict between China and Japan. The reporter is cut out mid-sentence and the channel flicks to advertisements. Felix and I look at each other in disbelief. Palpable, unashamed censorship. Who knows what happened to the reporter? Maybe he's fine; maybe he's locked up in a cell somewhere. More importantly for us, who knows what happens to traders when they get caught in this country? China has an unsettling reputation for making difficult people disappear. We're hardly political activists but we don't want to get on the wrong side of the law in a country where the existence of 1.3 billion people has inherently decreased the value put on human life and freedom.

Hence, I'm a little shifty as I take a seat in the tennis stand the next day. Not for the first time in my life, I'm the only Caucasian on court in a foreign country. I'm not the only trader, though. A Chinese lady sits a few rows back from me with a big pointed hat on, a scarf covering most of her face, and a magazine held up over her mouth to conceal the fact that she's talking into a hidden microphone and calling points. It takes me a while to realise but it would appear I have competition. This always motivates me to hit points quickly and remain vigilant with my trading.

We make a very healthy profit from our first match, and, as a result, I receive a nasty glare from the lady in the scarf. She's pissed off – most of that money probably belonged to her operation. That's the least of her worries, though. The head of security storms into the stand. My mirth is instantly frozen, and it feels like my balls have made their way into my ribcage somehow. Gripped with panic, I shrink into my seat and pray for deliverance. The security guard walks past me and straight to the lady in the scarf. Once again, her loss is my gain. While he's talking to her, I jump out of my seat and pin it towards the exit.

There's a security guard waiting for me with an official at the bottom of the stairs, though. Shit! They stop me and issue a barrage of harsh-sounding Chinese. I reply with dumb English. It's a stalemate. Neither of them speak any English and they could be speaking Chinese as far as I'm . . . oh, wait. I edge my way towards the exit. They motion at it with one final burst of what I assume to be aggressive Cantonese (the language they speak in the Guangdong region). I take this as my cue to leave and waste no time in doing so. But where does this leave me? Do I return later and risk seriously pissing them off? I'd pay good money to know what was actually said in that transaction. Ah, here's a chance to solve the puzzle. The Chinese lady is also being shown the exit. Maybe she can shed some light on this situation for me.

'Hi, excuse me. Do you speak any English?' I ask, holding up my thumb and forefinger lamely to signal my request for just a little of my own language.

I receive yet another spray of aggressive Cantonese. Fair play, really. I think we just took her for a couple of grand!

I learnt my lesson in Chennai. I've never forgotten Leo's tale of Malaysian imprisonment either. I will not be going back this week. Felix is ejected from the stands later in the day, which leaves us both at a loss and a loose end. Luckily, there is a lot to do and see in this mysterious city.

We hike up a local mountain to get a panoramic view of the city. We visit the Xiangjing amusement park and safari park (home to the largest population of tigers I've ever seen in captivity), and we play ping-pong at the local parks where permanent public tables line the streets. The metro system in 'G-town' is high-tech and impressive. Flashing lights, automatic doors, tokens and maps all help us on our way. As Felix and I ride an air-conditioned train one morning, we laugh at the kid sitting across from us. He's around three years old, and while sitting on his grandpa's lap manages to grab a cigarette out of his pop's shirt pocket, followed by a lighter. He then attempts to spark one up on the train. We laugh and he looks across at me inquisitively. I doubt a three-year-old boy from Guangzhou has seen many funny-looking Caucasians. I think we're both equally perplexed and amused. Felix and I also manage a few nights partying at the local nightclubs. It's interesting to see how people party in China. The clubs are huge. People seem to drink hot tea with vodka and play games of Roshambo to see who has to down the next shot. There are entertainers dancing on stage, and catwalks where models and dancers strut about to the music. Somehow, we manage to get into a game of Roshambo without actually understanding a single word of what is said.

One of the best things about China is how despicably cheap it is. As we stumble into a McDonald's at the end of the night, I order a large Big Mac Meal for around two and a half American dollars. This puts China at number four on the global Big Mac Index's affordability chart. (I haven't made that up, either; it's a list published by *The Economist*.)

*

From Guangzhou, we make a quick hop across the South China Sea to Bangkok. This time, it is only Felix and me. Neither of us can hope to match Archie or Mono in the maniacal drinking stakes, so the week ends up being a lot quieter than last year's effort. We visit the Grand Palace, eat good food and enjoy the hotel facilities.

It is also a lot less successful on the trading front. On the Monday, I am approached by a security crew, addressed by name, then ejected and banned from the venue. A year ago, this place was a cakewalk. It is just another example of how much things have changed. I am reduced to trading from the TV feed in our hotel room. For some matches, I sneak down to the venue and watch the big-screen-TV feed with a beer (it is marginally quicker than the televised coverage), but even then I have to keep an eye out for security personnel. I could still get myself into trouble just for being on the premises. Some drastic measures have to be taken – I decide to shave my head in the hope that I won't be recognised in future.

We enjoy the Thai food, massages, temples, kick-boxing matches and sights, but before we get settled we are returning to China. Getting a travel visa for China is tedious at best. Getting a double-entry visa for the second year in a row is even harder. Imagine if I'd tried to apply for a work visa! After jumping all the hurdles and ticking the boxes, I am allowed in the country again. This time, we are headed to Beijing.

The National Tennis Center, in Beijing, was built for the 2008 Olympic Games. It houses state of the art stadiums (centre court boasts an air-conditioned climate-control system) and draws in a crowd of tennis-mad Chinese spectators. Beijing is probably the biggest city I've ever been to. The population density, built-up metropolitan sprawl and traffic all converge to create a bustling city that never sleeps. We take advantage of our proximity to the Olympic site and visit the famous Bird's Nest stadium, along with the Cube (a colourful swimming complex).

Because play doesn't start until twelve each day, we use our mornings to visit famous sights in the centre of town. Unfortunately, it just so happens to be Golden Week. This means there is a seven-day public holiday in effect for the entire country. Not a good time to be visiting the most revered and popular sites of the country's capital – especially when that country boasts the largest population on earth. Our visit to the Forbidden Palace exposes us to the very definition of overpopulation. It is overwhelming. I've never seen so many people in one place in my life, and I hope I never do again. In situations like this, general convention is broken down and most people look out for themselves exclusively. With the help of a local student, we manage to push through the mosh pit of Chinese tourists and secure a few tickets. We scarcely make it into the site before tickets are sold out for the day. I'm not sure how many people are there but I've since read that Golden Week produced a record attendance at the Forbidden City – a whopping 182,000 people in a single day!

It seems every single person there wants a photo of us, too. As strange-looking foreigners with different-coloured skin and hair, we become an attraction in our own right. It's funny for the first few minutes as we high-five kids, pose for photos and say 'hello' over and over. But, when a line starts forming for people to photograph us, we realise it is time to move on.

Sadly in countries with such overpopulation, people inevitably suffer. Poverty, malnutrition and abortion are all rife in China. I see a truly heart-wrenching thing as we leave the Forbidden Palace. Disfigured beggars line the street. Most of them are missing limbs, and some are mutilated to unfathomable extents. I am devastated to see one of the beggars propped up against a tree, pretending to sing along to a tape he has playing. He has no arms or legs. His body is badly burnt and his face has been melted into a contorted, tortured mask. It is like a disturbing scene from a horror movie, to watch this person mime the words to a Chinese love song while his tarnished face twists inhumanly. The poor man is forced to humiliate himself in public just for the sake of a few yuan, thrown his way in heartbroken sympathy.

The problem is, where do you stop? This guy has been dealt a rough hand – worse than most people on earth. But there are hundreds of others all lining the street with similar predicaments. Men with no arms play flutes with their feet so they can busk to the masses. Some paint with a brush held in their mouth. Others play guitar from their wheelchair, and those who don't have family to set them up for the day, or resources they can busk with, simply beg. It is a hellish scene, and one of those moments where you realise just how very privileged you are to be alive and healthy.

This isn't the only time we encounter street beggars. Every time we go out, there are people harassing us in the street. Shameless mothers push their children into bars late into the night to beg for money. It's a horrible thing to turn your back on an innocent child and tell him or her to go away but there is no way any of us are going to reward this irresponsible parenting by giving the children money. The only comfort is that life in China is cheap. Hopefully, this helps those in need to get by. It is one of the cheapest countries I've ever been to. Taxis, food, drinks, attractions, electronics, you name it: they're all dirt-cheap. And, with 1.3 billion people there to produce them, they're available in abundance.

The Chinese also appear to have an obsession with producing and buying fake products, making (counterfeit) goods even cheaper. 'Marlboro' cigarettes, famous wines, electronics, brand-name clothing and even unofficial Apple Mac stores have all been well documented in China. Apparently, these replicas are so good that even the *employees* in the Apple stores don't realise they are working for a fake company!

In our spare time, Fitzy and I manage to visit the 798 Art Zone, the Summer Palace, a famous restaurant known for its delicious Beijing roast duck, and a food festival held at the Olympic site. We spend our time away from the tennis doing and seeing as much as possible. Once again, we are trying to distract ourselves from an inevitable truth – our industry is being strangled and we are helpless to stop it.

*

The Beijing tournament is a problematic affair. The scouts are present on court and there are plenty of police around the grounds. We aren't taking any risks here. Just to screw us right over, our connection is cripplingly limited in this new city. As a result, I spend most of my time on court reading a book and trying my hardest to blend in like a regular tennis fan. When I'm not doing that, I sneak off to the big screen and try to get a connection up and running, so I can trade from the safety of the food court.

Television trading can be incredibly boring, though – to the point where drinking beer becomes the most practical way to deal with the day. On Friday, I am watching the big screen with Doug and Dylan (two of the only traders left on the tour by this stage), and we are all nursing serious hangovers from the night before. Obviously, beers have to be ordered. After a few rounds, everyone is starting to feel better, and it becomes apparent that we'll be settling in for another session this evening.

A few matches and a fistful of beers later, we are now officially drunk at work. Our speed isn't up to scratch but we are keeping it together. Whenever a new round needs to be ordered, there is always the excuse of 'lost con' for a few minutes while one of us makes a trip to the bar. There is a fair crowd gathered around the TV by evening and the Chinese tunes are blasting. We don't need our chairs any more because we are up and dancing! We're getting among the crowd and cheering for our favourite players. Mistakes are made – that was always going to happen – but at least they aren't costly ones. By the time the matches finish, there are only three of us left in the grounds and we've had a fucking blast for a day of work!

Leaving the venue hammered, we manage to avoid the rip-off taxi drivers and somehow negotiate a ride home on the back of a local man's bicycle. He has one of those electric numbers with a little wooden cart attached to it. Doug agrees on a price with him in sign language and we manage to fit three grown men in the cart. We haven't exchanged a single word of comprehended conversation with the Chinese man, but once we show him the hotel card he laughs and starts riding. We even get a bit of speed up as the traffic buzzes past us from all directions.

Our chauffeur gets us home safely, so we get changed and hit the town already charged up and raring to go for a second night in a row. TV trading has its merits.

*

Did I mention I am rooming with Fitzy in Beijing? There's never a dull moment when rooming with this kid, and he lives up to his reputation in China. In a dingy bar, Fitzy discovers he's been ripped off while buying cigarettes. The darts are some shitty variation of tea-leaves rolled in pages from the Bible. 'Marlboro Reds, my arse,' he says. Fitzy's not happy, but when he tries to complain the locals behind the bar go ballistic. It escalates quickly and before we know it, a few glasses have been smashed and we're being pushed out the front door. Local reinforcements arrive and it looks like a fight is about to break out. As the Chinese gang prepares to charge across the road at us, Fitzy does the last thing imaginable: drops his pants and waves his Johnson around, giving them a good old-fashioned windmill.

'Get a load of this big old western one-eyed warrior!' he yells at the stunned would-be aggressors. They are literally stopped in their tracks. Nobody wants to scrap with the despicable naked caveman. Fitzy has discovered the ultimate anti-violence tactic. I have mentioned this dude is completely insane, right?

On Saturday morning, I awake to the sound of housekeeping knocking on my door.

'Excuse me, sir?' comes the meek and hesitantly spoken English from outside.

My head is pounding. It has been a big week and we finished it off with a massive evening out in the Sanlitun nightlife district. 'No thank you!' I shout from the refuge of my bed. I am not dealing with housekeeping right now.

'Sorry, sir, but . . . your friend!'

I jump up in bed. Fitzy is nowhere to be seen. He has a habit of passing out on the toilet or in the hallway but he's not there either. Oh dear, this could be bad.

I throw on a pair of shorts and step outside, rubbing sleep from my eyes. Seven hotel staff await. Yes, seven! The manager is there in a three-piece suit. They are all staring at a naked caveman sleeping in the foetal position on the floor of the hallway. It's Fitzy. I laugh, then look at the hotel staff and signal for them to wait a second. I run back into the room to grab my camera and snap a few shots of the disgrace while he snores belligerently on the dirty carpet. To the relief of the hotel staff, I shake him out of his slumber and drag him inside.

'Wake up, you fucking clown, we've got a train to catch!'

Two hours later, I wander back from the bathroom to find Fitzy passed out again. This time, it's on the tiles of the Beijing South Train Station departure area. His passport, ticket and work phone are all strewn across the floor in front of him. I shake my head in disbelief and give him a gentle kick to the ribs.

'Is he your friend?' a businessman asks me.

'Unfortunately, yeah,' I reply.

'Well, you should tell him to be more careful in future. Everything could have been stolen.'

'I know. Thanks for keeping an eye on him, pal. This kid is a liability today!'

Another hour later and we're on board a bullet train to Shanghai. Until recently, you had to take a flight to cover this distance. But the new lightning-fast rail system sits between 300 and 400 kilometres per hour for the duration of the journey.

If I had a choice, I'd take train travel every time over flying. Even if it takes a few hours longer, it eliminates the rigmarole of check-in, immigration and security screening. I'd rather spend those two hours relaxed, watching a movie or reading a book than standing in queues and being questioned. It was refreshing to take such a smooth ride at those sorts of speeds without the hassle of turbulence or baggage collection. As for flying . . . well, flying sucks. I'm well and truly sick of it by now and I don't even dislike it that much. Take-off is fun. I take turbulence better than most people – a good bout tends to make me laugh and rocks me off to sleep rather than stressing me out. But the whole lengthy process becomes painful and tedious after some time.

I'm not religious. I don't believe in God or any religious story I've ever heard. I do, however, believe in balance. I think the universe is governed by some undiscovered system that links all things to each other and ensures some sort of equilibrium. Jim Morrison, Kurt Cobain, Jimi Hendrix and Janis Joplin were all incredibly talented people. But they only got twenty-seven years to make the most of it. Stephen Hawking and John Nash (who Russell Crowe portrayed in *A Beautiful Mind*) were bequeathed with the greatest minds of our time, yet they were also burdened with torturous disability. The savant paradox is far too familiar and unfair. The best surf breaks in the world are always too crowded so you never get to enjoy them properly. Fresh powder only falls when foul weather presides. It seems to me that you can't have it all, and that's the way the universe intends it to be. It makes me wonder how much more I can milk from this wonderful life. Maybe that's why security issues have escalated at tennis venues. I've been blessed with such an incredible few years that I find it hard to imagine a better existence.

This is why I sometimes get nervous when I fly now. Sceptical is probably the best way to describe it. As I jet off to my next exotic location, I often wonder how many more of these unbalanced treats I'll get. Plane crashes are rare, so I'm never that stressed. I guess it's just an indicator of how good my job is – feeling like I'm cheating the universe by having such a great time. As for the safety of bullet trains, well, they haven't been around long, so I'm not sure, but mine delivers me to Shanghai without incident. Now, the question is, can I stay safe during my week here?

*

Now I am in the biggest city I've ever been to. With over twenty-three million inhabitants, Shanghai is one of the largest cities on earth. I just wish more of the locals would come to the tennis! I'm sitting on court and feeling like a sacrificial lamb once again. It's an impressive venue. I'm not impressed with my situation, though.

The scout has just walked past me off court. But I wasn't trading so there's nothing he can do, right? Negative. Like he gives a flying fuck – in his eyes, I'm incriminated by my presence at this event. He's seen my photo. He's had me kicked out in the past. It's straight-up profiling and discrimination. The security guard is not impressed when I tell him this.

'You were gambling,' he tells me.

'No, I wasn't,' I reply. I wasn't either. My phone was in my pocket the whole time. Intent to gamble? Sure, but that 'crime' doesn't even exist.

'Well, you've been caught doing it in the past and you're suspected of doing it here, so you're out,' he counters.

'This is fucking bullshit, man!' I explode. There are players and officials walking past as I'm photographed in the media area beneath the centre court. I don't even care any more, I'm sick of being demonised because a few people have decided, in their minds, that I'm doing the wrong thing.

'Hey!' In steps a large security officer. He's the head of security, I realise. 'You're either going to cooperate and give us your identification or we'll hand you over to the police. Fancy trying your luck with them?' He points towards a couple of armed officers standing nearby. Always with the ultimatums, these guys! I take a deep breath, swallow my anger and shake my head.

'Didn't think so. Identification, now!'

I go through the wringer again. I'm banned from yet another event and my week of work is over on Monday, again.

That's three Monday boots in four weeks. Which equals fuck all matches traded and a gaping hole in the profit column. I have no delusions; this signals the end for us. I'll see the rest of the year out but for once I'm not feeling optimistic about my luck changing.

When Fitzy arrives back at the hotel later that evening, he is rattled.

'Bad security encounter?' I ask.

'Nah, mate. Bad taxi encounter is more like it. Holy shit. This taxi driver just crashed straight into a scooter rider on the way back. He hit him at serious speed. The rider was thrown out onto the road and was in a bad way.'

'That is heavy!' I exclaim.

'Yeah. I tried to help but the taxi driver went off at me. He was pushing me away and signalling for me to fuck off, pretty much.'

'What? Was the person okay?'

'I dunno, mate. They would have needed to go to hospital after a crash like that. Your guess is as good as mine – I just hope the taxi driver didn't do a hit and run after I left.'

By the time we leave the country, I've had enough noodles and dumplings to last me a lifetime. China was fun but it was also a disaster. I failed to trade anything of note, and cemented my face as an immediate ejection with the officials. If it wasn't for the new culture and country to explore, I would have gone insane this week. The experience of the road is the very thing that made me take up this job in the first place. Unfortunately, it looks like the cultural experiences and international travel are well on their way to being shut down.

22

НИЧЕГО ОСОБЕННОГО

Family, friends and even random people I've just met are always asking me how they can score a job as a court-sider. Is my syndicate looking for anybody at the moment? Do I know any other people who will hire them? I can't blame them; that's how I got the job myself. My answer is pessimistic these days. It appears the trading industry is in its twilight. The police interviews are becoming more prevalent and some of us are now being turned away at ticket booths. Sandy even jumped out a window to escape police interrogation in Japan last week!

However, we can't just quit the tour with a snap of our fingers. Disregarding the fact that we're very reluctant to give it up, there's also the issue of pre-booked flights, tickets and hotels to consider. There's a fair sum of money tied up in these commitments and we need to do all we can to at least cover the expenses.

After Asia, we only have a few weeks remaining, so we decide to see the tennis year out. The remaining stops, however, do not look like they are going to be any easier to survive.

Moscow is the next destination for Freddy and me. Getting a Russian visa is almost as difficult as acquiring a Chinese one. The Russian bureaucratic labyrinth is incomprehensible to any foreigner. When I ask my Russian friend, Yelena, why her country is so convoluted and mysterious, she simply shakes her head and laughs.

'This is Russia,' she explains.

I drop my bags on the floor of our new Moscow hotel room and the phone rings.

'Hello?'

'Hello,' comes a husky Russian woman's voice, 'do you want sex?'

'Um, yeah!' I profess. But quickly remember what I've heard about Russian hotels.

'Oh, no wait. No, no, no, no I'm good, thanks!' I splutter before slamming the receiver down. Working girls frequent the bars and lobbies of many hotels and offer guests 'extra' services during their stay. If you sit at the hotel bar you'll inevitably be approached, like in some sleazy scene out of *Leaving Las Vegas*. That type of extra service is just not my thing!

Navigating Russia is not much easier than China, either. Once again, there's a different language, alphabet and culture to try to understand. If it wasn't for Yelena, I'm not sure I would have any joy in trying to collect my tennis tickets from the front office on Monday morning. Even with her present, it still takes fifteen minutes for the employees to piss about and get our tickets organised.

Sitting with a girl is a great way to blend into the crowd. Many traders have resorted to this technique in the past year to avoid profiling. Bringing a girl along always defies the initial sweep and can help you look like an average punter out on a date. One of the Italian traders follows the tour with his wife. He's never had any trouble because he's never even been looked at twice by security.

Yves, the ingenious Frenchman, even pays one of his friends a commission just for her to come and sit with him in the stands. This initiative has paid off many times over, as he's never had any problems and does extremely well in the profit margins as a result.

Now that Yelena has come to meet up with me in Moscow, I finally have a chance to try this manoeuvre out and will hopefully evade security for a change. The Moscow tennis venue was designed for the 1980 Olympics, and, like most things from the Soviet era, it's a little worse for wear. It's also a warren of hallways, and it takes another fifteen minutes before we find our way to our seats in a secluded little corner up the back. Yelena is happy to snap photos on her iPad, chat with me and learn about tennis while I trade with my phone hidden under my jacket. She's a typical Russian girl: sophisticated, elegant and gorgeous. She knows what I am doing, but I have to explain that there is a slight chance I might be confronted by security. She finds this quite amusing.

While mid-level female players battle it out on court, I scan the stands for any sign of threat. I must admit, mid-level women's matches bore me more often than not. The slower play, tactics and attitude of some of the players is just not very entertaining compared with quality matches. I don't mean any disrespect to WTA players – I'm in awe of the top female players and their talent – but some players are just not as captivating to trade. The generally higher prevalence of choking and double-faults often leads to good trading opportunities, though, with unexpected swings in momentum. Today is one of those days, and, while the going is slow, the profit potential is there.

Awkwardly, it turns out to be a more embarrassing than amusing day for Yelena and me. We only last two matches before the big, burly security duo approach. They know my name. Kind of. They keep addressing me by my middle name. It appears there has been some confusion during the translation. Either way they've been watching me and matching photos to my face. They would have some very recent ones too. It's amazing to think you can be in China one week and then Russia the next, yet still be recognised by a bunch of strangers just because of the damned 'folder' and orders from insistent officials.

When I stand up to be escorted to the exit, I turn to Yelena and ask her if she wants to stay. The head of security interrupts and says, 'No, she's leaving too.' The poor girl! She is getting kicked out of the Moscow Olympic stadium just for sitting next to me.

I feel bad for a number of reasons. Moscow marks my fifth Monday boot in a row. It is bloody Groundhog Day in the stands. This infuriates me, as I am now more adept in my job than I have ever been. I've been following the tour for almost two years now and have built an intimate knowledge of the tennis world. I know the players' abilities, mindsets and fitness levels inside out. I can predict the outcomes of most mental and physical battles between players. I know which surfaces and tournaments they are likely to perform well at. I am quick on the buttons and can read points better than ever. It is all for nothing, though; even a pretend girl-friend and a shaved head can't save me from being booted! There is no denying it – I am a marked man and my presence will not be tolerated at any tournaments from now on.

Outside, in the freezing Moscow weather, I manage to scalp a few of my tickets for some much-needed roubles. Moscow is one of the most expensive cities in the world and, now that I have the rest of the week to kill, I'll be doing my fair share of sightseeing and partying.

The city centre of Moscow is my favourite of any city on earth. I've been to Moscow before but it is still a special place to explore. I visit Red Square many times that week. There's the Kremlin with its sparkling gold spires and regal eagles sitting atop the national armoury – the headquarters of political activity for the country. Then there's St Basil's Cathedral – the 'ice-cream factory', as some people call it – with its colourful spires and unique architecture. According to legend, once the building was finished, Ivan the Terrible had the architect's eyes burnt out with a hot iron so he could never replicate its beauty. Easy to see how the guy got his name!

So you've got St Basil's at one end of Red Square, marking the point of the city centre, then at the other end is the Resurrection Gate and Iberian Chapel, rebuilt with red bricks in the nineties after centuries of historical importance. Red Square is considered by many to be the spiritual and physical heart of Russia. It is the origin point of all the major roads in the capital city, which, in turn, connect to all the major highways of the nation. Look it up on a map; it's quite fascinating to see. Lenin's mausoleum is situated in the square, and, if you're willing to line up between 10 a.m. and 1 p.m., you can catch a glimpse of his embalmed body. I say glimpse because the security team there are even stricter than those at the tennis. You're only allowed to linger for a few seconds before you are firmly moved on, and photos and videos are strictly forbidden.

The rest of the week is spent travelling on the Metro (which is a national treasure in its own right, adorned with grandiose marble sculptures, statues and chandeliers), checking out the sights and frequenting bars and shisha cafes. Russia is a strange animal. There are rickety old cars, roads and buildings from the Soviet era, all used by supermodel fit women with incredible fashion sense. Then there are fancy new hotels and shopping malls next to grand old Orthodox churches in the city centre. It's a unique landscape that depicts a superpower still trying to find its identity and strength after the fall of Communism.

Wandering down the street, Freddy G and I see a guy walking his . . . goat. Fred stops to pat it and it headbutts him in the leg! I snap a photo and laugh. I can't make head or tail of this strange place, but Freddy is loving it. He accosts random people on the street and tries to talk to them. Most cannot speak English at all but those who can are keen to practise it. The Russians are a friendly and hospitable bunch if you can break through the icy facade they unintentionally present to the world. People there will stare straight through you with piercing eyes that feel as cold as the weather, but it's simply a matter of difference in culture – eye contact is a sign of trust in Russia.

Freddy G is determined to get himself a Russian tattoo as a memento of this trip, so he asks our waitress if she will write out some words in Cyrillic for him.

'What did you have in mind?' she asks.

'Oh, nothing special,' he answers. It's obvious he hasn't given this idea much thought.

'Okay, that's kind of cool,' she replies, writing 'nothing special' – or, should I say, ничего особенного – down on a napkin.

'Oh . . . thanks,' stutters Freddy, realising what's just happened.

'You're welcome.' Our waitress smiles and heads to another table.

Fred and I burst into hysterics at this hilarious misinterpretation.

'You know what, mate?' he blurts out over his beer. 'I'm going to fucking get it!'

'You serious?' I ask.

'Yeah, why not? I wanted some Russian writing on me and now I've got a funny story to go with it.'

By the next tournament, he is sporting those very words on his arm. Classic.

*

It seems the tennis gods are willing to give me a parting gift for the year. Security doesn't even come close to getting me in Paris. I trade with my phone tucked into my leather jacket for the entire week and it's a welcome relief to finally do some bloody work!

The weather is shithouse and I keep things low-key. It's Paris. I've been here at least five times now. I'm sure most people would kill for a week off in Paris, staying in a boutique hotel, sampling fresh food from patisseries, visiting museums and watching the world go by from the traditional cafes that line the street. But, after the past two years on tour, it barely raises an eyebrow for me. I know what you're thinking – I'm a spoilt brat. It's been a long year, though, and, once again, all I can think about is the warm weather and golden beaches back home.

In no time, I'm back in Paris's Charles de Gaulle Airport, waiting for my final flight. It's 5 November 2012, and I'm looking forward to swapping three degrees with rain for twenty-seven and sunny. It's safe to say this has been the best year of my life. Sure, I put up with some shit and had some close calls, but that just adds to the excitement in the end. Somehow, I've managed to top last year. Snowboarding in Canada, jet skiing in Mexico, freediving in Thailand, backpacking through Israel, feasting on a range of the world's most delicious cuisine, and soaking up culture in new countries, not to mention about thirty other stops in-between. Then again, I've come to the same conclusion around this time of year for the past five years. That's how long I've been travelling now, and that's a pretty good point in my argument that travel is the most fulfilling thing a person can do.

I'm stoked to survive the trading week in Paris. At least this way I get to finish the road on my own terms. Despite my recent troubles, the undercover police who frequent the stands and the fact that Sandy (who's still a fresh face on the tour) got booted on the Monday, I made it through. It was a strange tournament in every way. All of the top players bowed out or withdrew early. David Ferrer won his first Masters title, and a young Polish guy named Jerzy Janowicz made a name for himself by defeating five of the top twenty en route to the final. We won a bucketload.

So, is this the end of the road for me? There's talk of us trading the Australian tournaments in January but that won't really be 'the road' for an Aussie. I'm not holding my breath (apart from when I practise my freediving exercises of a morning). In the meantime, there is a whole summer of waves waiting back home. Year two on tour is over, and it's time to put down my phone and pick up my surfboard.

23

THE LAST HURRAH

It's January in Queensland, and the weather is steamy and sunny. Most afternoons, crackling thunderclouds rip through the city, unleashing the pent-up precipitation from another humid day in the subtropics. It's the first week of the tennis calendar and the rapscallions are back together. I'm with Fitzy and Archie for our trading swansong on the Australian circuit. Brisbane, Sydney, Melbourne. I'm in my homeland, and I'm comfortable, but I certainly won't be complacent on court. There are snitches at every tournament now. Freddy G has already been caught and thrown out of the VIP area at the Heineken Open in Auckland, prompting the *New Zealand Herald* to run an article headlined 'Sport-betting spectators ejected'. Things are escalating very early in the year and these hired scouts are the reason.

The officials like to call us 'the rodents'. So what should we call the vermin who rat on the rodents? We despise these guys and vice versa. The hypocrisy of it all is that we're both here doing the same thing – getting paid to travel the world and watch live sport. Our battles are no longer with officials or umpires. The snitches are our main problem now. Which is frustrating because they're not even professionals. They're just young punks – friends and family of officials who have been hired by a large company that is making aggressive moves to ensure it owns the live scores exclusively. Somehow these young punks have lucked into a fun job that allows them to get paid, watch live sport and see the world. Sound familiar? Disguises, pre-emptive movement and covert trading are all necessary to outfox them. I thought *my* job was easy – all they have to do is spot me and call it in! I'm in the wrong line of work. The boys and I joke about becoming turncoats and wrangling a deal with the enemy. We'd be the best damn scouts possible, already knowing every face on tour and all. No chance! So this game of cat and mouse continues, unknown to the spectators, as the action unfolds on court in a new year of tennis.

It's just not the same now. The game has changed and the fun has been taken out of this job. I'm constantly pursued through the first few days at the Brisbane tournament, meaning I spend precious little time court-side trading. When I escape to a beer garden to trade the big-screen action from a beanbag, I'm pounced on, thrown out and banned from the event. Not even my home town is safe these days!

This is what my trading life has been reduced to – giving it a crack, getting spotted by a scout, booted by security, embarrassed in front of a crowd, and releasing my frustration by passing the rest of the week with borderline alcoholic antics. I want to get in there and get on court and watch some points and hit some buttons. I've been doing this for two years – I'm good at it, I'm used to it, and I'm pissed off that a set of rules has deemed me unworthy of entering the premises to continue my work.

At this point in time, January 2013, no trader has been prosecuted by the law. But a very large and influential company has purchased the rights for live score updates. They have a contract that guarantees them fast live updates directly from the umpires' chair. Quite amusing that the umpires who despise us so much have now become the ultimate court-siders! Moreover, how can anyone claim to *own* the score of a match?! It unfolds in the public eye. It is general public knowledge from start to finish. The idea seems a little preposterous to me. Yet they continue to vilify us with increasing malevolence. The hypocrisy of it all is that they're creating a lucrative monopoly by muscling the competition out under corporate demands for millions of dollars. It's okay for them to do it but if we try to trade then we're suddenly 'threatening the integrity of the sport'. Bullshit.

The back end are getting frustrated. Nowadays, they're trading most matches from inferior TV broadcasts because we're being kicked out. At home, in front of the computer, it's hard to understand just how impossibly tight venue security is. Every point we miss is a trading opportunity lost. The profit margins are dwindling and we can't continue to run a viable enterprise under these circumstances. Our trading lives have run their course, and it's time to admit defeat. Even fancy gadgets and fake moustaches can't help us these days. Nads, Fitzy and I have discussed our options and regretfully decided we'll be turning our phones in once the Australian leg is over. While our faces are now blacklisted, there will always be opportunities for new players to enter the trading game and try their luck. Some European traders may try to keep the dream alive, but, for the Aussies, retirement looms.

Sydney turns out to be an infuriatingly similar affair to Brisbane. On the second day, I see the snitch on court during my first game. I recognise the smug little prick from last year. Before I even have a chance to duck off court and give him the slip, he's called security. I'm trapped. Game over. I don't even wait for them to approach me. I meet them halfway down the stand and simply say, 'Let's do this.'

After being escorted from the grounds, I sit on a park bench and wait for the inevitable. They're on a blitz so it won't be long now. Lo and behold, within five minutes, Fitzy comes lumbering out the gates after also being banned from the grounds and read the *Trespass Act*. It sucks not being able to do your job. The time off is great, but you still feel like a failure.

The guilt washes away later that week at Bondi Beach. We see the inside of a fair few pubs, then meet up with old mates before bar-hopping all the way to Kings Cross and back. On Sunday morning Archie wakes up on a park bench with two hippy girls standing over him offering him croissants for breakfast. He gratefully accepts them, then runs home to wake us up so we can get organised for yet another taxi to yet another airport.

*

We were astonished that things were so dire Down Under. It was a sure sign of the times and an affirmation that we had made the right decision in letting the road go. We did, however, have high hopes for Melbourne. The Grand Slam crowd and massive venue would make life easier for us. With any luck, we might even be able to survive the two weeks.

Our flight from Sydney to Melbourne was the most entertaining flight I've ever been on in my life. In his post-hangover revelry, Fitzy decided he'd rather stay drunk and become the unofficial in-flight entertainment for the duration of the trip.

'Can I have your IDs, please?' the hostess had asked at check-in.

'Do you really need them?' Archie complained from below the counter as he rifled through his bag for his misplaced passport.

'Um, yes. Of course we do. You can't get on a plane without it,' the annoyed hostess answered. 'Also, I'm going to ask that all three of you boys go have a coffee and chew some gum before boarding, otherwise you may not be allowed on the flight.'

'Yeah, we might have had a few drinks last night,' I conceded.

'A few?' she scoffed. 'You stink like a brewery!'

Archie was still rustling around in his bag like a tragic hungover mess and the poor check-in lady was really starting to get frustrated.

'There are people waiting,' she reminded him. Although I think most people in the queue were amused rather than annoyed.

'Can you just put him in a separate seat from us?' Tim joked. 'He slept on a park bench last night so we'd rather not be near him.'

'Oh, fuck you,' Archie mumbled from his bag, finally finding his passport and jumping to his feet.

Amusingly, the hostess had quite liked Fitzy's suggestion and was in the process of allocating our seats. 'Okay, I've put you two together. Archie, you're a few rows back in a middle seat.'

'What? You're kidding me!' cried Archie. Tim and I burst into laughter and walked through the gate with our outraged and soon-to-be ostracised English mate.

This little manoeuvre turned out to be a blessing in disguise for me because it left a spare seat to my left. We enjoyed a mandatory hair of the dog and met up with Sandy and Freddy, who had recently turned up as reinforcements to trade the week out and were now flying to Melbourne with us.

We finished our morning beers (so much for coffee) and wandered down to the boarding gate. Tim and I chatted in our aisle, and I waited to see if I'd get some extra leg space. The plane was almost full and nobody had sat next to me. I was pretty happy with the result when I heard an enchanting Cambridge accent lean over and say, 'Excuse me, sorry, but that's my seat.' I looked up to meet the blue eyes of a very attractive blonde girl in her early twenties.

'Cool,' I replied, absolutely stoked with this outcome, and got up so she could buckle in. As I stood in the aisle, I looked back at Archie a few rows behind me. He'd seen the whole thing and was even more outraged than before. I shot him a cheeky grin and he shook his head as Fitzy and I sat down and introduced ourselves to our travel companion for the next hour. She was a friendly English girl named Emily who was backpacking around Australia and looking forward to seeing Melbourne.

Twenty minutes later, we had beers in our hands and were laughing about stories from the past few days. Fitzy was ordering rounds of beers and getting them delivered around the plane to our mates. The service was amazing for a budget flight and we were all having a great time, until the turbulence kicked in. I personally couldn't give a shit about turbulence, but Tim openly admits he's a massive pussy when it gets bumpy.

'Oh, nup, nup, this is not cool, man, fuck this shit, I'm not cool with this!' he started.

I laughed my arse off. I couldn't help it. The poor bastard was shitting himself and all I could do was laugh at him. I felt a smidgeon guilty but it was just too funny. I knew the plane was fine and that everything was under control, but Fitzy was not having a bar of it. He'd chosen the wrong line of work to get into.

After the bumps died down, the flight attendant returned to ask if we wanted more beers. 'I just had a feeling you fellas might like a few more before we land,' he said. Damn straight. Talk about service.

'Yep,' said Fitzy. 'Six more, thanks.'

'Well, I can't serve you more than one each, I'm afraid.'

'That's cool,' I interrupted. 'He's not having two. One's for Emily.'

The host looked at our attractive blonde friend as she nodded in agreement. She was a keeper. It was bullshit, of course; we all knew Fitzy just wanted two beers. He got them.

Then the stench hit us. Somebody on board had committed the lowest of airline faux pas – the dreaded pressure-sealed fart. It was a fucking stinker too! Fitzy was outraged and was drunk enough to let everyone know.

'That is fucking *not* on!' he yelled. Everyone around us was coughing and nodding in agreement as they covered their noses with T-shirts or hats. The small Asian man in front of us was, according to Fitzy, the major suspect.

He tapped the guy on the shoulder. 'That really stinks, mate.'

'Huh?'

'I said that really stinks, mate! Seriously, did you fart or what?'

The question went unanswered and the laughter and coughing slowly dispersed with the noxious gas.

Once it was safe, Freddy came up for a chat. In the process, he tripped up one of the hostesses serving food. She had such enormous fake boobs and lips that she could have started her own silicon factory. To me, it is not an attractive look. Apparently, this did not faze Fitzy.

'Sorry,' he apologised on Freddy's behalf, 'my friend is a bit retarded.'

'You!' – the hostess spun around – 'Are a menace.'

Tim laughed; it wasn't the first time he'd heard it, and, judging by her tone, it was more of a cheeky jab than an insult. Tim saw an opportunity and ran with it. He started chatting her up and pretty soon she was asking where he was off to next with his incredible job.

'Ahh, London, Montpellier, Amsterdam, Indian Wells, Miami,' he boasted, just getting into his stride. 'Monte Carlo, Madrid, Rome, Paris . . .' He knew full well, of course, that he wouldn't be going around this year.

'Okay, okay, that's enough,' she laughed in amazement. As a domestic hostess, she must have found this pretty impressive. 'How do I sign up?' she asked.

'Just have to know the right people,' Fitzy replied with a wink.

'Well, do you need a girlfriend then?' she joked.

Fitzy didn't miss a beat. 'Sure, throw me your phone number.'

She laughed and walked off to serve the next customers. 'You'll get me fired!' she yelled over her shoulder.

'Whatever,' Fitzy shouted down the aisle. 'Relax, it's called flirting!'

We drained our beers as the plane descended and started getting excited for a big night out with all the crew. At Grand Slams, the whole team comes together to work. They only roll around four times a year, so it's a great opportunity to catch up with everyone and party hard. Once the plane landed, we disembarked and made our way to baggage collection. In the process, the hostess handed Fitzy a napkin with her phone number on it, and I got Emily's number. High fives all round.

While we waited for our luggage, Fitzy befriended a Frenchman named Henri who was standing nearby. They started chatting about the tennis and Henri told us that he was a full-time hitting partner who worked closely with some of the top French players. We were quitting so we threw caution to the wind and told him we were there to trade. He was nonchalant about it all. In fact, he invited us to come and sit with him during the week and gave us his number.

Our luggage came drifting down the conveyor belt along with . . .

Sandy. Nobody had noticed him disappear a few seconds ago and now the idiot appeared out of nowhere as a joke.

'I've always wanted to do that!' he laughed as we grabbed our bags.

We caught a maxi cab into the city, dropping Henri and Emily off along the way, thanking them for their company and agreeing to meet up later in the week. We rendezvoused with the rest of the team and then the real fun began. They were staying in a hostel, and, while it might not have been as cosy as our boutique hotel down the road, it was certainly a lot more fun.

The hostel bar served cheap drinks with a big screen showing sport, along with a pool table and lounge space where we could entertain ourselves. We made great use of these facilities and downed jugs of beer like Prohibition was about to be reinstated. It was incredible to catch up with our team and hear their stories. It had been a few months since we'd all been together in the same place, and excitement levels were high. We all got tickets to a gig and celebrated with a cracking night out on the town.

*

On Monday morning, it's back to business. And, in the trader business, it doesn't get any bigger than a Grand Slam event. This isn't just any Slam, either – it's my personal favourite. The first and foremost of the calendar year. The one that gets the ball rolling and challenges every player with its scorching hot days and energetic crowd: the Australian Open. I might be biased, but I honestly think it's the best in every aspect. Wimbledon might have the history and prestige, the US might boast the biggest arena in the sport, and the French might be the only campaign fought on the 'red stuff', but for me the Aussie is the grandest slam.

Melbourne has been voted the most liveable city in the world on a number of occasions, and it's easy to see why. During January, the weather is incredible. Blue skies and greenery surround the vast venue, and the air is abuzz with activity and excitement. The CBD is a refreshingly navigable area, dotted with charming historic colonial buildings, girt by the Yarra River and serviced by Melbourne's iconic tram system. If that's not enough, there's the ritzy Crown Casino, the mammoth structure of the Melbourne Cricket Ground and Federation Square, where you can watch all the tennis action on a giant screen for free! Australians love their sport and there's no better time to celebrate it than in summer. You can walk from downtown along the river all the way to Melbourne Park and soak up the ambiance from numerous bars, pubs, buskers and cafes that energise the water's edge along the way.

But it's the atmosphere inside the venue that makes the Australian Open for me. No other tennis crowd in the world is as colourful and vocal as the Australian public. The outfits and warpaint people wear, the chants they make up, the signs for their favourite players and the constant support are what make the place. With such a multicultural population, there is no shortage of supporters from any competing nation – Serbians and Croatians are the most avid and emotional of them all, and they show up in hordes to support their players.

In my opinion, Margaret Court Arena is one of the greatest assets to the game of tennis. A 'free entry' court that anyone inside the grounds can get onto (provided they make it on before the queue explodes), it is often the site of gladiatorial battles. The crème de la crème will never play here – they're on one of the stadiums dishing out straight-set thrashings against lower-seeded players. However, the best of the rest are showcased and pitted against each other in their most important hours. Struggles for a berth in the next round and battles of will and skill take place. This is often the venue for these players' most desperate, most explosive and entertaining tennis. I once saw Marcos Baghdatis smash four racquets in a row on Margaret Court during an outburst of pent-up frustration. The crowd loved every second of it.

The bogans, diehard fans, loyal supporters and average punters all converge on this arena to witness some of the most hardfought tennis you could ever hope to see. With beer flowing steadily from midday to midnight, and chants booming across the grounds, the pregnant silences of Wimbledon and the umpire's omnipotent 'quiet please' become a distant memory. Mexican waves, pub songs and beach-ball games take precedence over ceremony. Archie once came up to me after his first Margaret Court Arena experience gushing, 'It was like a soccer match. The place was absolutely buzzing. I've never seen anything like it!' Every point becomes a spectacle. It's something special and unique in tennis, and in my eyes it epitomises the Australian Open: big, loud and rambunctious. While beer may not be as sophisticated as a genial Pimm's, it sure brews a more boisterous broth.

*

I realise that I've painted an alcohol-fuelled picture of our world here. Admittedly, we drink a lot more than your regular group of workmates. While most staff get together for Friday drinks, we have a talent for igniting massive and uncontrollable binges on any given day of the week. Put a bunch of good mates in their mid-twenties in a hotel after a long day at work and what do you expect? However, in saying that, I must admit we still have a hell of a lot of fun when we're sober – which, amazingly, is more often than when we are drunk. This week there are Snickers-eating competitions, arm-wrestles, dry-biscuit-eating races, pool games and numerous wagers taken on to make things even more interesting.

On Monday, Freddy is forced to relieve himself behind the stand because he can't leave court in fear of missing a pivotal point or injury. His match is still going on while he takes a rushed piss underneath a stand full of oblivious spectators. Not to be outdone, Nads goes one better in his hungover state by having an unanticipated spew over the railings while sitting in the stand. Nobody notices and he doesn't even have to leave his seat. Now that's dedication! These stories keep us all entertained during our boring days on court as they filter around via text message.

While standing out the front of the venue on Tuesday morning waiting for Felix to arrive with tickets, a bright orange and green bug a few centimetres long lands on Mono's neck. He has no idea but I've spotted it.

'Hold still,' I warn, while I pick the bug off him. 'I know how you English fellas are when it comes to creepy-crawlies.'

I am thinking specifically of an occasion when Mono had a hilarious run-in with a wasp on court in Estoril, Portugal. He darted back and forth in his seat, with his phone in his right hand, to no avail as the persistent wasp homed in on his face.

'Ah, get away! Get away!' was the failed mantra. The wasp continued to buzz around his face as the match went on and he was trying desperately to concentrate on the points being scored. The wasp would not let up, though, and after being pushed to the brink poor Mono snapped. 'Fuck off!' he yelled at the wasp, hurling his phone at it in desperation. It missed and clunked down the steps of the steel stand, making an absolute racket.

'Oh shit!' quickly followed as he realised what he'd just done.

The program on his phone was still running, as was the match. That meant gambling could still take place without his control. It was irresponsible trading at its best!

'Oh shit, oh shit, oh shit' became the new mantra as he ran down the stairs to retrieve his phone. Luckily, nothing drastic went down on court in that time and the wasp even left him alone after that.

But it's a simple fact: the English don't mix well with creepy-crawlies, and Mono is no exception.

'What are you talking about?' Mono asks, as I hold up the bug.

'Well, this little guy was crawling around on your neck, trying to give you a kiss,' I reply.

'Oh Jesus!' he cries, and recoils.

'He's all right, mate,' I tease. 'He just wants to say hello.'

I look at the colourful bug inquisitively as it crawls over my fingers and hand. I haven't seen one before so I have to admit it's a bit weird.

'Oh, you're so tough. Why don't you go and eat it then?' taunts Mono.

I think about it for a second and decide no. I have an idea who might, though. 'Umm, nah,' I reply, 'but you will, won't ya, Fitzy?' I offer him the bug.

All eyes turn to Tim. He contemplates the bug for a grand total of half a second before snapping it up in a single gulp.

'Oh my god!' laughs Mono.

'Ahhhh,' screams Archie in a slightly more intense response and runs for the hills.

We all laugh and watch him pull up about ten metres away, as if he's finally found safety.

'Archie, you clown,' yells Fitzy. 'What the fuck is wrong with you?'

'What's wrong with me?' he retorts. 'Orange and green, man! They're the danger colours! You never go for the orange and green.'

We all laugh as Felix turns up with the tickets. It is an entertaining start to the day.

*

The weather is great all week and so is the tennis. This is more like it. I am trading matches without the slightest hint of pressure from security. I am sitting in the stands, chatting to fellow spectators, enjoying the sunshine and loving my job once again. This week reminds me of the good old days, and it is a bittersweet way to end my trading career. However, it's not quite over yet, and we still have a great weekend to look forward to. Things are destined to end in typical bizarre trader style.

On Saturday, we start the morning with steaming hangovers from yet another hilarious night out. It is becoming hazardously familiar, but hair of the dog is the only palatable option. Fitzy and I arrive at the venue to witness the biggest crowd the Australian Open has ever seen. He can't even get on court. I grab a beer and take off to my court, just scraping in on time to find a seat. The crowd is amazing, and I thoroughly enjoy the atmosphere. There are Mexican waves, chants and songs all unfolding around the stadium. I trade the match out and have a break for the next few hours.

I message Tim to see how he has fared on Margaret Court. The line to get on has not moved. I find him in the same spot where I left him, albeit much drunker. To continue the trend, we grab more beers and blow the Margaret Court option off. It's our last weekend of trading and we're going to enjoy it.

Fitzy messages Henri, the Frenchman, to see if he wants to hang out. He replies immediately and invites us over to Hisense Arena to join him. We part ways; I head off to trade an epic five-setter on an outside court, and Fitzy heads to Hisense. It's not until Fitzy gets there that he realises they'll be sitting in the players' box. Is this a good idea? Fitzy is public-enemy number one as far as the tennis authorities are concerned. How will they react if they see him sitting on court among the French players? It will cause all kinds of uproar and controversy!

A number of players are in the box, along with coaching staff and hitting partners. They're curious to see what Fitzy is doing with this strange program on his phone. He explains it to them, and they're completely unfazed. They had no idea court-side trading existed, and, if anything, they're a little impressed and intrigued by this ingenuity. What a contrasting perspective to the officials'! The sad thing is, if these guys were to be seen sitting with Fitzy, they would probably be investigated by TIU and regarded with suspicion from that point onwards. It appears there's no danger of that happening, though, because they've sat on court for an entire match and nobody seems to care in the slightest. Not only does Fitzy get to meet and hang with most of the French team, he also gets to trade from one of the best seats in the house.

Meanwhile, in a juxtaposition of mammoth proportions, the most outrageous and unbelievable of all trading quandaries is unfolding on the other side of Melbourne Park. Archie has been working on centre court all day, so we haven't heard from or seen him for hours. It has been a stinking-hot day in Melbourne, so he has taken a hotel towel with him to put over his head and cool him down while sat in the sun. The problem with Melbourne is it can be boiling hot during the day and still end up freezing cold once night falls. The towel is the perfect accomplice for these days, because it doubles as a blanket once the cool air filters into the stadium.

Without thinking, Archie places this towel over his legs to keep him warm and hide his phone while he continues to trade.

He hasn't considered the fact that he is hitting buttons every point and moving his hand around an awful lot while it is concealed and positioned right by his crotch. You can imagine how that looks. It doesn't help that he is trading a women's match and sitting by himself up in the back row on a Saturday night, when any normal guy would be hanging out with his mates or girlfriend. To some spectators, he must look like a bona fide creep.

Without any notice, the police storm into the stand and grab Archie, dragging him out of the stadium and taking him aside for questioning. Although he is disappointed and a little rattled, Archie simply assumes this is a routine booting. He is wrong. The police take his details, search his items and start going through his phone. It appears they are particularly interested in searching through his photos, for some reason.

'Now, do you know what this is all about?' asks a female officer.

This is the usual question, and Archie counters with the usual response. 'No, I've got no idea what's going on here. What's the problem?'

'Well, mate, we've had complaints from people in the crowd that you've been up the back of the court playing with yourself.'

There is a moment of shocked silence as this sinks in.

'You WHAT?' Archie blurts out in bewilderment.

'Yeah, mate. Don't play dumb, either. We watched you on camera for a while and you were blatantly fiddling around down there with a towel hanging over your lap. Enjoy getting your rocks off to women's tennis, huh?'

'No, no, no. There's been a big misunderstanding here!' he starts.

'Save it, mate. We know what you are!' snaps the officer.

These words stun Archie. He's been typecast as a pervert. In their eyes, he is a total creep and there is nothing he can do about it . . . Well, there is one thing: tell the truth. But the truth is only a lesser evil and it would get him in trouble too. It would guarantee his ejection from the venue and there is still week two of the Open to trade. Decisions, decisions. And only a split second to make one while the police glare at him with misplaced disdain. Archie's shoulders slump in resignation as he decides to take this embarrassing predicament on the chin. Down to the very last tournament, he is loyal to the road and never gives himself up as a trader.

'I don't believe this.' He shakes his head in dismay.

'Well, you have two choices here,' says the copper. 'You can fight the accusation in court at a later date or you can take an on the spot fine and be on your way.'

'Really? Okay, how long will it take to go to court?'

'We can't say for certain but usually it takes a few weeks.'

Archie doesn't have weeks to spare. He is booked on a flight back to England in ten days' time.

'Right, just give me the fine then. Let's get this over and done with.'

He hates saying that – he is admitting to a creepy crime he hasn't committed. With the fine comes a twenty-four-hour ban from the venue. Let's think about that for a second. For trading on court, you get banned for life. For doing the five-knuckle shuffle in the stands, you get told to piss off for *one* day! That's not the only crazy thing about the punishment, though. When the policewoman hands Archie the fine, he is flabbergasted yet again. Five hundred and sixty dollars! He stops in his tracks and considers trying to fight it in court. Then he thinks about how much it would cost to change his flight home and accepts this horrible happenstance. He is a self-confessed public masturbator and there is nothing he can do about it!

He is fined for indecent public conduct and marched to the exit of Melbourne Park. At least he will be allowed to return next week and continue trading. He has learnt a valuable lesson from this caper – never again will he take a towel to the tennis.

*

The final week of the Australian Open and of our lives as travelling tennis traders was a thoroughly enjoyable one. We caught up with friends, enjoyed meals in restaurants and pubs, reminisced over beers on rooftop bars, and relaxed by the beach in St Kilda. I even met up with Emily from my flight the week before. It was the prelude to a normal Australian life, and, although it signalled the end of the road, it was a celebration more than anything. We said our farewells to the remaining traders left on tour (their numbers were thin these days), and finally the time came for us all to part ways. It was a sad but acceptable moment. We'd lived the dream but were ready to move on.

My flight home to Brisbane was a bumpy one. It seemed the airways had saved the best for last. Maybe my theory was right and I'd milked too much from this great ride. Wouldn't it be ironic if my final plane was the one to go down? For the first time in my life, I felt apprehensive about putting my faith in a metal capsule in the air. There was a cyclone approaching the coast and the gale-force winds were making life very difficult for our pilot. Our first landing was aborted as we burst through some extremely low-lying cloud to an abrupt and alarming view of a runway that was a lot closer than expected. I'd never been so ungrateful to have a window seat! Luckily, our second attempt was much more successful. A few moments later, I was on solid ground, thanking the pilot for his efforts. This is where the road ended for me, in the best place it possibly could: home.

24

CASH OUT

It's all over – the best two years of my life and the greatest job I've ever had. Since quitting and moving home, the volume on my life has been turned down about eighty-six decibels. Mundane normality rings in my ears like an incessant mosquito. As I attempt to shake off a five-year travel hangover, my mind drifts over the quixotic memories, and the whole experience already feels like a distant dream. What I've learnt during this journey is worth more than any university course could ever teach me. I will confidently step off a plane almost anywhere in the world knowing I can handle myself, find my way and have a good time regardless. A lot less fazes me these days after dealing with all the security issues and learning how to react and respond to different situations overseas.

The world has become a lot smaller to me. It's much more accessible. I have friends around the globe who speak different languages and embody completely different outlooks and cultures. I've met traders, volunteers, drug addicts, successful business-men, homeless people, diplomats, alcoholics and many more along the way. I judge none of them because, without these wily characters, our world would not be the diverse and extraordinary place it is.

Now, when I meet somebody from a foreign country, I can generally find some common ground with them. I can use a few token words in their tongue, understand some of their customs, fondly recall my favourite food, drink or beer from their country, and discuss the beauty of their landscapes or landmarks . . . and, if all else fails, I probably know of a good tennis tournament in their neck of the woods.

I've developed an appreciation and admiration for European class and style. I hope that some of it has rubbed off on me. I can say hello, goodbye, yes, no, please, and thank you in about ten different languages, hold a basic conversation in Spanish (enough to make sure I'm not going to jail, at least!), and I feel at ease in many different corners of the globe these days. I don't just have a second home (London), I have a third (San Diego), a fourth (Banff, Alberta), a fifth (Lagos, Portugal), and many, many more that I hold close to my heart and hope to visit again.

I know where to go at which times of the year to chase hobbies, wildlife or natural phenomena. I know how to behave in different countries, what their customs are and how to act acceptably. I have a better understanding of the disputes, attitudes and rifts in countries or religions because I've witnessed them first-hand. I've seen the impact that political leaders, pop-culture icons, fashion trends, musicians, architects and other artists have on our global landscape. Nowadays, I see photos in travel magazines and pulses of nostalgia will surge through me. Whenever I catch a plane, I always flip through the airline's in-flight magazine and take a trip down memory lane. Every second page is almost guaranteed to remind me of a funny story or a treasured memory.

During my travels, I've seen almost every artist or band I could ever want to see at some of the best venues, festivals and locations on earth. I've managed to collect enough souvenirs along the way and now have art hanging on the walls of my house from Havana, Shanghai, Waikiki, Luxor and Los Angeles. I also have mementoes from Mexico, Guatemala, Germany, the Czech Republic and Croatia, to name a few. My life has been shaped by experiences in different lands and I like being surrounded by these daily reminders of great times and amazing places.

I've watched a shitload of tennis during a golden era in the sport. I've been privileged to trade Federer, Nadal, Djokovic, Murray, Roddick, Hewitt, del Potro, Haas, both Willams sisters, Clijsters, Azarenka, Ivanovic, Sharapova and many more. I've seen enough tennis to love and hate it. I've seen enough of the players to both love and hate them too (love always prevails).

How many different beds have I slept in during my life? How many strange and foreign pillows have I laid my head upon? The sleeper trains, hostels, couches, floors, beaches and bungalows are an endless collection of fond memories. But now I'm able to rest my noggin on a soft, fluffy, familiar bag of feathers that I can call my own.

Although I've fallen in love with this lifestyle over the past two years, I've missed having my own place. It's satisfying to have a wardrobe I can hang my clothes in, a steady base to settle into, and a week passing by without having to hop on a plane or worry about being dragged from a stand by security personnel. It's addictive, the trader's existence, and I'll no doubt miss it.

I've lived without much responsibility or accountability over the past few years, but I've matured and grown in a way that many people never have the chance to. I'm content with and proud of my life thus far. Most importantly, I appreciate it all and love the fact that, no matter how far I wander on this earth, I'll always be able to come back to one of its most beautiful and peaceful places: Australia. The road may be amazing but home will always be home.

I still keep up to date with the tennis scores, and watch big matches when the time zones align. I can't help myself. It was such an intrinsic part of my life, it's proving hard to walk away from. One thing's for certain: I'll never be able to watch tennis like a normal spectator again.

Are there still traders out there, sitting in the stands, secretly calling points and making a living on the tour? Maybe. Maybe not. I'm not telling, but I sure hope so. More pertinently, will you be able to go out there and join their ranks as a newcomer? Sorry to burst your hopes – I'm afraid those chances are incredibly slim. But feel free to prove me wrong!

I doubt very much that I'll be attending any tennis tournaments in the near future. After all, I do have a framed letter from Wimbledon, banning me for life, on my wall. But I know I'll be back to enjoy the live action as a spectator one day (once my name and mugshots have long been forgotten). And to all those uptight umpires and officials, well, don't you fret; my trading days are behind me. I'll be sure to leave my phone at home.

People always say, 'You're so lucky that you went travelling and did all those things.' Well, for me, that's a matter of perspective. Luck definitely played a part in some of it. There were moments when things just clicked and opportunities fell into my lap. I made certain to seize them all with both hands. My view, however, is that none of those opportunities would have arisen had I never got up off the couch, booked myself a flight and put myself out there in the world. I think all traders would agree that while Lady Luck's help is always welcome in life, you can never expect any return if you don't make an investment and commit to something in the first place.

The mates I've made on this tour are the part I'll miss the most. I've made lifelong friends that share a special bond. We travelled, traded and partied together all over the world, celebrating our experiences and making the most out of our extraordinary opportunity while it lasted. Sadly, it was far too short for a fellow trader and a great friend of mine. He loved the road more than anyone, and it was all taken away from him far too soon. A true character and comic, he was alongside us for most of our shenanigans on tour. He was always up for a beer and a laugh, and was one of the most loved traders to ever pick up a phone. I've chosen to leave his tales out as a matter of respect – the irony is he was the greatest storyteller I've ever met. The only way I can reconcile his early passing from cancer is by knowing that he got to enjoy a privileged life and lived to the fullest while he could.

It was an incredible stage in all of our lives, and these times have no doubt forged memories that will be looked back upon in fondness for a lifetime to come. The majority of my trader friends live abroad, so I've no idea when I'll see them next. I'm so used to being in a perpetual state of transit and being able to catch up with people everywhere, this rooted stability will come as a shock to me. But waking up every morning and wandering down the beach with my surfboard under my arm comes second to nothing. I've been to over fifty countries, but I still love Australia over them all. I've been lucky enough to see more of the world than most people see in their lives, and I'm twenty-seven. What the hell do I do with myself now?

I've just recently learnt that one of Felix's friends has cycled from Bangkok to England to raise funds for charity. He's now running across Canada to continue his mission. Meanwhile, some of Fitzy's mates are riding motorbikes from Alaska down to Argentina to raise money in honour of friends and family who have been affected by cancer. Now that's a real trip.

I feel like it's time for me to start giving back. I'm not going to tell you to live every day as if it's your last or repeat some tired parable of inspiration. If you want to do something, do it. Life is short but it's also beautiful, and so is our world. So long live travel, tennis, good times and the good life. Go get among it.

EPILOGUE

I'm standing in the knee-deep water of Rainbow Bay, with the satisfying texture of gritty golden sand between my toes, watching Kelly Slater destroy waves in the final of the Quiksilver Pro. I live on Australia's Gold Coast with a bunch of mates, work from Monday to Friday, and even make my own bed and breakfast of a morning. It's a regular life, and that's fine by me because I get to surf every day in my favourite place on earth. Good waves, good weather and no flights on the weekend. I'm stoked.

I'm also glad to be out of the tennis stands.

In November 2013, Sandy was wrestled off court and dragged by the throat into an unmonitored room where two security guards beat the shit out of him. They punched him in the face repeatedly. One of the pricks even lined up his sovereign ring so it connected with Sandy's lip each time. They kicked him in the shins with steel cap boots and smacked him in the back of the head as he went down. Of course nobody saw anything and the incident will always be denied by those involved. When the head of security told Sandy nothing had happened, he spat a wad of blood at the man's feet and asked him, 'What the fuck do you call that then?'

As if that wasn't enough, on 14 January 2014, Dan Dobson was arrested at the Australian Open for court-siding. He was charged with 'engaging in conduct that would corrupt a betting outcome'. His employer (Sporting Data) released a clarifying statement, assuring the public that 'Sporting Data has never been and never will be involved in any type of match-fixing'. They insist that the new law 'is being applied entirely inappropriately'. Dan was not gambling himself, only relaying scores via his phone. The gambling and court-siding community were stunned, intrigued and apprehensive about this seemingly unwarranted arrest. A conviction would set an international precedent and greatly influence the future of court-siding.

However, on 6 March 2014, the prosecution dropped their charges due to a lack of evidence and no reasonable chance of conviction. It was a relieving and satisfying moment for Dan and for court-siders worldwide.

I always said to those angry officials, 'if it becomes illegal, I'll quit'. It sounds like you need a full-time lawyer to keep informed and out of trouble on tour these days. With new laws being enacted across so many different countries, who knows where court-siding will sit in a few years? Maybe I got out at the right time. I'm content to be chilling back home after five years abroad. I had a damn good run.

But back on the beach, as I watch Kelly hack spray off the lip of a reeling right-hander before pulling into a perfect blue barrel, I think about the amazing stops the pro surfing tour consists of. Places I've never even been to, like Tahiti, Fiji, South Africa and Brazil. And while I'm trying really hard to settle down at home, I can't stop myself from wondering . . . could there be a way to *trade* this heat?

Lightning Source UK Ltd.
Milton Keynes UK
UKOW06f0816191215

264997UK00004B/119/P